*James K. Luiselli, EdD, ABPP, BCBA*
*Charles Diament, PhD*
*Editors*

# Behavior Psychology in the Schools: Innovations in Evaluation, Support, and Consultation

*Behavior Psychology in the Schools: Innovations in Evaluation, Support, and Consultation* has been co-published simultaneously as *Child & Family Behavior Therapy*, Volume 24, Numbers 1/2 2002.

*Pre-publication REVIEWS, COMMENTARIES, EVALUATIONS . . .*

"STATE OF THE ART . . . MASTERFULLY COVERS THE RAPIDLY EXPANDING FIELD OF BEHAVIORAL SCHOOL CONSULTATION. Key topics of great interest to psychologists, teachers, parents, and administrators are clearly and comprehensively explored. The readings provided are crucial for understanding timely issues such as school-wide positive behavior support, prevention of problem behavior, systems analysis and change, sustainability of intervention effects, and community involvement."

**Edward Carr, PhD**
*Leading Professor,*
*State University of New York*
*at Stony Brook*

The Haworth Press, Inc.

# Behavior Psychology in the Schools: Innovations in Evaluation, Support, and Consultation

*Behavior Psychology in the Schools: Innovations in Evaluation, Support, and Consultation* has been co-published simultaneously as *Child & Family Behavior Therapy*, Volume 24, Numbers 1/2 2002.

# The *Child & Family Behavior Therapy* Monographic "Separates"

Below is a list of " separates," which in serials librarianship means a special issue simultaneously published as a special journal issue or double-issue *and* as a "separate" hardbound monograph. (This is a format which we also call a "DocuSerial.")

"Separates" are published because specialized libraries or professionals may wish to purchase a specific thematic issue by itself in a format which can be separately cataloged and shelved, as opposed to purchasing the journal on an on-going basis. Faculty members may also more easily consider a "separate" for classroom adoption.

"Separates" are carefully classified separately with the major book jobbers so that the journal tie-in can be noted on new book order slips to avoid duplicate purchasing.

You may wish to visit Haworth's Website at . . .

## http://www.HaworthPress.com

. . . to search our online catalog for complete tables of contents of these separates and related publications.

You may also call 1-800-HAWORTH (outside US/Canada: 607-722-5857), or Fax 1-800-895-0582 (outside US/Canada: 607-771-0012), or e-mail at:

## getinfo@haworthpressinc.com

---

***Behavior Psychology in the Schools: Innovations in Evaluation, Support, and Consultation***, edited by James K. Luiselli, EdD, ABPP, BCBA, and Charles Diament, PhD (Vol. 24, No. 1/2, 2002). *"STATE OF THE ART. . . MASTERFULLY COVERS THE RAPIDLY EXPANDING FIELD OF BEHAVIORAL SCHOOL CONSULTATION. Key topics of great interest to psychologists, teachers, parents, and administrators are clearly and comprehensively explored. The readings provided are crucial for understanding timely issues such as school-wide positive behavior support, prevention of problem behavior, systems analysis and change, sustainability of intervention effects, and community involvement." (Edward Carr, PhD, Leading Professor, State University of New York at Stony Brook)*

***New Developments in Behavior Therapy: From Research to Clinical Application,*** edited by Cyril M. Franks (Supp. #1, 1984). *"This comprehensive, neatly organized, and well-referenced text represents an invaluable resource for the rigorous clinician interested in research and its application in the field of behavior therapy." (The American Journal of Family Therapy)*

# Behavior Psychology in the Schools: Innovations in Evaluation, Support, and Consultation

James K. Luiselli, EdD, ABPP, BCBA
Charles Diament, PhD
Editors

*Behavior Psychology in the Schools: Innovations in Evaluation, Support, and Consultation* has been co-published simultaneously as *Child & Family Behavior Therapy*, Volume 24, Numbers 1/2 2002.

The Haworth Press, Inc.
New York • London • Oxford

*Behavior Psychology in the Schools: Innovations in Evaluation, Support, and Consultation* has been co-published simultaneously as *Child & Family Behavior Therapy*™, Volume 24, Numbers 1/2 2002.

The development, preparation, and publication of this work has been undertaken with great care. However, the publisher, employees, editors, and agents of The Haworth Press and all imprints of The Haworth Press, Inc., including The Haworth Medical Press® and Pharmaceutical Products Press®, are not responsible for any errors contained herein or for consequences that may ensue from use of materials or information contained in this work. Opinions expressed by the author(s) are not necessarily those of The Haworth Press, Inc. With regard to case studies, identities and circumstances of individuals discussed herein have been changed to protect confidentiality. Any resemblance to actual persons, living or dead, is entirely coincidental.

Cover design by Thomas J. Mayshock Jr.

### Library of Congress Cataloging-in-Publication Data

Behavior psychology in the schools: innovations in evaluation, support, and consultation/James K. Luiselli, Charles Diament, editors.
     p. cm.
    "Co-published simultaneously as Child & family behavior therapy, volume 24, No. 1/2 2002."
    Includes bibliographical references and index.
    ISBN 0-7890-1920-5 (hard: alk. paper)–ISBN 0-7890-1921-3 (pbk: alk. paper)
    1. School psychology. 2. Behavioral assessment. I. Luiselli, James K. II. Diament, Charles. III. Child & family behavior therapy.
LB1027.55. B44 2002
370.15´3--dc21                                     2002007430

# Indexing, Abstracting & Website/Internet Coverage

This section provides you with a list of major indexing & abstracting services. That is to say, each service began covering this periodical during the year noted in the right column. Most Websites which are listed below have indicated that they will either post, disseminate, compile, archive, cite or alert their own Website users with research-based content from this work. (This list is as current as the copyright date of this publication.)

Abstracting, Website/Indexing Coverage . . . . . . . . . Year When Coverage Began

- *Behavioral Medicine Abstracts* . . . . . . . . . . . . . . . . . . . . . . . . . . . . . . **1991**

- *Cambridge Scientific Abstracts <www.csa.com>* . . . . . . . . . . . . . . . **1992**

- *Child Development Abstracts & Bibliography <www.ukans.edu>* . . . **1991**

- *CINAHL (Cumulative Index to Nursing & Allied Health Literature),*
  *in print, EBSCO, and Silver Platter, Data-Star,*
  *and PaperChase <www.cinahl.com>* . . . . . . . . . . . . . . . . . . . . . . . **2000**

- *CNPIEC Reference Guide: Chinese National Directory*
  *of Foreign Periodicals* . . . . . . . . . . . . . . . . . . . . . . . . . . . . . . . . . **1995**

- *Criminal Justice Abstracts* . . . . . . . . . . . . . . . . . . . . . . . . . . . . . . . . . **1991**

- *Current Contents/Social & Behavioral Sciences*
  *<www.isinet.com>* . . . . . . . . . . . . . . . . . . . . . . . . . . . . . . . . . . . . . . **1991**

- *Developmental Medicine & Child Neurology* . . . . . . . . . . . . . . . . . . . **1994**

- *Educational Research Abstracts (ERA) <www.tandf.co.uk>* . . . . . . . **2002**

- *e-psyche, LLC <www.e-psyche.net>* . . . . . . . . . . . . . . . . . . . . . . . . . **2001**

- *ERIC Clearinghouse on Counseling*
  *and Student Services (ERIC/CASS)* . . . . . . . . . . . . . . . . . . . . . . . **1995**

(continued)

(continued)

*Special Bibliographic Notes related to special journal issues*
*(separates) and indexing/abstracting:*

- indexing/abstracting services in this list will also cover material in any "separate" that is co-published simultaneously with Haworth's special thematic journal issue or DocuSerial. Indexing/abstracting usually covers material at the article/chapter level.
- monographic co-editions are intended for either non-subscribers or libraries which intend to purchase a second copy for their circulating collections.
- monographic co-editions are reported to all jobbers/wholesalers/approval plans. The source journal is listed as the "series" to assist the prevention of duplicate purchasing in the same manner utilized for books-in-series.
- to facilitate user/access services all indexing/abstracting services are encouraged to utilize the co-indexing entry note indicated at the bottom of the first page of each article/chapter/contribution.
- this is intended to assist a library user of any reference tool (whether print, electronic, online, or CD-ROM) to locate the monographic version if the library has purchased this version but not a subscription to the source journal.
- individual articles/chapters in any Haworth publication are also available through the Haworth Document Delivery Service (HDDS).

# Behavior Psychology in the Schools: Innovations in Evaluation, Support, and Consultation

## CONTENTS

# ABOUT THE EDITORS

**James K. Luiselli, EdD, ABPP, BCBA,** is Vice President, Applied Research and Peer Review at The May Institute, Inc., and also maintains a private practice in educational, clinical, and behavioral consultation. He is a licensed psychologist, a certified health provider, Diplomate in behavioral psychology from the American Board of Professional Psychology (ABPP), and a board certified behavior analyst. He holds appointments as a clinical affiliate in psychology at McLean Hospital; a clinical assistant professor in the Department of Counseling Psychology, Rehabilitation, and Special Education at Northeastern University; and a clinical instructor in psychology in the Department of Psychiatry at Harvard Medical School. Within The May Institute, Inc., he serves on the core faculty of the predoctoral clinical psychology internship training program.

Dr. Luiselli has authored more than 180 publications, including several books and has been the senior editor of three thematic journal issues published in *Behavior Modification, Mental Health Aspects of Developmental Disabilities,* and the *Journal of Developmental and Physical Disabilities.* He serves on the editorial boards of seven peer-reviewed journals and as an editorial consultant to several other professional publications. In 1999, he was selected to the national Expert Consensus Panel for the Treatment of Psychiatric and Behavioral Problems in Mental Retardation for the guideline series published by *The American Journal on Mental Retardation.*

**Charles Diament, PhD,** is a licensed psychologist practicing with children and their families for over twenty years. He has served as Director of the psychology internship program, Chairperson of the Department of Psychology and Director of Training at Children's Psychiatric Center-CMHC (currently CPC Behavioral Healthcare). He was also Managing Partner of Princeton Evaluation and Treatment Services, the provider of psychological services and evaluations at the Carrier Foundation in Princeton, New Jersey. Dr. Diament is the associate editor of *Child & Family Behavior Therapy,* a quarterly professional journal. He is also a psychological evaluator for the Physician's Health Program of the Medical Society of New Jersey, assessing potentially impaired physicians. Dr. Diament is the consulting psychologist at Ranney School and is currently in private practice in Red Bank, New Jersey, providing forensic, evaluative, consultative, and direct clinical services to children and their families, schools and adults.

# Introduction

## James K. Luiselli

As a graduate student I had the good fortune to participate in several research projects that were conducted in public schools. Our university teams were responsible for observation, data collection, and teacher training that addressed students who had learning disabilities and/or conduct problems. In selected cases we also were requested to consult with school staff regarding children and adolescents who posed serious challenging behaviors. Upon entering professional practice I did not expect to spend a significant amount of time in public schools. However, within a few years, and in response to several consultations, the referrals rolled in at an increasing rate. This level of involvement was dominated by behavioral assessment and intervention with individual students but gradually included programming for entire classrooms, in-service training for teachers, and guidance around policy decision making. I ultimately left full-time private practice and at that time, about 80% of my work was devoted to public school consultation.

In contrast to my early experiences, the scope and direction of behavioral consultation in public school settings has changed considerably. In an attempt to capture these developments I organized this publication first by having colleagues identify seminal topic areas. Important key sources in this respect also were reviewed (Kratochwill & Stoiber,

James K. Luiselli, EdD, ABPP, BCBA, is Vice President of Applied Research and Peer Review, The May Institute Inc., Norwood, MA.

Address correspondence to: Dr. James K. Luiselli, The May Center for Applied Research, The May Institute Inc., One Commerce Way, Norwood, MA 02062 (E-mail: jluiselli@mayinstitute.org).

[Haworth co-indexing entry note]: "Introduction." Luiselli, James K. Co-published simultaneously in *Child & Family Behavior Therapy* (The Haworth Press, Inc.) Vol. 24, No. 1/2, 2002, pp. 1-3; and: *Behavior Psychology in the Schools: Innovations in Evaluation, Support, and Consultation* (ed: James K. Luiselli, and Charles Diament) The Haworth Press, Inc., 2002, pp. 1-3. Single or multiple copies of this article are available for a fee from The Haworth Document Delivery Service [1-800-HAWORTH, 9:00 a.m. - 5:00 p.m. (EST). E-mail address: getinfo@haworthpressinc.com].

2000; Stoiber & Kratochwill, 2000; Ysseldyke, Dawson, Lehr et al., 1997). Next, based on their expertise and active roles as clinicians, educators, and researchers, selected authors were invited to write about specific areas. The stipulation was that they present salient issues, summarize key points, discuss impressions, and offer recommendations to improve professional service delivery. A prerequisite in preparing manuscripts is that the authors focus discourse on the practical ("real world") aspects of consultation.

Although the topics in this special issue are diverse, it is encouraging to see the common themes raised by the authors and the consensus of opinion that emerged. First, state and federal legislation has been instrumental in increasing consultant-delivered technical assistance to public schools. Second, there has been greater recognition of prevention-oriented interventions to ameliorate risk factors affecting students and the need to overcome discipline problems before they occur. Third, the emphasis on prevention has shifted the dominant activity of behavioral consultation from single-student interventions to classroom-wide and whole-school programs that embrace the entire student population. Fourth, practice standards have been defined for consultants and school personnel, stressing:

a. functional behavioral assessment,
b. positively constructed behavior support plans,
c. social skills building,
d. multiple source, data-based efficacy evaluation.

And fifth, effective practice hinges on particular competencies (knowledge and interpersonal) acquired by the consulting professional.

There are additional points raised by the authors worthy of consideration. As noted in several articles, behavioral consultation to public schools must attract community involvement to be sensitive to the multiple influences on students and to design the most comprehensive and effective interventions. A uniform finding from clinical and research endeavors is that teachers usually do not implement academic remediation and behavior support plans consistently when consultation is terminated. Therefore, another concern is how to ensure that the work of consultants has follow through and can be maintained long-term in the absence of ongoing assistance. Several authors offered the caveat that although we have good evidence-based outcomes from behavioral consultation, understanding the full impact of service models remains elusive. To this I would add that we have more to learn about how best to train consultative skills during graduate education and internship supervision. Finally, even with the adoption of consensus standards, procedures must find wider application and generality across student populations, grade levels, and diverse (e.g., inner city versus suburban) school settings.

I am indebted to Dr. Cyril Franks (Editor) and Dr. Charles Diament (Associate Editor) of *Child & Family Behavior Therapy* for advocating publication of this volume and lending assistance along the way. The project would not have been possible without the support of The Haworth Press. I am, of course, most grateful to the authors, all of whom worked diligently in preparing informative articles that I believe will advance our field. My thanks go to Dr. Pete Christian, President and CEO of The May Institute and my colleagues, Drs. Bob Putnam, Joe Ricciardi, and Dennis Russo, for making the Institute such a special place to work and learn. Most of all, I dedicate this project to my wife, Dr. Tracy Evans Luiselli, and my children, Gabrielle and Thomas, for lighting the candles and showing me the way.

## REFERENCES

Kratochwill, T. R., & Stoiber, K. C. (2000). Empirically supported interventions and school psychology: Conceptual and practical issues–Part II. *School Psychology Quarterly, 15*, 233-253.

Stoiber, K. C., & Kratochwill, T. R. (2000). Empirically supported interventions and school psychology: Rationale and methodological issues–Part I. *School Psychology Quarterly, 15*, 75-105.

Ysseldyke, J., Dawson, C., Lehr, C., Reschly, D., Reynolds, M., & Telzrow, C. (1997). *School psychology: A blueprint for training and practice II*. Bethesda, MD: National Association of School Psychologists.

# Focus, Scope, and Practice of Behavioral Consultation to Public Schools

James K. Luiselli

**SUMMARY.** Public school districts frequently seek professional consultation to improve educational services. This article is an overview of the focus, scope, and practice of behavioral consultation to public schools. A four-stage process of consultation is described, followed by a discussion on the expanding role of behavior support intervention. Next, the involvement of consultants in the design of individual-student, classroom-wide, and whole-school programs is considered. Contemporary approaches to consultation are presented such as positive behavior support, functional behavioral assessment, and efficacy evaluation that targets natural data sources. A concluding section sets forth recommendations for the successful practice of public school behavioral consultation. *[Article copies available for a fee from The Haworth Document Delivery Service: 1-800-HAWORTH. E-mail address: <getinfo@haworthpressinc.com> Website: <http://www.HaworthPress.com> © 2002 by The Haworth Press, Inc. All rights reserved.]*

**KEYWORDS.** Public school consultation, applied behavior analysis, practice standards

---

James K. Luiselli, EdD, ABPP, BCBA, is Vice President of Applied Research and Peer Review, The May Institute Inc., Norwood, MA.

Address correspondence to: Dr. James K. Luiselli, The May Center for Applied Research, The May Institute Inc., One Commerce Way, Norwood, MA 02062 (E-mail: jluiselli@mayinstitute.org).

[Haworth co-indexing entry note]: "Focus, Scope, and Practice of Behavioral Consultation to Public Schools." Luiselli, James K. Co-published simultaneously in *Child & Family Behavior Therapy* (The Haworth Press, Inc.) Vol. 24, No. 1/2, 2002, pp. 5-21; and: *Behavior Psychology in the Schools: Innovations in Evaluation, Support, and Consultation* (ed: James K. Luiselli, and Charles Diament) The Haworth Press, Inc., 2002, pp. 5-21. Single or multiple copies of this article are available for a fee from The Haworth Document Delivery Service [1-800-HAWORTH, 9:00 a.m. - 5:00 p.m. (EST). E-mail address: getinfo@haworthpressinc.com].

Behavioral consultation is a problem-solving approach that has been implemented effectively to improve service delivery in the areas of education, mental health, and business (Bergan & Kratochwill, 1990). Similar to other consultative models, a behavioral orientation has conceptual foundations that guide practice implementation. As contrasted to other models, a critical feature of behavioral consultation is the commitment toward protocol-driven methodologies and empirical efficacy evaluation. This article discusses the focus, scope, and practice of behavioral consultation to public schools.[1]

## DESCRIPTION AND COMPONENTS

Gutkin and Curtis (1982) stated that, "At its most basic level, consultation is an interpersonal exchange" such that "the consultant's success is going to hinge largely on his or her communication and relationship skills" (p. 822). In effect, a professional with technical competencies (the consultant) works with one or more persons (the consultee) who are responsible for the care of a "client." The consultant provides services indirectly through exchanges with the consultee. In behavioral consultation, these exchanges occur as a series of interviews and meetings that define the referral problems, analyze contributory influences, apply solutions, and evaluate outcome. Relative to public schools, the recipients of consultation would be teachers, principals, administrators, parents, and ancillary therapists.

Bergan, Kratochwill, and associates have written extensively about the process of behavioral consultation (Bergan & Kratochwill, 1990; Kratochwill & Bergan, 1990; Kratochwill, VanSomeren, & Sheridan, 1989). They specified four stages of implementation, summarized in Table 1, and described more fully below.

*Stage 1: Problem Identification.* The first stage of consultation is to identify the areas of concern that will be the focus of evaluation and intervention. The consultant meets with relevant staff to pinpoint behavioral targets, define them operationally, and develop a measurement system (data collection). The problem identification interview (PII) frequently will require several meetings between consultant and consultees to reach consensus about the objectives of consultation. In particular, the consultant must guide staff toward a common understanding of how to describe goals (dependent measures) objectively. Most persons who seek consultation, for example, are not familiar with data-based measurement and, instead, articulate behavior and academic concerns in

## TABLE 1. Stages of Behavioral Consultation

*Stage 1: Problem Identification*

Identify challenging behaviors and competencies

Define target behaviors operationally

Design baseline data collection procedures

Initiate baseline assessment

*Stage 2: Problem Analysis*

Complete functional behavioral assessment

Develop behavior hypotheses

Formulate and design behavior support plan

*Stage 3: Intervention Plan Implementation*

Implement behavior support plan

Provide staff training

Refine and modify intervention

Introduce maintenance facilitating strategies

*Stage 4: Intervention Plan Evaluation*

Evaluate intervention effects

Assess collateral behavior-change

Gather social validity measures

nonspecific terms such as, "Billy is anxious all the time," or, "Mary is not motivated to learn." Although extra time may be required to "fine tune" behavioral definitions with staff, it pays dividends for later intervention implementation.

The data collection methods developed at this stage ideally should be incorporated in a baseline phase of evaluation. Gathering baseline data yields an objective measure to compare with effects of intervention. It also is desirable to institute interobserver agreement (IOA) assessments to measure the reliability of data collection. Reliability is essential to verify that the staff responsible for data collection actually document the same responses. Such assessment can be accomplished by having two staff members (e.g., a teacher and classroom assistant) simultaneously collect data during scheduled times or by having the consultant serve as the second source of data collection during her or his school visits.

*Stage 2: Problem Analysis.* At this stage the objective is to gather information through a functional behavioral assessment (FBA). The purpose of a FBA is to isolate conditions that set the occasion for (antecedents) and reinforce (consequences) challenging behaviors. Biological, environmental, and interpersonal influences represent three main categories that should be addressed through assessment. FBA methodology also should be extended to non-problem behaviors, that is, desirable academic and interpersonal skills. More recently, the role of establishing operations (EOs) has been a point of emphasis for FBA (McGill, 1999). An EO is a manipulation that momentarily alters the reinforcing effectiveness of consequence events and the frequency of behaviors producing those events.

The use of indirect and descriptive methods of FBA (Iwata, Vollmer, & Zarcone, 1990) generally is well suited to the exigencies of public school settings, although a more rigorous experimental-analog approach can be implemented with integrity (Northrup, Wacker, Berg, Kelly, Sasso, & DeRaad, 1994). Indirect procedures include semi-structured interviews and rating checklists such as the Motivation Assessment Scale (Durand & Crimmins, 1988). Descriptive methods of assessment consist of A-B-C (antecedent-behavior-consequence) evaluations that are extracted from systematic data collection. For example, a classroom teacher might be taught how to record the frequency of disruptive behavior displayed by a student, and, in addition, the conditions associated with their occurrence (e.g., type of instructional activity, time of day, academic requirement). This information would be used to identify behavior-function. Direct observations of students and staff, of course, also would be performed by the consultant at the problem analysis phase.

When the FBA has been completed, the final step is to formulate one or more "hypotheses" about the "causes" of the challenging behaviors. One usual outcome from this activity is the preparation of a behavior support plan (BSP) that includes intervention procedures matched to the hypothesis-derived formulation (Drasgow, Yell, Bradley, & Shriner, 1999). To illustrate, if the purported influence on a student's challenging behavior was the social attention he or she received contingently, a BSP would be prepared which features differential positive reinforcement (social praise and approval) for desirable behaviors and "planned ignoring" (withdrawal of attention) as a consequence procedure. Or, if it were determined that a student did not attend consistently to classroom assignments because she or he were too "demanding," an antecedent manipulation such as reducing the response requirement, allowing the student to request work "breaks," or providing extra instructional support might be considered. The results of subsequent intervention confirm the correctness of the purported hypotheses.

*Stage 3: Intervention Plan Implementation.* After a BSP has been formulated, it is implemented under the supervision of the consultant. At this stage, the consultant trains staff members to apply procedures and supervises their intervention. Direct observation by the consultant, while providing "hands on" direction and feedback to staff, is critical during initial implementation. Importantly, the presence of the consultant in the early phase of intervention is a potent source of stimulus control and it enables staff to acquire skills via modeling, performance feedback, and rehearsal.

At Stage 3, behavioral interventions typically are modified and refined based upon the review of data. On this note, Sugai and Luiselli (1989) indicated that alterations to programming are necessary when

a. the intervention has failed to effect the desired change in the target problem,
b. the assessment procedures being used do not yield reliable or valid data, or
c. the staff encounters problems that interfere with the implementation of programming. (p. 210)

The consultant also should be responsible for documenting "treatment integrity." That is, staff performance must be monitored closely and with regularity to ensure that procedures are applied in accordance with the planned intervention.

*Stage 4: Intervention Plan Evaluation.* The design and use of various data collection procedures before, during, and following intervention enables the consultant to evaluate the effects from behavior support plans. At this stage of consultation the concern is to document that a desirable outcome has occurred and, ideally, to confirm that the result is attributable to the planned intervention. Plotting data in the form of simple graphs and charts allows for visual inspection of response trends within baseline and intervention phases. Presented as time-series analyses, the data display reveals the direction and magnitude of behavior-change subsequent to intervention. Whenever possible, single-case design strategies should be incorporated into the evaluation process (Barlow & Hersen, 1984).

Two other evaluation methods merit consideration. First, measurement of collateral behavioral effects from intervention should be recorded to demonstrate changes in non-target responses or generalization of clinical gains to other settings. And second, social validity assessment (Schwartz & Baer, 1992) should be conducted to document intervention acceptability by teachers, administrators, and parents. Another objective of social validity assessment is to quantify clinical significance by referencing the degree of obtained change against a normative standard.

## THE EXPANDING ROLES OF BEHAVIORAL CONSULTATION TO PUBLIC SCHOOLS

Behavioral consultation to public schools has expanded greatly during the preceding 15 years, in part due to several trends. First, the evolution of "inclusive" schooling and federal legislation governing "free and appropriate public education" (FAPE) requires that students who have developmental disabilities, cognitive impairments, and behavior disorders have the opportunity to attend their local schools with "typical" peers. Before the meaningful implementation of the regular education initiative (REI), it was common for this population to be enrolled in private programs or other educational settings outside the public schools. Because of the increased enrollment of students with "special needs," public schools have recognized the benefits of working with behavior consultants to improve academic instruction and reduce discipline problems. This fertile ground produces many referrals to professionals who provide consultation as psychologists or "behavior specialists" affiliated with a private practice, clinic, or human services agency.

A second influence on the expanding role of behavioral consultation to public schools is the 1997 re-authorization of the Individuals with Disabilities Education Act (IDEA). This act requires that "in the case of a child whose behavior impedes his or her learning or that of others, the child's IEP team must consider, when appropriate, strategies, including positive behavioral intervention strategies and supports, to address that behavior" [IDEA Amendments, 20 U.S.C. § 1414 (d) (3) (B) (I)]. In addition to decreasing challenging behaviors, the educational team must focus on teaching social skills. Conducting a FBA, writing a positively oriented BSP, and identifying measurable goals for outcome evaluation also must be a focus of attention. However, most public school personnel do not have the knowledge to fulfill requirements such as a FBA or other stipulations set forth in IDEA 1997 (Nelson, Roberts, Mathur, & Rutherford, 1999). It should be expected, therefore, that many referrals for behavioral consultation will be made by public school districts in their efforts to adhere to these new policies and to equip staff with requisite skills.

Finally, our public schools continue to struggle with student discipline problems (Dwyer, Osher, & Warger, 1998; Rose & Gallup, 1998). Many schools are plagued with violence, vandalism, threats to personal safety, and similar antisocial behavior. As a result, academic achievement is compromised, the learning environment is disrupted, and "at-risk" students are more susceptible to negative peer pressures. Many professionals have described behavioral approaches to effective school discipline practices, with an emphasis on skill-building and preventive interventions (Lewis, Sugai, & Colvin, 1998; Luiselli, Putnam, & Handler, 2001; Mayer, 1995; Walker, Horner, Sugai, Bullis, Sprague, Bricker, & Kaufman, 1996). Behavioral consultation that encompasses whole-school and district-wide applications can contribute greatly to prevention and the systematic evaluation of comprehensive discipline practices.

## INTERVENTION FOCUS AND SCOPE

Sugai, Sprague, Horner and Walker (2000) described a three-tiered model of school-wide discipline strategies, which is germane to the focus and scope of behavioral consultation. *Universal* interventions represent school-wide systems of behavior support that are applicable to all students. These interventions are intended to prevent challenging behaviors and, as proposed by Sugai et al. (2000), affect approximately 85-90% of a school's population. This approach rests with the assumption that most students entering school have the interpersonal and academic skills to ensure success. Effective prevention enables these students to avoid at-risk influences and to serve as exemplary peer models. Whole-school programs of behavior support include many components but generally emphasize collaborative team building among students and staff, teaching prosocial skills, reducing imposition of negative (punitive) consequences as a method of discipline, and achieving early academic competencies (Lewis et al., 1998).

The second intervention focus described by Sugai et al. (2000) is termed *selective* and is reserved for students who are at risk for, or display, challenging behaviors. Involving between 7-10% of a school population, these interventions frequently are designed for specialized classroom implementation. For example, behavioral consultation might involve training a teacher to manage better several students who are disruptive during instruction. As an illustration, Putnam, Luiselli, Handler and Jefferson (2001) reduced the number of student discipline referrals in a fifth-grade classroom through:

a. increased teacher monitoring,
b. designation of positively worded classroom "rules,"
c. formation of classroom teams that received "points" for adhering to rules,
d. public posting of "point" earnings,
e. exchange of "points" for daily and weekly preference activities.

Clearly, selective interventions are more intensive and student-specific than those that constitute a universal orientation.

In approximately 3-5% of cases, students require more complex and individualized supports beyond their exposure to universal and selective interventions. According to the scheme by Sugai et al. (2000), *targeted/intensive* interventions are designed for high-profile students, namely those with chronic challenging behaviors and poor school adjustment. Ideally, these students should receive a FBA that will help formulate intervention guidelines matched to the unique presentation of each student. In the study by Putnam et al. (2001) cited previously, for example, one student did not respond favorably to the classroom-wide intervention. A behavior support plan was written for him that included:

a. individualized academic support during "high demand" activities that appeared to set the occasion for disruptive behaviors,
b. a self-monitoring chart to document prosocial responses,
c. increased teacher praise,
d. noncontingent "breaks" from academic assignments,
e. access to preferred activities as a consequence for accurate self-monitoring.

This multicomponent plan eliminated discipline referrals for the student.

In summary, behavioral consultation to public schools spans the continuum of primary, secondary, and tertiary prevention. Experience suggests that most referrals for consultation are made to address students who pose significant behavior challenges or are at risk for developing such problems. This group is a small percent of the total student population at a school but requires the greatest investment of time and professional resources. It is for this reason that consultation services are increasingly devoted to whole-school and district-wide implementation of behavior support practices. That is, consultants will continue to write intervention plans for individually referred students but also contribute meaningfully by formulating "constructive discipline" models which are preventive and embrace all students (Luiselli et al., 2001; Mayer, 1995).

## CONTEMPORARY APPROACHES IN BEHAVIORAL CONSULTATION

Effective behavioral consultation to public schools requires the dedicated delivery of "best practice" approaches. Research that is subjected to peer review, replicated, and refined produces evidence-based strategies that inform and direct practices. In recent years, consensus has emerged among many behaviorally-aware professionals concerning critical elements that comprise successful consultation.

### *Positive Behavioral Support*

Positive behavioral support, or PSB, reflects the evolution of behavior-change interventions from circumscribed, frequently punishment oriented, procedures to more multicomponent programs that emphasize skill-building, positive reinforcement, and lifestyle components. Sugai, Horner, Dunlap et al. (2001) commented that "PSB is not a new intervention package or a new theory of behavior, but an application of a behaviorally based systems approach to enhance the capacity of schools, families, and communities to design effective environments that improve the fit or link between research-validated practices and the environments in which teaching and learning occur" (p. 133). Integral features of PSB are:

a. an emphasis on functional determinants of challenging behaviors,
b. context-derived intervention plans,
c. outcome-based assessment,
d. consideration of social validity (satisfaction and acceptability) as a measure of efficacy. (Haring & DeVault, 1996)

Further delineation of the foundations comprising PBS was presented by Sugai et al. (2001). They discussed the link between PSB and learning theory explanations of behavior-change. PSB interventions stress the "contextual fit" among challenging behaviors, environments, and support strategies. Important to this distinction is developing interventions that are efficient and considerate of stakeholders by:

   a. involving recipients of PSB in the design of behavior support plans,
   b. considering the values of recipients and implementers of PSB,
   c. considering the skills of implementers of PSB,
   d. securing the approvals and endorsements of recipients and implementers of PSB,
   e. considering the resources and administrative supports needed to implement strategies,
   f. providing the supports needed to sustain the use of effective strategies over time. (p. 135)

Lifestyle outcomes also are stressed in that the effects from behavior support intervention should be comprehensive, durable, and relevant. The fourth critical element articulated by Sugai et al. (2001) concerns a "systems perspective" that encompasses school, family, and community foci, a team-based approach, and administrative support at the local school (e.g., principal, child study groups) and district-wide (e.g., superintendent, school committee) levels.

### Functional Behavioral Assessment (FBA)

   The role of FBA in behavioral consultation to public schools was cited earlier in this article. To reiterate, the purpose of a FBA is to identify influences that set the occasion for and reinforce challenging behaviors, as well as conditions associated with the non-occurrence of problems and the display of acceptable alternatives. Thus, this assessment includes both antecedent (discriminative stimuli, establishing operations) and consequence (positive and negative reinforcement) sources of control. By isolating behavior-function, intervention plans can be tailored to maintaining variables. In the absence of such assessment, intervention selection is arbitrary and ill defined.

   Most research on FBA emerged from treatment studies of seriously challenging behaviors among people with developmental disabilities using an experimental-analog methodology (Iwata, Dorsey, Slifer, Bauman, & Richman, 1982). In recent years, increased attention has been focused on FBA in the public schools, in part driven by consensus-determined approaches to behavior support and the mandate of IDEA 1997. Several developments are noteworthy:

   1. To be most effective, FBA must be adapted to the practical constraints of public school settings. In essence, assessment methods

must be "user friendly" because they are simple to understand and do not distract from routine academic instruction.

2. Although behavioral consultants may be called upon to complete a FBA for students, a dominant concern is that teachers, counselors, and school psychologists learn the skills to conduct these assessments independently. Various models of technical assistance consultation will be required to build the necessary competencies among school staff (Drasgow et al., 1999; Northrup et al., 1994).

3. FBA has been used most often with students who have severe developmental and intellectual disabilities, and, infrequently, with those who have mild, high incidence disorders such as learning disabilities and emotional problems. Although the extension of FBA to this population appears promising (Broussard & Northrup, 1995; Dunlap, White, Vera, Wilson, & Panacek, 1996; Kamps, Ellis, Mancina, Wyble, Greene, & Harvey, 1995), clear standards do not exist concerning FBA procedures for students who are at-risk or have mild disabilities (Scotti, Meers, & Nelson, 2000). The increased involvement of behavioral consultants in the public schools will help refine functional assessment so that it is relevant and adaptable to students that present with diverse challenges.

For a more detailed description of how to conduct FBA in public schools, including recommendations for writing an assessment-derived BSP, the reader is referred to Drasgow et al. (1999) and Sugai et al. (2000).

## *Measurement and Evaluation*

Data-based evaluation is a defining characteristic of applied behavior analysis. Objective measurement of outcome is critical in judging the effects from intervention and making clinical decisions. For behavioral consultation to be accepted and supported by public school administrators, there must be evidence of its efficacy in order that the allocation of personnel and financial resources can be justified.

Apropos to other applied settings, data collection in public schools is performed by practitioners who have multiple and, many times, conflicting, responsibilities. In most situations, classroom teachers are not able to integrate traditional behavioral assessment methods into their daily routines (e.g., frequency counts, interval recording). For consultants, the question is how to introduce data collection systems that yield reliable and valid measures that are also practical and efficient. One option, presented by several investigators (Putnam et al., 2001; Skiba, Peterson, & Williams, 1997; Sugai et al., 2000) is to target natural data sources such as office discipline referrals, in-school detentions, and suspensions. Typically, these events are recorded in public schools and can serve as a useful metric in several ways. First, such data can be analyzed to establish a profile of the discipline practices at a school. Contextual and functional influences on behavior potentially can be gleaned from distribution patterns, for example, the frequency of office discipline referrals according to grade level, individual classrooms, and type of rule infraction. Intervention effectiveness can be evaluated by examining corresponding trends in these measures. Lastly, and as proposed by Sugai et al. (2000), discipline data enable schools to pinpoint the selection of universal, selective, and targeted/intensive interventions.

The gathering of behavior reduction data need not exclude the domain of skill acquisition, particularly since the emphasis of preventive intervention and PBS is the strengthening of academic and interpersonal competencies. In keeping with the preceding discussion about natural data sources, representative measures would be grades, test scores, and the completion and accuracy of academic assignments. Again, these are permanent product measures that are monitored regularly in public schools and, in most cases, would be sensitive to individual student, classroom-wide, and whole-school behavior supports. The utility of curriculum-based measurement (CBM) also should be considered in this regard (Denno, 1992).

The value of social validity assessment cannot be overemphasized. Soliciting opinions from the recipients of behavioral consultation improves the "packaging" and dissemination of programmed interventions. For example, a teacher may report satisfaction with the outcome from a classroom-wide behavior support plan but describe it as being too burdensome and effort-intensive. Attention then would be devoted to refining aspects of the plan so that it is received better by future teachers. Similarly, consultants should strive to measure and evaluate the *process* of service delivery by having teachers and other school personnel report satisfaction and acceptability ratings. Some indicators here would be how staff view the professional abilities of the consultant, the manner in which consultation was delivered (e.g., meetings, training sessions), the responsiveness of the consultant when problems were encountered, and so forth. Other process variables such as the time spent on specific tasks (e.g., telephone calls, report writing) and the associated fee-for-service charges also can serve as measures of consultation efficiency.

Measurement and evaluation issues should extend beyond the immediate effects from behavioral consultation to include the long-term outcome of intervention. The study of maintenance, or generalization over time, has been underreported in the published literature (Luiselli, 1999) but is integral to clinical success. By demonstrating that intervention plans lead to durable change months and years following consultation, schools are more likely to continue investing resources and support. Furthermore, maintenance evaluation can reveal when modifications must be made to programming, as in situations where there is a deterioration in previously effective plans or additional procedures should be added to bolster progress further. Although few in number, several reports suggest that maintenance of whole-school behavior support interventions can be achieved over the course of multiple academic years (Luiselli, Putnam, & Sunderland, 2001; Nakasato, 2000; Taylor-Greene & Kartub, 2000).

## *Factors Associated with Successful Behavioral Consultation*

In concluding this overview of the focus, scope, and practice of behavioral consultation to public schools, several recommendations are presented to increase successful implementation. Certainly, the technical skills, knowledge, academic training, and experience of the consultant are paramount in determining effective practice. However, harking back to the earlier statement by Gutkin and Curtiss (1982), interpersonal skills are equally important. This factor relates to how a consultant applies her or his skills, as well as the "business of getting things done."

1. The role and responsibilities of the consultant should be articulated clearly at the onset of service delivery. Staff who receive consultation should understand why a referral was made for specialty services and what the intended outcome is intended to be. In as much detail as possible the consultant should describe the activities that she or he will undertake, the requests that will be made of the staff, and the typical course when addressing learning and behavior challenges.
2. Consultants should defer to school personnel as the "local experts" concerning individual student, classroom-wide, and whole-school objectives of behavior support. Teachers, therapists, counselors, and administrators interact daily with the school population and, as such, are the most knowledgeable people to inform the consult-

ing professional. The collaborative problem solving approach that defines behavioral consultation focuses naturally on the expertise and contributions of the consultee. Maintaining a high regard for the input given by consultees is the foundation upon which successful consultation is built.

3. Regularity of contact between consultant and staff is another key to successful practice. The consultant should determine a schedule of in-school visits with staff, being specific about the hours spent on site, frequency of contact (e.g., weekly, biweekly, monthly), and activities such as classroom observations, staff meetings, and review of data. Establishing a routine schedule means that the consultant has a predictable and visible presence in the school. The resulting effect is that staff can prepare for the tasks assigned during previous visits, for example, summarizing recording forms or updating student progress during case review.

4. Oral and written communications with staff should avoid jargon-laden technical language, which in most cases does not contribute positively to procedural implementation. Thus, the consultant's educated opinion about establishing operations relative to student disruptive behavior is best posited as a simple explanation of "motivation." Language that is clear, easily understood, acceptable, and adapted to the context of the listener will facilitate success at all levels of the consultation process.

5. Because a consultant makes many requests of school staff, she or he likewise should attend fastidiously to mutual tasks. Telephone calls from consultees should be returned promptly, written reports should be submitted in a timely manner, scheduling should be arranged to accommodate the priorities of the school, and there should be easily-accessed contact with the consultant in "crisis" situations. School staff respect professionals who "do what they say they will do" and demonstrate this behavior during every interaction with them.

6. As a final recommendation, consultants should have knowledge about the administrative hierarchy and policies of public school districts. The function of a local school committee, the direction of school reform in a community, the governing responsibilities of the teacher's union, and the involvement of parent advisory councils all are germane to working productively in public schools. At the level of the individual school, consultants should establish a strong relationship with the building principal who, in most cases, will be responsible for sanctioning team decisions. Just as

the consultant must educate staff in the effective delivery of instructional and behavior support strategies, she or he must be educated about the operation of the receiving environment to realize meaningful and lasting change.

## NOTE

1. The information presented in this article is geared primarily to professionals within the United States. It is recognized that many of the issues and discussion points may include similar, but not necessarily identical, concerns that arise in other developed countries such as the United Kingdom, Australia, and New Zealand.

## REFERENCES

Barlow, D. H., & Hersen, M. (1984). *Single case experimental designs: Strategies for studying behavior change*. New York: Pergamon.

Bergan, J. R., & Kratochwill, T. R. (1990). *Behavioral consultation and therapy*. New York: Plenum Press.

Broussard, C. D., & Northrup, J. (1995). An approach to functional assessment and analysis of disruptive behavior in regular education classrooms. *School Psychology Quarterly, 10*, 151-164.

Deno, S. L. (1992). The nature and development of curriculum based measurement. *Preventing School Failure, 36*, 5-10.

Drasgow, E., Yell, M. L., Bradley, R., & Shriner, J. G. (1999). The IDEA amendments of 1997: A school-wide model for conducting functional behavioral assessments and developing behavior intervention plans. *Education and Treatment of Children, 22*, 244-266.

Dunlap, G., White, R., Vera, A., Wilson, D., & Panacek, L. (1996). The effects of multi-component, assessment-based curricular modifications on the classroom behavior of children with emotional behavior disorders. *Journal of Behavioral Education, 6*, 481-500.

Durand, V. M., & Crimmins, D. B. (1988). Identifying the variables maintaining self-injurious behavior. *Journal of Autism and Developmental Disorders, 18*, 99-117.

Dwyer, K. P., Osher, G., & Warger, W. (1998). *Early warning, timely response: A guide for safe schools*. Washington, DC: U.S. Department of Education.

Gutkin, T. B., & Curtis, M. J. (1982). School-based consultation: Theory and techniques. In C. R. Reynolds & T. B. Gutkin (Eds.), *The handbook of school psychology* (pp. 796-828). New York: Wiley.

Haring, N. G., & De Vault, G. (1996). Family issues and family support: Discussion. In L. K. Keogel, R. L. Koegel, & G. Dunlap (Eds.), *Positive behavioral support: Including people with difficult behavior in the community*. Baltimore, MD: Brookes.

Individuals With Disabilities Education Act (IDEA) Regulations, 34 C.F.R. § Part 300 (1999).

Iwata, B. A., Dorsey, M., Slifer, K. J., Bauman, K. E., & Richman, G. S. (1982). Toward a functional analysis of self-injury. *Analysis and Intervention in Developmental Disabilities*, *2*, 3-20.

Iwata, B. A., Vollmer, T. R., & Zarcone, J. R. (1990). The experimental (functional) analysis of behavior disorders: Methodology, applications, and limitations. In A. C. Repp & N. N. Singh (Eds.), *Perspectives on the use of nonaversive and aversive interventions for persons with developmental disabilities* (pp. 301-330). Sycamore, IL: Sycamore Publishing.

Kamps, D. M., Ellis, C., Mancina, C., Wyble, J., Greene, L., & Harvey, D. (1995). Case studies using functional analysis for young children with behavior risks. *Education and Treatment of Children*, *18*, 243-260.

Kratochwill, T. R., & Bergan, J. R. (1990). *Behavioral consultation in applied settings: An individual guide*. New York: Plenum Press.

Kratochwill, T. R., VanSomeren, K. R., & Sheridan, S. M. (1989). Training behavior consultants: A competency-based model to teach interview skills. *Professional School Psychology*, *4*, 41-58.

Lewis, T. J., Sugai, G., & Colvin, G. (1998). Reducing problem behavior through a school-wide system of effective behavioral support: Investigation of a school-wide social skills training program and contextual interventions. *School Psychology Review*, *27*, 446-459.

Luiselli, J. K. (1999). Maintenance of behavioral interventions. *Mental Health Aspects of Developmental Disabilities*, *1*, 69-76.

Luiselli, J. K., Putnam, R. F., & Handler, M. W. (2001). Improving discipline practices in public schools: Description of a whole-school and district-wide model of behavior analysis consultation. *The Behavior Analyst Today*, *2*, 18-27.

Luiselli, J. K., Putnam, R. F., & Sunderland, M. (2001). *Brief report: Longitudinal evaluation of behavior support intervention in a public middle school*. Manuscript submitted for publication.

Mayer, G. R. (1995). Preventing antisocial behavior in the schools. *Journal of Applied Behavior Analysis*, *28*, 467-478.

Nakasato, J. (2000). Data-based decision making in Hawaii's behavior support effort. *Journal of Positive Behavior Interventions*, *2*, 247-251.

Nelson, J. R., Roberts, M. L., Mathur, S., & Rutherford, R. (1999). Has public policy exceeded our knowledge base? A review of the functional behavioral assessment literature. *Behavioral Disorders*, *24*, 169-179.

Northrup, J., Wacker, D. P., Berg, W. K., Kelly, L., Sasso, G., & DeRaad, A. (1994). The treatment of severe behavior problems in school settings using a technical assistance model. *Journal of Applied Behavior Analysis*, *27*, 33-47.

Rose, L. C., & Gallup, A. M. (1998). The 30th annual Phi Delta Kappa/Gallup poll of the public's attitudes toward the public schools. *Phi Delta Kappan*, *80*, 41-56.

Schwartz, I. S., & Baer, D. M. (1992). Social validity assessments: Is current practice state of the art? *Journal of Applied Behavior Analysis*, *24*, 189-204.

Scott, T. M., Meers, D. T., & Nelson, C. M. (2000). Toward a consensus of functional behavioral assessment for students with mild disabilities in public school contexts: A national survey. *Education and Treatment of Children*, *23*, 265-285.

Skiba, R. J., Peterson, R. L, & Williams, T. (1993). Office referrals and suspensions: Disciplinary intervention in middle schools. *Education and Treatment of Children*, *20*, 295-315.

Sugai, D., & Luiselli, J. K. (1989). Behavioral medicine consultation. In J. Luiselli (Ed.), *Behavioral medicine and developmental disabilities* (pp. 199-225). New York: Springer-Verlag.

Sugai, G., Horner, R. H., Dunlap, G., Hieneman, M., Lewis, T. J., Nelson, C. M., Scott, T., Liaupsin, C., Sailor, W., Turnbull, A. P., Turnbull, H. R., Wickham, D., Wilcox, B., & Ruef, M. (2000). Applying positive behavior support and functional behavioral assessment in schools. *Journal of Positive behavior Interventions*, *2*, 131-143.

Sugai, G., Sprague, J. R., Horner, R. H., & Walker, H. M. (2000). Preventing school violence: The use of office discipline referrals to assess and monitor school-wide discipline interventions. *Journal of Emotional and Behavioral Disorders*, *8*, 94-101.

Taylor-Greene, S. J., & Kartub, D. T. (2000). Durable implementation of school-wide behavior support: The high five program. *Journal of Positive Behavior Interventions*, *2*, 233-235.

Walker, H. M., Horner, R. H., Sugai, G., Bullis, M., Sprague, J. R., Bricker, D., & Kaufman, M. J. (1996). Integrated approaches to preventing antisocial behavior patterns among school-age children and youth. *Journal of Emotional and Behavioral Disorders*, *4*, 193-256.

# The Evolution of Discipline Practices: School-Wide Positive Behavior Supports

George Sugai
Robert Horner

**SUMMARY.** In response to public requests to improve the purpose and structure of discipline systems, schools have increased their emphases on "school-wide" positive behavior support. The thesis of this paper is that the current problem behavior of students in elementary and middle schools requires a preventive, whole-school approach. The foundation for such an approach lies in the emerging technology of positive behavior support. The features of positive behavior support are defined, and their application to whole-school intervention articulated. Finally, the steps that have been used to implement school-wide positive behavior support in over 500 schools across the nation are described. *[Article copies available for a fee from The Haworth Document Delivery Service: 1-800-HAWORTH. E-mail address: <getinfo@haworthpressinc.com> Website:*

George Sugai, PhD, and Robert Horner, PhD, are Professors of Special Education and co-direct the Center on Positive Behavioral Interventions and Supports at the University of Oregon.

Address correspondence to: George Sugai and Robert Horner, Educational and Community Supports, 1235 University of Oregon, Eugene, OR 97403-1235.

The authors express their appreciation to Claudia Vincent for her invaluable support and contribution to the final version of this paper.

The Center is supported by a grant from the Office of Special Education Programs, with additional funding from the Safe and Drug Free Schools Program, US Department of Education (H326S980003).

Opinions expressed herein are those of the authors and do not necessarily reflect the position of the US Department of Education, and such endorsements should not be inferred.

[Haworth co-indexing entry note]: "The Evolution of Discipline Practices: School-Wide Positive Behavior Supports." Sugai, George, and Robert Horner. Co-published simultaneously in *Child & Family Behavior Therapy* (The Haworth Press, Inc.) Vol. 24, No. 1/2, 2002, pp. 23-50; and: *Behavior Psychology in the Schools: Innovations in Evaluation, Support, and Consultation* (ed: James K. Luiselli, and Charles Diament) The Haworth Press, Inc., 2002, pp. 23-50. Single or multiple copies of this article are available for a fee from The Haworth Document Delivery Service [1-800-HAWORTH, 9:00 a.m. - 5:00 p.m. (EST). E-mail address: getinfo@haworthpressinc.com].

**KEYWORDS.** School-wide positive behavior support, school discipline, prevention

In 1968, the publication of Issue #1, Volume I of the *Journal of Applied Behavior Analysis* (*JABA*) marked an important point at which the experimental analysis of behavior extended the application of behavioral principles to the study of human behavior. In this seminal issue, Baer, Wolf, and Risley (1968) laid the foundation for the application of applied behavior analysis (ABA) to the study and improvement of human behavior. Subsequent papers in *JABA* and other behavior-related journals demonstrated functional relations between changes in adult and child behaviors, both academic and social.

Now, 33 years after the publication of the first issue of *JABA,* attention on behavioral practices and processes in classrooms and schools has increased. Most significantly, amendments to the Individuals with Disabilities Education Act (IDEA) (1997) codified "positive behavioral interventions and supports," "functional behavioral assessment" (FBA), and "positive behavior supports" (PBS) into policy and practice and into the business of discipline and classroom and behavior management in every school in America. The purpose of this paper is to describe the status of discipline practices in the context of school-wide PBS and its ABA roots. This discussion is organized into four sections:

   a. need and context for school-wide PBS;
   b. whole-school as the unit of analysis;
   c. defining features of school-wide PBS;
   d. implementation steps for school-wide PBS.

### *NEED AND CONTEXT FOR SCHOOL-WIDE POSITIVE BEHAVIOR SUPPORT*

Although American schools are one of the safest places for children, demands for safer schools have increased because of more attention on acts of school violence, playground "bullies," and student victimization. In fact, concerns about discipline and problem behavior in schools are not new. Over the past 20 years, fighting, violence, vandalism, truancy, lack of discipline, and drug use have been among the top concerns of the general public and teachers (1998 Kappan/Gallup Poll). In addition, efforts to improve educational services and opportunities for students with disabilities and problem behavior have increased, especially in general education settings (P.L. 94-142, IDEA 1997, US Department of Education). Thus, management and control of problem behavior regardless of whether the student does or does not have a disability has drawn increased attention from schools, families, and communities.

However, debates continue regarding where, how and whether students with severe antisocial behavior should be educated in general education settings. When teachers experience situations in which students are violent toward their peers or adults, are insubordinate and noncompliant, run away from school, or disrupt the learning of others, their basic reaction is to engage in actions that decrease or avoid such aversive situations (Gunter, Denny, Jack, & Shores, 1993; Gunter, Jack, DePaepe, Reed, & Harrison, 1994; Jack, Shores, Denny, Gunter, DeBriere, & DePaepe, 1996; Shores, Jack, Gunter, Ellis, DeBriere, & Wehby, 1993). Most school conduct codes and discipline handbooks detail consequence sequences designed to "teach" these students that they have violated a school rule, and that their "choice" of behaviors will not be tolerated. When occurrences of rule-violating behavior increase in frequency and intensity,

a. monitoring and surveillance are increased to "catch" future occurrences of problem behavior,
b. rules and sanctions for problem behavior are restated and reemphasized,
c. the continuum of punishment consequences for repeated rule-violations are extended,
d. efforts are direct toward increasing the consistency with which school staff react to displays of antisocial behavior,
e. "bottom-line" consequences are accentuated to inhibit future displays of problem behavior.

Ironically, when these types of solutions are used with students with established histories of severe antisocial behavior, increases in the intensity and frequency of antisocial behavior are likely (Mayer, 1995; Mayer & Butterworth, 1979; Mayer, Butterworth, Nafpaktitis, & Sulzer-Azaroff, 1983).

At the school and district levels, reactive responses to occurrences of antisocial behavior also are likely. For example, when significant acts of school violence are experienced (e.g., shooting, bomb threats, illegal drug activity), schools direct attention toward:

a. establishing zero tolerance policies;
b. hiring security personnel;
c. adding surveillance cameras and metal detectors;
d. adopting school uniform policies;
e. using in- and out-of-school detention, suspension, and expulsion;
f. establishing alternative school placements and programs. (US Department of Health and Human Services, 2001)

Ironically, the effectiveness of these policy and structural responses has not been adequately studied, demonstrated, and validated.

Increases in the uses of these reactive individual teacher and school responses are predictable because they often are associated with relatively immediate (albeit short-term) reductions in serious problem behavior (McCord, 1995; Patterson, Reid, & Dishion, 1992). However, alone they have been ineffective in creating more sustained positive school climates that prevent the development and occurrence of antisocial behavior in schools. In the long term, reactive and punishment-based responses create a false sense of security. Environments of authoritarian control are established. Antisocial behavior events are inadvertently reinforced. Most importantly, the school's primary function to provide opportunities for teaching and academic engagement is decreased.

By themselves, these reactive responses are insufficient to meet the challenge of creating safe schools and positive school climates, and maximizing teaching time and learning opportunities. Numerous sources have advocated for the adoption of more proactive (positive and preventive) approaches to shape individual and school-wide discipline responses (e.g., Center for the Study and Prevention of School Violence, Center for Positive Behavioral Interventions and Supports, Institute on Violence and Destructive Behavior, American Psychological Association, Center on Effective Collaboration and Practice, Office of Safe and Drug Free Schools, Office of Special Education Programs). For example, a recent report on the prevention of school violence published by the Office of the US Surgeon General and prepared by the US Department of Health and Human Services recommends that schools emphasize prevention-based strategies that, for example,

a. break-up the contingencies that maintain antisocial behavior networks,
b. increase rates and opportunities for academic success,
c. establish and sustain positive school and classroom climates,
d. give priority to an agenda of primary prevention. (US Department of Health and Human Services, 2001)

Similar recommendations for a prevention-based response to school violence have been put forth by leading researchers (Elliott, Hamburg, & Williams, 1998; Gottfredson, 1987; Gottfredson, Gottfredson, & Hybl, 1993; Gottfredson, Gottfredson, & Skroban, 1996; Guerra & Williams, 1996; Mayer, 1995; Skiba & Deno, 1991; Walker, Horner, Sugai, Bullis, Sprague, Bricker, & Kaufman, 1996).

Incongruously, classroom practices and behavior management strategies that support a prevention agenda have been known for over 40 years. For instance, Madsen, Becker, Thomas and colleagues published a series of studies demonstrating the importance of establishing and approving appropriate classroom rules and behavior to achieve positive classroom atmospheres (Becker, Madsen, Arnold, & Thomas, 1967; Madsen, Becker, & Thomas, 1968; Thomas, Becker, & Armstrong, 1968). In addition, in the 1970s educators and psychologists (Berliner, 1985; Brophy, 1979; Brophy & Good, 1986; Emmer, Evertson, & Anderson, 1980; Evertson & Emmer, 1982; Kounin, 1970; Rosenshine, 1985; Rosenshine & Stevens, 1986) highlighted the importance of academic engagement and success in managing and preventing disruptive classrooms.

Although less empirically supported, the importance and features of a prevention agenda at the school-wide level also have solid historical and applied foundations. For example, Mayer, Sulzer-Azaroff, and colleagues (Mayer, 1995; Mayer et al., 1983; Sulzer-Azaroff & Mayer, 1994, 1986) have demonstrated improvements in social behavior and school climate by adopting constructive disciplinary practices (e.g., teaching and encouraging school expectations and behaviors) which led to reductions of vandalism, assaults, and other antisocial behavior (Mayer & Butterworth, 1979; Mayer et al., 1983). Ron Nelson and his colleagues have replicated similar positive outcomes in reducing rates of disruptive behavior and office discipline referrals (Nelson, 1996; Nelson, Johnson, & Marshand-Martella, 1996; Nelson, Martella, & Galand, 1998; Nelson, Martella, & Marchand-Martella, in press). Finally, recent efforts have demonstrated improvements in school discipline patterns when a positive and preventive approach is emphasized (Colvin, Kame'enui, & Sugai, 1993; Taylor-Greene, Brown, Nelson, Longton, Gassman, Cohen, Swartz, Horner, Sugai, & Hall, 1997).

In sum, research support for responding to concerns about school violence, problem behavior, and lack of discipline has a long history. As schools have moved beyond simply excluding children with problem behavior to a policy of active development of social behaviors, expectations for discipline systems have changed. Research indicates that

a. punishment and exclusion are ineffective when used without a proactive support system (Gottfredson, Karweit, & Gottfredson, 1989; Mayer, 1995; Tolan & Guerra, 1994),
b. behavioral principles exist for organizing successful support for individual students with problem behavior (Alberto & Troutman, 1999; Kazdin, 1982; Kerr & Nelson, 1983; Vargas, 1977; Wolery, Bailey, & Sugai, 1988),
c. effective instruction is linked to reduced behavior problems (Becker, 1971; Heward, Heron, Hill, & Trap-Porter, 1984; Jenson, Sloane, & Young, 1988; Lee, Sugai, & Horner, 1999; Sulzer-Azaroff & Mayer, 1986), and
d. school-wide systems of behavior support can be an efficient system for reducing the incidence of disruptive and antisocial behavior in schools (Chapman & Hofweber, 2000; Colvin & Fernandez, 2000; Horner & Sugai, 2000; Lohrman-O'Rourke et al., 2000; Nakasato, 2000; Nelson, in press; Nersesian et al., 2000; Sadler, 2000; Taylor-Greene et al., 1997; Taylor-Greene & Kartub, 2000; Walker et al., 1996)

## WHOLE-SCHOOL AS THE UNIT OF ANALYSIS FOR POSITIVE BEHAVIOR SUPPORT

From these behavioral foundations and research validations, systemic efforts to implement and sustain effective behavioral interventions have evolved. These efforts focus on taking specific behavioral strategies, practices, and processes beyond the behavior of the individual. The effect has been an increased emphasis on the collective behaviors, working structures, and routines of educators and focusing on the whole school as the unit of analysis (Colvin, Kame'enui, & Sugai, 1993; Colvin, Sugai, & Kame'enui, 1994; Lewis & Sugai, 1999; Sugai & Horner, 1999; Sugai, Horner, Dunlap, Hieneman, Lewis, Nelson, Scott, Liaupsin, Sailor, Turnbull, Turnbull, Wickham, Reuf, & Wilcox, 2000). By focusing on the whole school as the unit of analysis, efforts to arrange learning and social environments for the adoption and sustained use of research-validated practices have become increasingly important in addressing the social behavioral needs of all students in schools. Thus, schools are being asked to organize their resources, activities, and initiatives in ways that efficiently occasion high quality and sustained improvements and positive change in teacher and student behavior.

With the focus on schools to improve school cultures, research-validated strategies and practices remain an important part of the school-wide discipline and behavior management picture. However, systemic factors, like administrative support, team-based problem solving, and data-based decision making, assume even greater importance. This expanded view of school-wide discipline has caused behavior analysts to expand their unit of study to include systems or organized collections of adult behavior. The result has been the evolution of school-wide "positive behavior support" (PBS). Positive behavior support is the combination of four key elements:

   a. outcomes (e.g., academic achievement, social competence, employment options) that are uniquely defined and "valued" by stakeholders (e.g., students, families, teachers, employers),
   b. a behavioral and biomedical science of human behavior that provides fundamental principles for the design of support,
   c. empirically validated practices for achieving identified outcomes in applied contexts,
   d. the implementation of validated practices in the context of the systems change needed for durable and generalized effects. (Sugai et al., 2000)

Thus, PBS has been described as the broad range of systemic and individualized strategies for achieving important social and learning outcomes while preventing problem behavior (OSEP Center on Positive Behavioral Interventions and Supports, 2001).

## *DEFINING FEATURES OF SCHOOL-WIDE POSITIVE BEHAVIOR SUPPORT*

Given this definition and characterization, whole-school PBS can be operationalized by its

   a. integration of four critical elements,
   b. multi-systems perspective,
   c. continuum of behavior support.

### *Integration of Four Crtical Elements*

Schools are learning that the "tricks" (i.e., strategies, practices, interventions) of behavior and classroom management are insufficient to achieve meaningful and sustained improvements in student behavior, especially when the problem behaviors are chronic and intense. More importantly, the behavior management capacity of the school is not enhanced when the focus is on reacting to one situation at a time. Thus, schools are integrating effective practices with four critical elements (see Figure 1).

First, school-wide PBS is guided by a careful acknowledgement and consideration of outcomes (e.g., academic achievement, social competence, career/work opportunities) that are valued by significant stakeholders (e.g., students, family members, teachers, employers). Schools must be able to articulate measurable student and staff outcomes if they are to be successful and efficient in

  a. selecting and presenting relevant curriculum,
  b. conducting meaningful educational assessments and evaluations,
  c. utilizing dwindling resources,
  d. creating positive school climates.

Second, school-wide PBS is based on the adoption and sustained use of research-validated practices and curricula that maximize achievement of student and teacher outcomes. Schools must resist the "impulsive" and reactive temptation to discard proven practices whenever a

FIGURE 1. Four Elements of School-Wide Positive Behavior Support

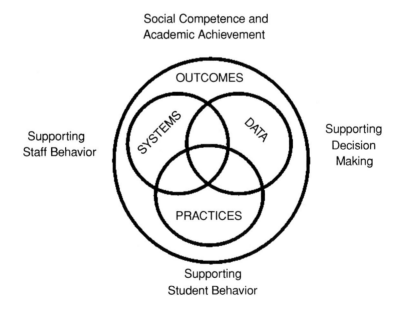

new initiative, curriculum, or strategy is presented. Consideration of new or different practices should be guided by questions of trustworthiness, effectiveness, efficiency, and relevance (Carnine, 1997, 1995, 1992; Peters & Heron, 1992; Sugai & Horner, 1999), for example:

a. Are educationally and/or socially relevant outcomes specified?
b. Will the efficiency of outcome achievement be improved (e.g., time, effort)?
c. Is research accessible and supportive?
d. Are adoption costs (e.g., training, purchase) justifiable?
e. Are sound conceptual and theoretical foundations indicated?
f. Are successful local applications available?
g. Does evidence exist to support a change in current practice?
h. Have previous practices been implemented with high fidelity?
i. Are supports in place to occasion and sustain implementation?

Third, school-wide PBS relies on data to guide decision making (Lewis-Palmer, Sugai, & Larson, 1999; Sugai, Sprague, Horner, & Walker, 2000). Data-based decision making is applied at many levels (i.e., individual, classroom, school), with multiple individuals (i.e., student, teacher, administrator, support staff), across contexts (e.g., general vs. special education, school vs. home), and with multiple outcomes (e.g., reading, grades, attendance, discipline referrals). As indicated above, data should be used to guide the selection of new practices. In addition, data must be collected to evaluate the effectiveness and quality of implementation of current practices (individual or system), characterize and understand a situation (e.g., student's performance, school setting, teacher instruction), guide the development of new or modification of current practices, and monitor student or program progress.

Finally, school-wide PBS considers the systems (e.g., processes, routines, working structures, administrative supports) that are needed to ensure consideration of valued outcomes, research validated practices, and data-based decision making. Systems refer to the effectiveness, efficiency, and relevance, for example, of:

a. organizational working structures (e.g., committees),
b. policies and guiding principles (e.g., mission statement, school purpose),
c. operating routines (e.g., faculty meetings, communications, problem solving, action planning),
d. resource supports (e.g., families, special education, counseling),
e. staff/professional development structures and opportunities,
f. administrative leadership (e.g., participation, visibility, decision making).

### Multi-Systems Perspective

Together the four above elements of school-wide PBS emphasize the need for schools to improve the effectiveness, efficiency, and relevance with which they do the business of supporting student behavior. However, this task can be daunting unless schools organize their work around a four systems perspective:

a. school-wide,
b. classroom,
c. non-classroom,
d. individual student. (Lewis & Sugai, 1999; Sugai & Horner, 1999; Sugai et al., 2000) (See Figure 2.)

*School-Wide Discipline Systems.* A review of the published research and demonstrations of school-wide discipline implementations (Comer, 1985; Gottfredson, 1987; Gottfredson, Gottfredson, & Skroban, 1996; Knoff, 1995; Mayer, Butterworth, Nafpaktitis, & Sulzer-Azaroff, 1983; Sprick & Nolet, 1991; Sulzer-Azaroff & Mayer, 1994; Weissberg, Caplan, & Sivo, 1989) indicates six common features:

1. *Statement of Purpose* that expresses the explicit objective of and rationale for a school-wide discipline structure. This statement should
   a. be positively phrased;
   b. focus on all staff, all students, and all school settings;
   c. link academic and behavioral outcomes.

For example, *George Ikuma School is a community of learners. We are here to learn, grow, and become good citizens.*
2. *Clearly Defined Expectations and Behavioral Examples* that permit consistent communications and establish an effective verbal community for all staff and students and across all settings. Five or fewer positively stated expectations are expressed in a few common words, for example, Respect Ourselves, Respect Others, Respect Environment, Respect Learning.
3. *Procedures for Teaching Expectations and Expected Behaviors* that staff can use to ensure students know and understand school-wide rules, expectations, routines, and positive and negative consequences. Basically, the same procedures that are used to teach academic skills and concepts are applied:

   a. teach directly (tell/show, practice, test),
   b. supervise use,
   c. provide positive and/or corrective feedback.

4. *Procedures for Encouraging Expected Behaviors* that are organized and provided along a continuum of:

    a. tangible to social forms of feedback,
    b. staff to student administered,
    c. high to low frequency,
    d. predictable to unpredictable presentations.

5. *Procedures for Preventing Problem Behavior* that are organized and provided along a continuum of:

    a. minor to major rule violations
    b. increasing intensity and aversiveness of responses.

These procedures should provide clear definitions and examples of rule-violating behaviors, focus on preventing future occurrences of problem behavior by teaching and strengthening prosocial replacement behaviors, consider the contextual function (purpose) of rule-violating behavior, and delineate between teacher versus administrator managed problem behaviors.

6. *Procedures for Record Keeping and Decision Making* that allow for regular (weekly and monthly) feedback to staff about the status of school-wide discipline implementation efforts. Teams should be able to examine patterns at least across students, time, locations, behavior types (appropriate and inappropriate), consequences, and staff members to improve the effectiveness, efficiency, and relevance of their efforts.

*Classroom Setting Systems.* Behavior management practices and routines in classrooms have many parallels to the six features of school-wide discipline systems. However, teachers also must organize their classrooms in ways that support the presentation and use of academic instruction and curriculum (Colvin & Lazar, 1997, Gettinger, 1988; Kame'enui & Darch, 1995; Martens & Kelly, 1993; Northwest Regional Education Laboratory, 1984; Smith & Misra, 1992). For example, teachers must directly teach students expectations and routines for typical classroom activities (e.g., large vs. small group instruction, whole vs. independent activities, making transitions between activities) such as:

    a. being prepared (e.g., materials, taught the features and expectations of typical routines),
    b. asking for assistance,
    c. getting teacher attention,
    d. solving problems.

Direct instruction on these expectations and routines should occur at critical times of the year (e.g., first day and first week, just prior to and following grading periods or vacation breaks) and practiced and reviewed regularly (e.g., daily/weekly) (Paine et al., 1983; Sprick, Sprick, & Garrison, 1992; Wong & Wong, 1991).

Teachers also must maximize their use of fundamental behavior management practices. For example, teachers must engage in active supervision (e.g., move, scan, interact) so that students learn that teachers are monitoring and evaluating their social behaviors. Teachers must have frequent positive contacts with students individually and as groups. Latham (1992) recommends that teachers maintain a ratio of six to eight positive social engagements for every negative interaction to promote a positive social classroom climate and to support instructional success. Teachers must organize their classroom environments in ways

FIGURE 2. Multiple Systems of School-Wide Positive Behavior Support

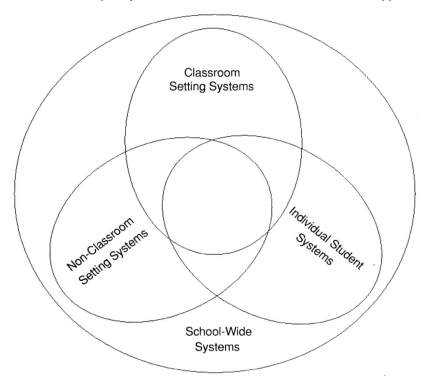

that communicate the importance of teaching and learning (e.g., student work, current events), prompt socially desirable behaviors (e.g., posted rules, positive reinforcers), and maximize the delivery of instruction (e.g., curriculum, seating arrangements, supplies).

Teachers must adopt and sustain their use of curriculum that is empirically supported, culturally and developmentally appropriate, modifiable to accommodate individual differences, and outcome-oriented. Finally, teachers must have opportunities to develop and maintain fluency with the delivery of the above practices through, for example, regular staff development experiences, formative collection and review of student progress, and constructive supervisory feedback.

*Non-Classroom Setting Systems.* School settings, like hallways, restrooms, parking lots, and cafeterias present a different set of behavior management challenges. Typically, these settings are characterized by large numbers of students, strong social or student-to-student interaction emphasis, relatively minimum adult presence in number and influence, and limited interpersonal relationships between adults and students. Behavior management in these non-instructional contexts must emphasize supervision that is overt, active and efficient (Colvin & Lazar, 1997; Colvin, Sugai, Good, & Lee, 1997; Kame'enui & Darch, 1995; Lewis, Colvin, & Sugai, in press; Sprick, Sprick, & Garrison, 1992). First, students must be taught directly how school-wide expectations relate to the specific expected behaviors and routines for specific non-classroom settings, and they must have regular opportunities to practice these expected behaviors and routines.

Second, all staff members must engage in active supervision when assigned to a non-classroom setting or when moving through these environments. Active supervision can be operationalized as:

a. scanning–keeping head up and looking for rule following and violating behaviors,
b. moving–routinely move through locations where expected behaviors are more difficult for students to demonstrate or where large numbers of students congregate or transition,
c. interact–make prosocial (positive and preventive) contacts with as many different students as possible (Latham's 6-8 to 1 rule).

Third, all staff members must provide "precorrections" (Colvin, Sugai, & Patching, 1991) in situations where rule-violating behaviors are likely or with individual students in situations where problem behaviors are probable. Precorrections are structured reminders or practice that are presented *before* a student or group of students enter into a situation in which problem behaviors have been displayed in the past. For example, teachers precorrect students about appropriate ways to use playground equipment as they move from their classrooms to recess. Bus drivers remind students about acceptable hallway behaviors as they exit the bus and enter the school. Supervisors give students verbal reminders about keeping their hands and feet to themselves as they move from the playground into the hallways and into their classrooms.

Finally, if all staff members do not provide positive reinforcement for student displays of rule- and expectation-following behaviors, they cannot expect displays of these behaviors in the future, especially when competing problem behaviors receive reinforcement from peers and when adult presence is insufficient to inhibit problem behaviors. Colvin, Sugai, Good, and Lee (1997) demonstrated that student behavior is functionally related to supervisor behavior. In settings where active supervision was absent, problem behaviors were more likely to be observed regardless of the number of staff members who were present. Given the competing factors that occasion and maintain unacceptable behaviors, staff must provide overt and high rates of specific and general positive reinforcement for rule-following behaviors. Students must learn that expectation-following behaviors are important and valued by adults.

*Individual Student Support Systems.* Systems of PBS for students whose behaviors have proven to be unresponsive to general school- and classroom-wide systems must be more specialized, comprehensive, and individualized, and of higher intensity (Sugai et al., 2000). Individual student systems of PBS have been characterized as having, for example:

a. a team-based approach to problem solving,
b. a "function-based" approach to behavioral assessment and behavior intervention planning,
c. a person-centered approach to comprehensive intervention and service planning,
d. an emphasis on individualized and targeted social skills and self-management instruction,
e. an overt link with school-wide academic and behavioral expectations,
f. an early identification and intervention philosophy. (Horner, 1994; O'Neill et al., 1997; Sugai, Lewis-Palmer, & Hagan-Burke, 1999-2000)

To ensure that these characteristics are implemented with high fidelity, behavioral competence must be available daily and within the schools in which behavioral programming is required. A sample of areas of behavioral competencies related to individual student support is listed below:

1. School-wide PBS systems, practices, outcomes, and data-based decision making.
2. Functional behavioral assessment-based behavior intervention planning.
3. Multi-disciplinary team-based problem solving and facilitation.
4. Case management facilitation and evaluation.
5. Coordination of cross-disciplinary planning and intervention implementation.
6. Staff training and implementation support.
7. Specialized design of instruction, curriculum accommodations, and instructional delivery strategies.
8. Family support and communication.

### *Continuum of Behavior Support*

Finally, PBS relies on a continuum of behavior support in which the intensity of behavior support necessarily increases relative to increases in the behavioral needs and challenges of the student (Walker et al., 1996) across the above four systems (see Figure 3). This continuum also iterates how a prevention based perspective is applied across all students within a school. The goal of primary prevention is to inhibit the development of problem behavior by emphasizing the teaching and encouraging desired social behaviors, maximizing academic success, and removing the factors that promote and sustain problem behavior. Secondary prevention strategies focus on removing or reducing the impact of risk factors (e.g., poverty, unsafe neighborhoods, lack of supervision) that students bring to school by bolstering the availability of protective factors (e.g., specialized community and/or school supports, remedial programming, family assistance). Tertiary prevention is focused on reducing the complexity, intensity, severity of problem behaviors that become well-established in the behavioral repertoire of individual students.

When the interplay among outcomes, practices, systems, and data; multiple systems; and continua of behavior supports are considered collectively, the importance of the "school-as-the-unit of analysis" becomes more apparent and important. Educators will need to look beyond basic behavior and classroom management and toward the collective functioning of the members of the school community.

FIGURE 3. Continuum of School-Wide Positive Behavior Support

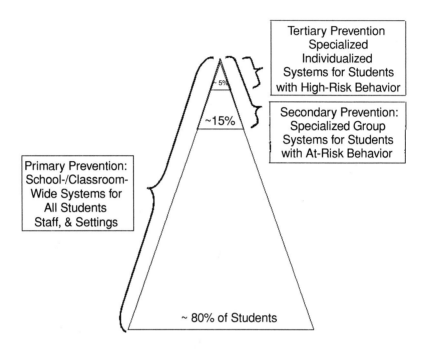

Tertiary Prevention
Specialized
Individualized
Systems for Students
with High-Risk Behavior

~5%

~15%

Secondary Prevention:
Specialized Group
Systems for Students
with At-Risk Behavior

Primary Prevention:
School-/Classroom-
Wide Systems for
All Students
Staff, & Settings

~ 80% of Students

## *IMPLEMENTATION OF SCHOOL-WIDE POSITIVE BEHAVIOR SUPPORT*

When schools experience challenging situations, a common response is to organize staff development events in which "experts" in the area of concern validate and describe the problems or concerns, present a range of possible solutions, and encourage staff to consider the adoption of one or more proposed solutions. When these events are completed, the assumption is that staff members will adopt and implement a solution. Unfortunately, depending on the capacity of the staff and the level of available supports, the quality and sustainability of the implementation can be highly variable and short-lived (Latham, 1988; Slavin, 1989). The school-wide PBS approach has combined its behavior analytic roots with the adoption of practices and principles of organizational behavior management (Axelrod, 1991; Binder, 1991; Gilbert, 1978; Gilbert & Gilbert, 1992; Lindsley, 1992) to improve a school's capacity to respond. In particular, schools simultaneously must consider outcomes, data-based decision making, research-validated practices, and systems in their staff development efforts. The goal is to establish "host environments" that provide the processes and supports that increase a school's capacity to adopt and sustain the use of evidence-based practices (Zins & Ponte, 1990). Five basic steps characterize the establishment of these host environments and implementation of a school-wide PBS approach (see Figure 4).

### Step 1. Establish Leadership Team

Individual staff members cannot affect change that substantially improves the manner in which systems function. School-wide leadership teams are needed to guide the implementation of school-wide PBS. This team should be composed of individuals who are respected by their colleagues, are representative of the school (e.g., by grade level or department), collectively have behavioral competence, have a regular and efficient means of communicating with the school staff as a whole, and are endorsed actively and vigorously by their principal. Principals must be members of this team because they have unique leadership capacities and decision making authority. Parents also are recommended to serve as team members because they can provide a voice and link to the school for families and community members. This team should meet regularly (at least monthly), and its meetings should be guided by data and a proactive problem solving approach.

Schools should not "add" this team to their administrative organizations without first assessing what team or committee structures already exist. From an efficiency perspective, schools should endorse and activate leadership teams that have clearly and uniquely described

    a. purpose statements,
    b. target groups,
    c. measurable outcome/progress indicators,
    d. memberships,
    e. relationships with school improvement goals and objectives.

Whenever possible, the number of committees and teams should be minimized to avoid redundancies and inefficiencies, and a single school-wide leadership role should be established regarding all behavior related initiatives, actions, and decisions. This team has the responsibility for reviewing school needs and establishing staff and school improvement action plans, including staff development activities.

FIGURE 4. Implementation Steps for School-Wide PBS

Establishing a School-Wide Positive Behavior Support System

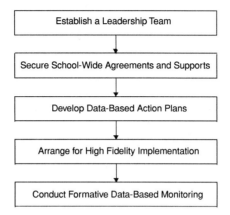

## Step 2. Secure School-Wide Agreements and Supports

If schools are to establish the capacity to support the efficient adoption and sustained use of evidence-based practices, leadership teams must secure staff agreements regarding the

a. nature and priority of staff development efforts and needs,
b. long term (3-4 year) commitment and investment in the effort,
c. importance of taking a preventive and instructional approach to behavior management and school-wide discipline.

To maximize the impact of action plan efforts, we recommend that action plans not be put into full implementation until more than 80% of the staff support these agreements.

In addition to staff agreements, adequate resource support is needed to maximize achievement of outcomes. Fiscal supports, implementation materials, ongoing training opportunities, time, etc., are needed. Much of this support is arranged and/or provided by school administrators who continuously make decisions about resource allocations, monitor and occasion compliance to agreements, and staffing arrangements.

## *Step 3. Develop Data-Based Action Plan*

After the leadership team has secured general school-wide agreements and supports, data are collected and reviewed to determine which school practices need to be adopted, maintained, improved, and/or eliminated within each of the four school-wide systems. A variety of data types should be reviewed, for example:

a. attendance and tardy patterns;
b. office discipline referrals;
c. detention, suspension, and expulsions rates; and
d. behavioral incidence data.

In addition, valuable information can be obtained from school staff through self-assessment inventories, surveys, or checklists. For example, Sugai and colleagues have developed a self-assessment instrument (Effective Behavior Support Survey) that guides school personnel through a process to identify the extent to which key practices and processes are "in place" and need "to be improved" across school-wide, classroom, nonclassroom, and individual student systems (Lewis & Sugai, 1999; Sugai, Horner, & Todd, 2000). Based on a review of response patterns across the entire staff and an examination of school discipline data, an action plan is developed. A sample of items from the EBS Survey and from each of the four systems is given in Figure 5.

An action plan usually focuses on efforts to improve one system-related objective at a time. Typical of most action plans, PBS action plans indicate

a. measurable outcomes,
b. a 1-3 year timeline of events,
c. participating and leadership staff members,
d. specific activities that lead to measurable outcomes,
e. staff development and training activities,
f. resource and support needs.

As emphasized in the EBS Survey, PBS action plans should focus on the identification, adoption, and sustained use of research-validated and best practices. Most teams begin with an action plan that focuses on establishing or enhancing the school-wide discipline system that is foundational for the other three systems and can involve all staff, all students, and all settings. However, consideration should be directed toward all four of the systems described previously:

a. school-wide,
b. non-classroom settings,
c. classrooms,
d. individual students.

### Step 4. Arrange for High Fidelity of Implementation

A school could purchase or develop the best available school-wide discipline curriculum and write the best lesson plans for teaching classroom expectations, and still fail to achieve its action plan outcomes. This failure is not necessarily because interest and motivation are lacking but because the capacity to implement the features of their action plan with high fidelity (accuracy) over time is lacking.

Schools should not attempt to implement any action plan without high confidence that *all* staff are fluent with the skills and strategies of the plan, adequate supports are available to sustain staff member implementation efforts, and appropriate leadership is in place to guide the implementation effort. For example, before the practices and strategies of any action plan are implemented fully, school-wide PBS systems strive toward

a. team-based leadership and implementation,
b. agreements from at least 80% of the staff to implement,
c. active and strong administrative leadership and support,
d. high skill fluency before implementation by any staff member (i.e., opportunities to practice),
e. practical and efficient aides for implementation (e.g., scripts, checklists),
f. adequate professional development and training opportunities,
g. high levels of positive reinforcement for staff implementation efforts and successes.

### Step 5. Conduct Formative Data-Based Monitoring

One of the best positive reinforcers to support school-wide PBS implementation efforts is knowledge that action plan outcomes are being achieved. However, to be able to judge whether adequate progress is being made, data systems must be in place. A variety of data types can be collected, for example, attendance and tardy rates, suspensions and expulsions. One of the best naturally available data sources is behavioral incidents data that usually are collected in the form of office discipline referrals (ODR). Like any data source, ODR data are only as good as the systems that are in place to determine when to give and process them.

FIGURE 5. Sample of Items from the EBS Survey and from Each of the Four Systems

| School-Wide Systems Items: |
| --- |
| 2. Expected student behaviors are taught directly. |
| 3. Expected student behaviors are rewarded regularly. |
| 6. Distinctions between office vs. classroom managed problem behaviors are clear. |
| 10. School administrator is an active participant on the behavior support team. |
| 11. Staff receives regular (monthly/quarterly) feedback on behavior patterns. |
| 14. School-wide behavior support team has a budget for (a) teaching students, (b) ongoing rewards, and (c) annual staff planning. |

| Non-Classroom Setting System Items: |
| --- |
| 2. School-wide expected student behaviors are taught in non-classroom settings. |
| 3. Supervisors actively supervise (move, scan, and interact) students in non-classroom settings. |
| 4. Rewards exist for meeting expected student behaviors in non-classroom settings. |
| 7. Staff receive regular opportunities for developing and improving active supervision skills. |
| 8. Status of student behavior and management practices are evaluated quarterly from data. |

| Classroom Setting System Items: |
| --- |
| 3. Expected student behavior and routines in classrooms are taught directly. |
| 4. Expected student behaviors are acknowledged regularly (positively reinforced) (> 4 positives to 1 negative). |
| 6. Procedures for expected and problem behaviors are consistent with school-wide procedures. |
| 8. Instruction and curriculum materials are matched to student ability (math, reading, language). |
| 9. Students experience high rates of academic success ($\geq$ 75% correct). |
| 11. Transitions between instructional and non-instructional activities are efficient and orderly. |

| Individual Student Support System Items: |
| --- |
| 1. Assessments are conducted regularly to identify students with chronic problem behaviors. |
| 3. A behavior support team responds promptly (within 2 working days) to students who present chronic problem behaviors. |
| 5. Local resources are used to conduct functional assessment-based behavior support planning (~10 hrs/week/student). |
| 6. Significant family and/or community members are involved when appropriate and possible. |
| 8. Behavior is monitored and feedback provided regularly to the behavior support team and relevant staff. |

Every ODR is representative of the decisions and actions of three entities: the student who engages in a rule-violating behavior, the staff member who observes the rule-violating behavior and initiates the ODR, and the administrator who processes the ODR. Each one of these individuals influences whether an ODR is counted, and what is highlighted in the referral.

Thus, to increase confidence in the data that are used to monitor a school-wide PBS system, three conditions must be satisfied. First, "good" (reliable and valid) information must be collected and entered. For example, for school-wide discipline systems, clear and discriminating definitions for the range of rule-violating behaviors must be developed, efficient steps for processing ODRs must be specified, a range of consequences should be specified, etc. Schools should only collect information that will be used to answer questions, evaluate progress, and improve action plan practices. Collecting data without a clear reason is likely to hinder the sustained use of general data-based decision making.

Second, mechanisms and processes should be in place for storing, manipulating, and summarizing data. Usually, a staff member assumes responsibility for entering ODR information into a spreadsheet or database software program and "builds" macros and formulas for creating tables and graphs. Unfortunately, the level of expertise required to operate this system is high, and the speed with which reports and graphs can be produced is not sufficient for daily or weekly decision making. A number of data management developers are attempting to address these efficiency and relevance questions. One example is a Web-based program called the "School-Wide Information System" (SWIS) (go to *www.swis.org* for information). SWIS allows school staff to enter password protected ODR information (e.g., problem behavior type, location, time of day, grade, possible motivation) through any platform that can access the Internet and produce immediately a number of standard tabular and/or graphic displays (e.g., # of referrals/day/month, # by location, # by time of day) or customizable displays (e.g., by individual student, by grade, by teacher). Staff members are more likely to engage in data-based decision making if the effort, processes, and technical skills for data collection, summarization, and presentation are not excessively time-consuming, effortful, or complicated.

Third, structures and processes must be in place to occasion and facilitate data-based decision making. For example, a schedule for bi-weekly data presentations and reviews to all staff should be in place. A team-based data review process should precede presentation to all staff. Specific actions or steps should evolve from each data-review activity. Being able to see change in student performance can be an effective and relevant positive reinforcer for sustaining staff implementation efforts.

## CONCLUSION

The purpose of this paper is to describe how school-wide PBS has evolved out of a need for a more proactive approach to school discipline and safety and from a strong behavior analytic tradition of studying and improving human behavior. PBS is defined in terms that reflect this need and tradition, and features of school-wide PBS are summarized. Most importantly, a central message is that PBS is not a collection of behavior modification practices. Rather, PBS represents a balanced integration of four key features:

a. clearly defined and socially important outcomes for students and their families and teachers,
b. research-validated practices,
c. data-based decision making processes,
d. systems that support high fidelity implementation.

Finally, a generic five-step implementation process for school-wide PBS is proposed as a way to operationalize these four features. Central to this process is a strong bias toward establishing structures and processes that increase the capacity of a school to adopt and sustain use of relevant research-validated practices that address the unique characteristics and needs of individual schools. Clearly, schools will need to work collaboratively with families, businesses, local and state agencies, and researchers, but much can be done in and by schools to improve school climate, maximize academic and social outcomes, and create safer school environments. However, schools will need to work smarter in identifying important outcomes and implementing what they know works best in achieving these outcomes.

## REFERENCES

Albert, P., & Troutman, A. (1999). *Applied behavior analysis for teachers.* (5th ed.). Columbus, OH: Merrill.

Axelrod, S. (1991). The problem: American education. The solution: Use behavior analytic technology. *Journal of Behavioral Education, 1,* 275-282.

Baer, D.M., Wolf, M.M., & Risley, T.R. (1968). Some current dimensions of applied behavior analysis. *Journal of Applied Behavior Analysis, 1,* 91-97.

Becker, W. C. (1971). *An empirical basis for change in education: Selections on behavioral psychology for teachers.* Chicago: Science Research Associates.

Becker, W. C., Madson, C.H., Jr., Arnold, C.R., & Thomas, D.R. (1967). The contingent use of teacher attention and praise in reducing classroom behavior problems. *Journal of Special Education 1967,* 287-307.

Berliner, D. C. (1985). Effective classroom teaching: The necessary but not sufficient condition for developing exemplary schools. In G. R. Austin & H. Garber (Eds.), *Research on exemplary schools.* Orlando, FL: Academic Press.

Binder, C. V. (1991). Marketing measurably effective instructional methods. *Journal of Behavioral Education, 1,* 317-328.

Brophy, J. E. (1979). Teacher behavior and student learning. *Educational Leadership*, *37*, 33-38.

Brophy, J., & Good, T. L. (1986). Teacher behavior and student achievement. In M. C. Wittrock (Ed.), *Handbook of research on teaching* (3rd ed.) (pp. 328-3375). New York: MacMillan.

Carnine, D. (1992). Expanding the notion of teacher's rights: Access to tools that work. *Journal of Applied Behavior Analysis*, *25*, 13-19.

Carnine, D. (1995). Trustworthiness, useability, and accessibility of educational research. *Journal of Behavioral Education*, *5*, 251-258.

Carnine, D. (1997). Bridging the research-to-practice gap. *Exceptional Children*, *63*, 513-521.

Center on Positive Behavioral Interventions and Supports (2001). Defining positive behavior support. Unpublished manuscript. Author.

Chapman, D., & Hofweber, C. (2000). Effective behavior support in British Columbia. *Journal of Positive Behavior Interventions*, *2*, 235-237.

Colvin, G., & Fernandez, E. (2000). Sustaining effective behavior support systems in an elementary school. *Journal of Positive Behavior Interventions*, *2*, 251-253.

Colvin, G., & Lazar, M. (1997). *The effective elementary classroom: Managing for success*. Longmont, CO: Sopris West.

Colvin, G., Kame'enui, E. J., & Sugai, G. (1993). Reconceptualizing behavior management and schoolwide discipline in general education. *Education and Treatment of Children*, *16*, 361-381.

Colvin, G., Sugai, G., Good, R., & Lee, Y. (1997). Effect of active supervision and precorrection on transition behaviors of elementary students. *School Psychology Quarterly*, *12*, 344-363.

Colvin, G., Sugai, G., & Kame'enui, E. J. (1994). *Proactive schoolwide discipline: Implementation manual*. Project PREPARE. Behavioral Teaching and Research, College of Education, University of Oregon. Eugene.

Colvin, G., Sugai, G., & Patching, W. (1991). Pre-correction: An instructional strategy for managing predictable behavior problems. *Intervention in School and Clinic*, *28*, 143-150.

Comer, J. (1985). The Yale-New Haven primary prevention project: A follow-up study. *Journal of the American Academy of Child Psychiatry*, *24*, 154-160.

Elliot, D.S., Hamburg, B.A., & Williams K.R. (1998). *Violence in American schools: A new perspective*. Cambridge: Cambridge University Press.

Emmer, E., Evertson, C., & Anderson, L. (1980). Effective classroom management at the beginning of the school year. *Elementary School Journal*, *80*, 219-231.

Evertson, C.M., & Emmer, E.T. (1982). Effective management at the beginning of the school year in junior high classes. *Journal of Educational Psychology*, *74*, 485-498.

Gettinger, M. (1988). Methods of proactive classroom management. *School Psychology Review*, *17*, 227-242.

Gilbert, T.F. (1978). *Human competence: Engineering worthy performance*. New York: McGraw Hill.

Gilbert, T. F., & Gilbert, M. B. (1992). Potential contributions of performance science to education. *Journal of Applied Behavior Analysis*, *25*, 43-49.

Gottfredson, D.C. (1987). An evaluation of an organization development approach to reducing school disorder. *Evaluation Review*, *11*, 739-763.

Gottfredson, D.C., Gottfredson, G.D., & Hybl, L.G. (1993). Managing adolescent behavior: A multiyear, multischool study. *American Educational Research Journal, 30*, 179-215.

Gottfredson, D.C., Gottfredson, G.D., & Skroban, S. (1996). A multimodel school based prevention demonstration. *Journal of Adolescent Research, 11*, 97-115.

Gottfredson, D.C., Karweit, N.L., & Gottfredson, G.D. (1989). *Reducing Disorderly Behavior in Middle Schools*. (Report No. 47). Baltimore, MD: John Hopkins University, Center of Research on Elementary and Middle Schools.

Guerra, N.G., & Williams, K.R. (1996). *A program planning guide for youth violence prevention: A risk-focused approach*. Center for the Study and Prevention of Violence. University of Colorado, Boulder.

Gunter, P.L., Denny, R.K., Jack, S.L., Shores, R.E., & Nelson, C.M. (1993). Aversive stimuli in academic interactions between students with serious emotional disturbance and their teachers. *Behavioral Disorders, 19*, 265-274.

Gunter, P.L., Jack, S.L., DePaepe, P., Reed, T.M., & Harrison, J. (1994). Effects of challenging behaviors of students with EBD on teacher instructional behavior. *Preventing School Failure, 38*, 35-46.

Heward, W. L., Heron, T. E., Hill, D. S., & Trap-Porter, J. (1984). *Focus on behavior analysis in education*. Columbus, OH: Merrill.

Horner, R. H. (1994). Functional assessment: Contributions and future directions. *Journal of Applied Behavior Analysis, 27*, 401-404.

Horner, R. H., & Sugai, G. (2000). School-wide behavior support: An emerging initiative (special issue). *Journal of Positive Behavioral Interventions, 2*, 231-232.

Individuals with Disabilities Education Act Amendments of 1997, 20 U.S.C §1400 *et seq.* (1997).

Jack, S.L., Shores, R.E., Denny, R.K., Gunter, P.L., DeBriere, T., & DePaepe, P. (1996). An analysis of the relationship of teachers' reported use of classroom management strategies on types of classroom interactions. *Journal of Behavioral Education, 6*, 67-87.

Jenson, W. R., Sloane, H. N., & Young, K. R. (1979, 1988). *Applied behavior analysis in education: A structured teaching approach*. Englewood Cliffs, NJ: Prentice Hall.

Kame'enui, E. J., & Darch, C. B. (1995). *Instructional classroom management: A proactive approach to behavior management*. White Plains, NY: Longman.

Kazdin, A. E. (1982). Applying behavioral principles in the schools. In C. R. Reynolds & T. B. Gutkin (Eds.), *The handbook of school psychology*. (pp. 501-529). New York: Wiley.

Kerr, M. M., & Nelson, C. M. (1983). *Strategies for managing behavior problems in the classroom*. Columbus, OH: Merrill.

Knoff, H. M. (1995). Best practices in facilitating school-based organizational change and strategic planning. In A. Thomas & J. Grimes (Eds.), *Best practices in school psychology-III*. Silver Spring, MD: National Association of School Psychologists.

Kounin, J. (1970). *Discipline and group management in classrooms*. New York: Holt, Rinehard, & Winston.

Langland, S., Lewis-Palmer, T., & Sugai, G. (1998). Teaching respect in the classroom: An instructional approach. *Journal of Behavioral Education, 8*, 245-262.

Latham, G. (1992). Interacting with at-risk children: The positive position. *Principal, 72*(1), 26-30.

Latham, G.I. (1988). The birth and death cycles of educational innovations. *Principal*, *68* (1), 41-44.

Lee, Y., Sugai, G., & Horner, R. (1999). Effect of component skill instruction on math performance and on-task, problem, and off-task behavior of students with emotional and behavioral disorders. *Journal of Positive Behavioral Interventions, 1*, 195-204.

Lewis, T. J., Colvin, G., & Sugai, G. (in press). The effects of pre-correction and active supervision on the recess behavior of elementary school students. *School Psychology Quarterly*.

Lewis, T. J., & Sugai, G. (1999). Effective behavior support: A systems approach to proactive school-wide management. *Focus on Exceptional Children, 31*(6), 1-24.

Lewis-Palmer, T., Sugai, G., & Larson, S. (1999). Using data to guide decisions about program implementation and effectiveness. *Effective School Practices, 17*(4), 47-53.

Lindsley, O. R. (1992). Why aren't effective teaching tools widely adopted? *Journal of Applied Behavior Analysis, 25*, 21-26.

Lohrman-O'Rourke, S., Knoster, T., Sabatine, K., Smith, D., Horvath, B., & Llewellyn, G. (2000). School-wide application of PBS in the Bangor Area School District. *Journal of Positive Behavior Interventions, 2*(4), 238-240.

Madsen, C.H. Jr., Becker, W.C., & Thomas, D.R. (1968). Rules, praise, and ignoring: Elements of elementary classroom context. *Journal of Applied Behavior Analysis 1*, 139-150.

Martens, B. K., & Kelly, S. Q. (1993). A behavioral analysis of effective teaching. *School Psychology Quarterly, 8*, 10-26.

Mayer, G. (1995). Preventing antisocial behavior in the schools. *Journal of Applied Behavior Analysis, 28*, 467-478.

Mayer, G. R., & Butterworth, T. (1979). A preventive approach to school violence and vandalism: An experimental study. *Personnel and Guidance Journal, 57*, 436-441.

Mayer, G. R., Butterworth, T., Nafpaktitis, M., & Sulzer-Azaroff, B. (1983). Preventing school vandalism and improving discipline: A three year study. *Journal of Applied Behavior Analysis, 16*, 355-369.

McCord, J. (Ed.) (1995). *Coercion and punishment in long-term perspective*. New York: Cambridge University Press.

Nakasato, J. (2000). Data-based decision making in Hawaii's behavior support effort. *Journal of Positive Behavior Interventions, 2*, 247-251.

Nelson, J. R. (1996). Designing schools to meet the needs of students who exhibit disruptive behavior. *Journal of Emotional and Behavioral Disorders, 4*, 147-161.

Nelson, J. R., Johnson, A., & Marchand-Martella, N. (1996). Effects of direct instruction, cooperative learning, and independent learning practices on the classroom behavior of students with behavioral disorders: A comparative analysis. *Journal of Emotional and Behavioral Disorders, 4*, 53-62.

Nelson, J. R., Martella, R., & Galand, B. (1998). The effects of teaching school expectations and establishing a consistent consequence on formal office disciplinary actions. *Journal of Emotional and Behavioral Disorders, 6*, 153-161.

Nelson, J.R., Martella R.M., & Marchand-Martella, N. (in press). Maximizing student learning: The effects of a comprehensive school-based program for preventing problem behaviors. *Journal of Emotional and Behavioral Disorders*.

Nersesian, M., Todd, A., Lehmann, J., & Watson, J. (2000). School-wide behavior support through district-level system change. *Journal of Positive Behavior Interventions, 2*, 244-247.

Northwest Regional Education Laboratory (1984). *Effective schooling practices: A research synthesis*. Portland, OR: Author.

O'Neill, R.E., Horner, R.H., Albin, R.W., Sprague, J.R., Storey, K., & Newton, J.S. (1997). *Functional assessment and program development for problem behavior: A practical handbook*. Pacific Grove, CA: Brookes/Cole.

Paine, S. C., Radicchi, J., Rosellini, L. C., Deutchman, L., & Darch, C. B. (1983). *Structuring your classroom for academic success*. Champaign, IL: Research Press.

Patterson, G. R., Reid, J. B., & Dishion, T. J. (1992). *Antisocial boys*. Eugene, OR: Castalia Press.

Peters, M. T., & Heron, T. E. (1993). When the best is not good enough: An examination of best practice. *Journal of Special Education, 26*, 371-385.

Rose, L. C., & Gallup, A. M. (1998). The 30th annual Phi Delta Kappan/Gallup poll of the public's attitude toward the public schools. *Kappan, 79*, 41-56.

Rosenshine, B. V. (1985). Synthesis on research on explicit teaching. *Educational Leadership, 43*, 60-69.

Rosenshine, B., & Stevens, R. (1986). Teaching functions. In M. C. Wittrock (Ed.), *Handbook of research on teaching* (3rd ed.) (pp. 376-391). New York: MacMillan.

Sadler, C. (2000). Effective behavior support implementation at the district level: Tigard-Tualatin School District. *Journal of Positive Behavior Interventions, 2*(4), 241-243.

Shores, R.E., Jack, S.L., Gunter, P.L., Ellis, D.N., DeBriere, T.J., & Wehby, J.H. (1993). Classroom interactions of children with behavior disorders. *Journal of Emotional and Behavior Disorders, 1*, 27-39.

Skiba, R. J., & Deno, S. J. (1991). Terminology and behavior reduction: The case against punishment. *Exceptional Children, 57*, 293-313.

Slavin, R.E. (1989). PET and the pendulum: Faddism in education and how to stop it. *Phi Delta Kappan* June 1989, 752-759.

Smith, M. A., & Misra, A. (1992). A comprehensive management system for students in regular classrooms. *Elementary School Journal, 92*, 353-371.

Sprick, R. S., & Nolet, V. (1991). Prevention and management of secondary-level behavior problems. In G. Stoner, M. R. Shinn, & H. M. Walker (Eds.), *Interventions for achievement and behavior problems* (pp. 519-538). Silver Spring, MD: National Association of School Psychologists.

Sprick, R., Sprick, M., & Garrison, M. (1992). *Foundations: Developing positive school-wide discipline policies*. Longmont, CO: Sopris West.

Sugai, G., & Horner, R. H. (1999). Discipline and behavioral support: Preferred processes and practices. *Effective School Practices, 17*, 10-22.

Sugai, G., Horner, R. H., Dunlap, G., Hieneman, M., Lewis, T. J., Nelson, C. M., Scott, T., Liaupsin, C., Sailor, W., Turnbull, A. P., Turnbull, H. R., III, Wickham, D., Reuf, M., & Wilcox, B. (2000). Applying positive behavioral support and functional behavioral assessment in schools. *Journal of Positive Behavioral Interventions, 2*, 131-143.

Sugai, G., Horner, R.H., & Todd, A.W. (2000). Effective Behavior Support (EBS Survey): Assessing and planning behavior support in schools. University of Oregon. Eugene.

Sugai, G., Lewis-Palmer, T., & Hagan-Burke, S. (1999-2000). Overview of the functional behavioral assessment process. *Exceptionality, 8*, 149-160.

Sugai, G., Sprague, J. R., Horner, R. H., & Walker, H. M. (2000). Preventing school violence: The use of office discipline referrals to assess and monitor school-wide discipline interventions. *Journal of Emotional and Behavioral Disorders, 8*, 94-101.

Sulzer-Azaroff, B., & Mayer, G. R. (1986). *Achieving educational excellence: Using behavioral strategies.* New York: Holt, Rinehart & Winston.

Sulzer-Azaroff, B., & Mayer, G. R. (1994). *Achieving educational excellence: Behavior analysis for achieving classroom and schoolwide behavior change.* San Marcos, CA: Western Image.

Taylor-Greene, S., Brown, D., Nelson, L., Longton, J., Gassman, T., Cohen, J., Swartz, J., Horner, R. H., Sugai, G., & Hall, S. (1997). School-wide behavioral support: Starting the year off right. *Journal of Behavioral Education, 7*, 99-112.

Taylor-Greene, S.J., & Kartub, D.T. (2000). Durable implementation of school-wide behavior support: The high five program. *Journal of Positive Behavior Interventions, 2*, 233-235.

Thomas, D.R., Becker, W.C., & Armstrong, M. (1968). Production and elimination of disruptive classroom behaviors by systematically varying teacher's behavior. *Journal of Applied Behavior Analysis, 1*, 35-45.

Tolan, P., & Guerra, N. (1994). What works in reducing adolescent violence: An empirical review of the field. Center for the Study and Prevention of Violence. University of Colorado, Boulder.

US Department of Health and Human Services (2001). *Youth violence: A report of the surgeon general.* Washington, DC: Office of the Surgeon General.

Vargas, J. S. (1977). *Behavioral psychology for teachers.* New York: Harper Row.

Walker, H. M., Horner, R. H., Sugai, G., Bullis, M., Sprague, J. R., Bricker, D., & Kaufman, M. J. (1996). Integrated approaches to preventing antisocial behavior patterns among school-age children and youth. *Journal of Emotional and Behavioral Disorders, 4*, 193-256.

Weissberg, R. P., Caplan, M. Z., & Sivo, P. J. (1989). A new conceptual framework for establishing school-based social competence promotion programs. In L. A. Bond & B. E. Compas (Eds.), *Primary prevention and promotion in the schools.* (pp. 255-296). Newbury Park, CA: Sage.

Wolery, M. R., Bailey, D. P., Jr., & Sugai, G. (1988). *Effective teaching: Principles and procedures of applied behavior analysis with exceptional students.* Boston, MA: Allyn & Bacon.

Wong, H. K., & Wong, R. T. (1991). *The first days of school: How to be an effective teacher.* Sunnyvale, CA: Harry K. Wong.

Zins, J. E., & Ponte, C. R. (1990). Best practices in school-based consultation. In A. Thomas and J. Grimes (Eds.), *Best practices in school psychology–II* (pp. 673-694). Washington, DC: National Association of School Psychologists.

# Academic Remediation: Educational Applications of Research on Assignment Preference and Choice

Christopher H. Skinner
Monica A. Wallace
Christine E. Neddenriep

**SUMMARY.** Within educational settings students can choose to engage in assigned academic activities or other, sometimes disruptive behaviors. In the current paper recent research on assignment preference, choice, and choosing is reviewed. Results of these studies show how educators can enhance students' academic behaviors (e.g., on-task behavior), decrease disruptive behaviors, and improve academic performance by (a) allowing students to choose assignments, (b) assigning higher preference academic activities, (c) strengthening reinforcement for engaging in academic activities, and (d) altering assignments to make them more acceptable to students. *[Article copies available for a fee from The Haworth Document Delivery Service: 1-800-HAWORTH. E-mail address: <getinfo@haworthpressinc.com> Website: <http://www.HaworthPress.com> © 2002 by The Haworth Press, Inc. All rights reserved.]*

Christopher H. Skinner, PhD, is Professor and Coordinator of School Psychology Programs at The University of Tennessee.

Monica A. Wallace, MA, and Christine E. Neddenriep, MS, are School Psychology PhD students at The University of Tennessee.

Address correspondence to: Christopher H. Skinner, The University of Tennessee, College of Education, Claxton Complex A 525, Knoxville, TN 37996-3400.

[Haworth co-indexing entry note]: "Academic Remediation: Educational Applications of Research on Assignment Preference and Choice." Skinner, Christopher H., Monica A. Wallace, and Christine E. Neddenriep. Co-published simultaneously in *Child & Family Behavior Therapy* (The Haworth Press, Inc.) Vol. 24, No. 1/2, 2002, pp. 51-65; and: *Behavior Psychology in the Schools: Innovations in Evaluation, Support, and Consultation* (ed: James K. Luiselli, and Charles Diament) The Haworth Press, Inc., 2002, pp. 51-65. Single or multiple copies of this article are available for a fee from The Haworth Document Delivery Service [1-800-HAWORTH, 9:00 a.m. - 5:00 p.m. (EST). E-mail address: getinfo@haworthpressinc.com].

**KEYWORDS.** Assignment choice, preference, reinforcement, interspersal procedure, effort

Within educational settings, students are not typically allowed to select their academic activities. Instead, teachers assign specific activities (e.g., complete assignments, respond to recitation questions, read silently, conduct laboratory experiments). However, students do have options. Students can choose to engage in assigned academic activities or a variety of other behaviors including passive off-task behaviors (e.g., orienting oneself to an assignment while day dreaming) or disruptive behaviors (Shapiro, 1996).

Lindgren and Suter (1985) suggest that teachers focus on what students need to do in order to learn, as opposed to what educators need to do to teach. For students to acquire and master skills (e.g., become fluent or automatic with skills, learn to generalize and adapt those skills) they must engage in academic behaviors (Skinner, 1998). Researchers have shown that students who engage in more academic responding become more automatic in the use of those skills and are better able to apply and adapt those skills (Greenwood, Delquadri, & Hall, 1984; Skinner, 1998). Thus, getting students to choose to engage in academic behaviors is often a necessary pre-requisite for skill development.

In the current paper, research on student choice behavior will be reviewed. Specifically, the paper focuses on research where students are given a choice of assignments and variables that impact assignment choice and preference including consequence variables and variables associated with the assignments themselves.

## PROVIDING A CHOICE OF ACADEMIC ASSIGNMENTS

Although students always have the option of choosing to engage in assigned academic activities or other behaviors, researchers have investigated the effects of allowing students to choose from a variety of assignments on students' academic behavior (e.g., on-task behavior), inappropriate behavior (e.g., disruptive behavior), and academic performance (e.g., accuracy). As it is beyond the scope of this paper to provide a comprehensive review of the literature on choice, readers should refer to Kern et al. (1998).

Dunlap et al. (1994) investigated the impact of allowing students to choose assignments, on-task engagement, and disruptive behavior in two boys with emotional disabilities in a special education classroom. The students were exposed to alternating choice and no-choice conditions. During choice conditions students could choose from six to ten spelling or English independent seatwork assignments. During the no-choice condition, students were given a specific assignment. Results show higher levels of task engagement and lower levels of disruptive behavior under the choice condition. Students were also exposed to a no-choice yoked condition where the identical assignments selected by the students during the choice condition were assigned by the teacher. Similar levels of disruptive behavior were found across both no-choice conditions. This suggests that the process of choosing accounted for the decrease in disruptive behavior and the increase in on-task behavior during the choice condition.

Although increasing task persistence (i.e., on-task) and decreasing misbehavior are important goals, improvement in these behaviors does not necessarily mean that students' academic performance is enhanced (Lentz, 1988). Cosden, Gannon, and Harring (1995) conducted a study of choice and measured the quality of students' academic work. Results show higher levels of accuracy under the choice conditions. However, in this study students chose both assignments and reinforcers. Although offering a choice of reinforcers had a relatively consistent impact on accuracy, for some students offering a choice of assignments appears to have much less effect on academic performance.

Research suggests that providing choices is particularly important for lower-preference assignments. Killu and Clare (in press) compared task engagement under choice and no-choice conditions with higher-preference and lower-preference academic assignments. For higher-preference assignments, small and inconsistent differences were found across choice and no-choice conditions. However, for lower-preference assignments, two of three participants showed higher levels of engagement when allowed to choose their assignments. In another study, Vaughn and Horner (1997) found that providing a choice of lower-preference tasks yielded a small reduction in problem behaviors.

## Application of Providing Assignment Choices

Other researchers have demonstrated that providing choice of assignments can enhance performance and behaviors across students (e.g., preschool, kindergarten and middle school students, students with mental retardation or emotional disturbances) and settings (e.g., residential facility, special education classroom, clinic assessment). Additionally, studies have shown that providing choices is effective across tasks including textbook assignments, spelling seatwork, and storybook reading (Cosden et al., 1995; Dunlap, Kern-Dunlap, Clark, & Robbins, 1991; Dunlap et al., 1994; Dyer, Dunlap, & Winterling, 1990).

These studies suggest that choice-making as an antecedent intervention has several practical applications for educators. First, when feasible, educators may find that providing choices can enhance students' academic performance and classroom behaviors. Additionally, allowing students to make choices may contribute to their sense of personal control and dignity (Dunlap et al., 1994). After students choose an assignment they tend to begin working on that assignment immediately. Thus, instead of an immediate teacher-student confrontation at the onset of a work session, the teacher is provided with an opportunity to deliver positive reinforcement. This immediate engagement occasioned by providing a choice may create the momentum for longer periods of appropriate academic behaviors (Belfiore, Lee, Vargus, & Skinner, 1997). If teachers are able to spend less time modifying disruptive behaviors they may get to spend more time teaching. Thus, providing choices may enhance class-wide student achievement.

Although choice-making can be an effective antecedent procedure, such procedures should not be used in all situations. There are some academic assignments that students should not be allowed to avoid (e.g., avoid engaging in narrative writing assignments by choosing to do grammar worksheets). Additionally, students may choose tasks that consistently result in lower levels of learning. For example, a student may consistently choose a spelling crossword assignment over other spelling assignments. Thus, educators should monitor student learning that is associated with each task to ensure that providing choices does not reduce learning rates.

## PREFERENCE:
## VARIABLES THAT INFLUENCE STUDENT CHOICE

In some instances it may be possible to allow students to avoid specific assignments by allowing them to choose to engage in other academic assignments that they prefer. However, providing multiple options can require time and resources. Furthermore, students with skill deficits may find assignments that require them to employ underdeveloped skills particularly aversive because they require much time and effort to complete. If students are allowed to avoid these aversive assignments, they are likely to fall farther behind in their skill development and mastery (Binder, 1996; Skinner, 1998; Stanovich, 1986).

Many general theories and specific variables have been identified that may explain why students prefer or choose to engage in assigned academic behavior or other behaviors (e.g., staring out the window). However, several variables appear to effect choice behavior or preference across behavior options, environments, and organisms with such precision that they have been incorporated into theories of choice behavior that have become known as laws [see research on Fitts Law, e.g., Fitts (1954) and Herrnstein's (1961) Matching Law]. Below we will review applied research on these consequence variables and antecedent assignment variables.

## *Reinforcement Procedures*

Herrnstein's (1961) Matching Law incorporates consequence variables that may impact student choice behaviors. This research suggests that one way to enhance student perceptions of tasks and increase the probability of them choosing to engage in assigned academic activities is to provide higher rates of reinforcement, more immediate reinforcement, and higher quality reinforcers (Myerson & Hale, 1984).

*Rate of reinforcement.* Several applied studies have demonstrated that when students are given a choice between two tasks, they distribute their time between these tasks at a rate equivalent to the rate of reinforcement provided for these tasks (Mace, McCurdy, & Quigley, 1990; Mace, Neef, Shade, & Mauro, 1996; Martens & Houk, 1989; Martens, Lochner, & Kelly, 1992; Neef, Mace, & Shade, 1993; Neef, Mace, Shea, & Shade, 1992). This match between a respondent's behavior and the level of reinforcement provided is described by Herrnstein's (1961) Matching Law. For example, Martens and Houk (1989) demonstrated that Herrnstein's Matching Law accurately described the relationship between a student's behavior and the classroom teacher's attention. The level at which the student engaged in on-task versus disruptive behavior was proportional to the teacher's attention provided for these two competing behaviors. Thus, to increase the probability of students choosing to engage in assigned academic behaviors, educators can increase the rate of reinforcement for desired academic behavior and/or decrease the rate of reinforcement for other competing behaviors (Myerson & Hale, 1984).

In other studies, researchers allowed students to make frequent choices between two assignments and assessed the impact of consequence variables on choice behavior (i.e., time engaged in each assignment). For example, Mace et al. (1990) provided a student with division and multiplication problems. When the schedules or rates of reinforcement were equal across assignments (i.e., VR-2 or reinforcing on average every two responses across both assignments) the student showed no preference for one assignment over another. However, when the schedule of reinforcement for one assignment was doubled (CRF or reinforcement for every response) the student increased his responding to the CRF assignment, matching the rate of reinforcement on both tasks (i.e., spending about twice as much time working on the assignment that was reinforced at twice the rate). In a second experiment, Mace et al. (1990) found similar results where the tasks involved assembling pens and packaging silverware.

*Reinforcement delay.* Another consequence variable influencing choice is reinforcement delay. Neef et al. (1993) provided two students with two mathematics assignments (i.e., math problems in two stacks of note cards). These two stacks were on concurrent variable interval (VI) schedules of reinforcement (VI 30/60-second and VI 120-second). Students were provided nickels for completing problems for either assignment. During the equal-delay condition, the nickels were made available within 2 seconds of a correct response from either assignment. During the unequal-delay condition, the students received one nickel for every 30 or 60 seconds working on this assignment. However, the nickels were not given to the students until 1 to 3 weeks later. For the other assignment, students were required to work for 120 seconds in order to receive a nickel, but the nickels were delivered within 2 seconds. The results showed that students chose to complete the mathematics problems associated with more immediate reinforcement, even though this yielded overall lower levels of reinforcement (i.e., fewer nickels).

*Reinforcer quality.* In the previous studies, equivalent reinforcers were used across choice behaviors. Others have used different reinforcers and measured the impact on student choice behavior. For example, Neef et al. (1992) investigated the impact of reinforcer quality on student choice behavior. Three students were provided with two mathematics assignments (again math problems in two stacks of note cards). The two assignments were on concurrent schedules of reinforcement (VI 30-second and VI 120-second) with high quality reinforcers (nickels) and low quality reinforcers (program money) delivered. During the unequal-quality reinforcer condition, the respondent was provided the opportunity to earn the lower quality reinforcer four times as often as his opportunity to earn the higher quality reinforcer. The results show that reinforcer quality significantly impacted choice behavior.

*Interactive effects.* Applied studies have also attempted to discern the interactive effects of quality, rate, delay, and effort (represented by problem difficulty) on a student's choice behavior. For example, Neef et al. (1993) also studied the combination of rate, quality, and delay of access to reinforcement. For one student, the quality of the reinforcer had a larger influence on choice behavior or assignment preference than rate or reinforcement delay. For another student, reinforcement delay influenced choice behavior more than quality or rate of reinforcement. In a similar study, Mace et al. (1996) investigated the interaction between reinforcer quality, rate, and problem or assignment difficulty. Results show that choice behaviors were more influenced by quality and rate of reinforcement than assignment difficulty.

## Applications of Enhancing Reinforcement

The tightly controlled experimental studies previously reviewed show how rate, quality, and delay of reinforcement can influence the probability of students choosing to engage in academic assignments. In most educational settings, systems are designed to reinforce students for learning. Thus, students receive grades based on their test performance that demonstrate their learning (e.g., a weekly spelling test administered on Friday). While reinforcing test performance may indirectly reinforce learning behaviors (e.g., completing spelling assignments on Monday and Tuesday), this reinforcement for engaging in assigned work is delayed. Thus, one procedure for increasing the probability of students engaging in assigned academic activities is to directly and immediately reinforce these behaviors that account for their learning and strong performance on tests. Examples include reinforcement for completing daily assignments and homework.

To increase reinforcement rates, reinforcement can be provided contingent upon smaller units of academic behavior. An example of this is Classwide Peer Tutoring (Greenwood, Delquadri, & Carta, 1997). During spelling, students earn discrete reinforcers (i.e., points as part of a game) for each word spelled correctly as opposed to reinforcement for completing an entire assignment (e.g., grade for individual seatwork). Furthermore, peers are able to evaluate discrete academic responses and immediately deliver reinforcement and feedback contingent upon the response. Thus, rather than waiting for the teacher to grade a worksheet and provide feedback, this program incorporates both immediate and high rate reinforcement. Computers can be used to provide similar immediate, high rate reinforcement for discrete academic responses (e.g., Johns, Skinner, & Nail, in press; Neef, Shade, & Miller, 1994).

Providing reinforcers that are of higher quality than those provided for competing behaviors can prove challenging to many educators. One solution is to employ interdependent group oriented contingencies where the entire class receives access to reinforcement when they meet their group goals (Skinner, Cashwell, & Dunn, 1996). Because reinforcement is delivered to all or none of the students, these contingencies allow educators to use high quality, inexpensive, activity reinforcers that can be difficult to deliver to some students (i.e., those who earned it) and not others (i.e., those who didn't earn it). For example, listening to music during independent seat-work or receiving 10 minutes of extra recess are easy to deliver to an entire class. Additionally, because each student is more likely to gain access to reinforcement when his/her classmates do well, interdependent reinforcement procedures may also cause peers to encourage and praise each other's successful academic behaviors. This social praise from peers may be a particularly potent high-quality reinforcer.

## ALTER ACADEMIC ASSIGNMENTS: CHOICE AND PREFERENCE

To increase the probability of students engaging in assigned work educators can assign preferred activities. A variety of reasons may explain why students prefer one assignment over another. However, one variable that appears to effect choice behavior or preference across behavior options is the effort required to complete the task (Fitts, 1954; Herrnstein, 1961).

### Altering Assignments: Effort Reduction

Researchers have shown that, when given a choice of two assignments and all else is held constant, students are likely to choose, prefer, or rate more favorably assignments that are less difficult and require less time and effort to complete (e.g., Cates, Skinner, Watkins, & Rhymer, in press; Cooke, Guzaukas, Pressley, & Kerr, 1993; Horner & Day, 1991; Kern, Childs, Dunlap, Clarke, & Falk, 1994; Martin, Skinner, & Neddenriep, in press). Thus, one way to increase the probability of students choosing to engage in assigned academic behaviors, as opposed to off-task or disruptive behaviors, is to reduce the time and effort required to complete assignments. This can be accomplished by making the assignments briefer (e.g., reducing the number of mathematics problems on an assignment, see Cates et al., in press) and/or easier (e.g., removing difficult tasks within an assignment, changing assignments completely, or removing some difficult and time-consuming tasks and replacing them with easier, brief tasks, see Cooke et al., 1993).

### *Application of Effort Reduction Procedures*

Students who have academic skill deficits often require more time and effort to complete assigned work. Thus, reducing assignment length or demands may be more likely to improve their academic behavior (e.g., increase on-task and decrease off-task behavior) and perceptions of assignments (Martin et al., in press; Skinner, 1998; Stanovich, 1986). However, making assignments briefer or easier may also reduce learning rates. Thus, although these procedures may improve student behavior, they may also result in students who already have academic skill deficits falling farther and farther behind as teachers continue to alter their assignments by reducing academic demands or "watering down the curriculum" (Cates et al., in press; Martin et al., in press; Roberts & Shapiro, 1996; Roberts, Turco, & Shapiro, 1991).

In some instances it may be possible to reduce time and effort required to complete assignments without reducing opportunities to respond. For example, researchers have shown that altering the response topography (requiring students to verbally report academic responses as opposed to writing them) can decrease the time and, most likely, the effort required to complete academic tasks (Skinner, Belfiore, Mace, Williams, & Johns, 1997; Skinner, Ford, & Yunker, 1991).

### *Adding and Interspersing Briefer Problems: Increasing Response Rates*

Reducing assignment length or replacing difficult problems with easier problems may reduce the time and effort required to complete an assignment and make assignments more preferable. Recently, researchers have shown how educators can enhance students' perceptions of assignments and academic behaviors by lengthening assignments (Johns et al., in press; Logan & Skinner, 1998; McCurdy, Skinner, Grantham, Watson, & Hindman, 2001; Skinner, Fletcher, Wildmon, & Belfiore, 1996; Skinner et al., 1999; Skinner, Robinson, Johns, Logan, & Belfiore,

1996; Wildmon, Skinner, McCurdy, & Sims, 1999; Wildmon, Skinner, & McDade, 1998).

Skinner, Robinson et al. (1996) allowed college students to work on two mathematics assignment. The control assignment contained 15 3-digit by 2-digit computation problems (e.g., $489 \times 67 =$ ). The experimental (i.e., interspersal) assignment contained 15 similar matched problems plus six 1-digit by 1-digit problems ($4 \times 6 =$ ) interspersed following every third target problem. After working on both assignments, significantly more students chose the experimental assignment for homework and rated it as requiring less time and effort to complete even though it contained more problems. Furthermore, adding these brief problems did not reduce problem completion rates or accuracy levels on target $3 \times 2$ problems. Subsequent studies showed that interspersing additional brief problems had a similar impact on sixth-grade students (Logan & Skinner, 1998) and college and secondary students working on mathematics word problems (Wildmon et al., 1999; Wildmon et al., 1998).

### Applications of the Interspersal Procedure

Previously described research showed that the interspersal procedures enhanced student perceptions of assignments without decreasing their opportunities to respond to target problems or the speed and accuracy of their responses to these problems. Subsequent studies showed that interspersing additional brief problems caused students to prefer assignments with more, longer target problems (Cates & Skinner, 2000; Cates et al., in press). For example, Cates and Skinner (2000) exposed remedial mathematics secondary students to control assignments with 15 $3 \times 2$ problems and experimental assignments with 18 and 21 $3 \times 2$ problems and 1 $\times$ 1 problems interspersed following every third $3 \times 2$ problem. Results show that interspersing these additional problems caused these remedial mathematics students to select or rate more positively the assignments that contained 20% and 40% more longer (i.e., $3 \times 2$) problems. Thus, rather than "watering down the assignment," these studies show how assignments could be enhanced or "thickened," and students would still choose and prefer these assignments.

Research was also conducted to determine if adding and interspersing brief problems influenced task persistence (i.e., on-task behavior). McCurdy et al. (2001) found that a second grade student engaged in higher levels of on-task behavior during independent seatwork when additional brief problems were added and interspersed. Skinner, Hurst,

Teeple, and Meadows (under review) found that interspersing brief problems also increased on-task levels in students with emotional disorders.

Researchers have also attempted to determine why the interspersal procedure is effective. Although it may appear that this procedure is effective because the interspersed problems are easier, research suggests that students prefer interspersal assignments because adding these problems increases their discrete task completion rates (Skinner, Fletcher et al., 1996; Skinner et al., 1999; Skinner, Robinson et al., 1996; Wildmon et al., 1999; Wildmon et al., 1998). Thus, this procedure is most likely to be effective when (a) assignments contain discrete tasks, (b) interspersed problems require much less time to complete than the target tasks, and (c) interspersed problems are extremely brief so they do not substantially increase the effort associated with the tasks.

While working on independent seatwork assignments with many discrete tasks, the completion of each task may be a conditioned reinforcer (Logan & Skinner, 1998). Thus, by interspersing additional brief problems, educators may increase rates of problem completion and rates of reinforcement (Skinner et al., 1999). This theory may account for findings related to the interspersal procedure. Also, this theory may explain why increasing student rates of responding by increasing the pace of teacher led instruction (Darch & Gersten, 1985) or implementing explicit timing procedures (Carnine, 1976) has been shown to (a) increase on-task behavior, (b) reduce inappropriate behavior, and (c) improve accuracy of academic responding. Finally, this theory suggests that increasing discrete task completion rates and delivering additional reinforcement for accurate task completion may result in even greater changes in academic and disruptive behaviors (see Horner, Day, Sprague, O'Brien, & Heathfield, 1991).

## CONCLUSION

Students may engage in inappropriate behaviors in order to escape or avoid engaging in assigned academic activities (Sprague, Sugai, & Walker, 1998). One solution for remedying this problem is to deliver aversive consequences contingent upon these inappropriate behaviors. However, such procedures may not increase the probability of students choosing to engage in assigned academic activities (Lentz, 1988). Thus, these procedures may not enhance learning.

In the current paper we reviewed several procedures that can be used to increase the probability of students choosing to engage in assigned work including:

a. allowing students to choose assignments,
b. assigning higher preference academic activities,
c. enhancing reinforcement for engaging in assignments,
d. altering assignments to increase assignment completion or problem completion rates.

Researchers should continue to investigate such procedures as they may:

a. decrease disruptive behaviors,
b. increase the amount and quality of students' academic behavior,
c. increase learning rates,
d. improve students' perceptions of academic assignments,
e. allow educators to spend more time teaching and less time addressing disruptive behaviors.

## REFERENCES

Belfiore, P. J., Lee, D. L., Vargus, A. U., & Skinner, C. H. (1997). The effects of high probability single digit mathematics problem completion on multiple digit mathematics problem performance. *Journal of Applied Behavior Analysis, 30*, 327-330.

Binder, C. (1996). Behavioral fluency: Evolution of a new paradigm. *The Behavior Analyst, 19*, 163-197.

Carnine, D. W. (1976). Effects of two teacher presentation rates on off-task behavior, answering correctly, and participation. *Journal of Applied Behavior Analysis, 9*, 199-206.

Cates, G. L., & Skinner, C. H. (2000). Getting remedial mathematics students to prefer homework with 20% and 40% more problems: An investigation of the strength of the interspersing procedure. *Psychology in the Schools, 37*, 339-347.

Cates, G. L., Skinner, C. H., Watkins, C. E., & Rhymer, K. N. (in press). Effects of interspersing additional brief math problems on student performance and perception of math assignments: Getting students to prefer to do more work. *Journal of Behavioral Education.*

Cooke, N. L., Guzaukas, R., Pressley, J. S., & Kerr, K. (1993). Effects of using a ratio of new items to review items during drill and practice: Three experiments. *Education and Treatment of Children, 16*, 213-234.

Cosden, M., Gannon, C., & Haring, T. (1995). Teacher-control versus student-control over choice of task and reinforcement for students with severe behavior problems. *Journal of Behavioral Education, 5*, 11-27.

Darch, C., & Gersten, R. (1985). The effects of teacher presentation rates and praise on LD students' oral reading performance. *British Journal of Educational Psychology, 55*, 295-303.

Dunlap, G., DePerzcel, M., Clark, S., Wilson, D., Wright, S., & Gomez, A. (1994). Choice making to promote adaptive behavior for students with emotional and behavioral challenges. *Journal of Applied Behavior Analysis, 27*, 505-518.

Dunlap, G., Kern-Dunlap, L., Clarke, S., & Robbins, F. (1991). Functional assessment, curricular revision, and severe behavior problems. *Journal of Applied Behavior Analysis, 24*, 387-397.

Dyer, K., Dunlap, G., & Winterling, V. (1990). Effects of choice making on the serious problem behaviors of students with severe handicaps. *Journal of Applied Behavior Analysis, 23*, 515-524.

Fitts, P. M. (1954). The information capacity of the human motor system in controlling the amplitude of movement. *Journal of Experimental Psychology, 47*, 381-391.

Greenwood, C. R., Delquadri, J. C., & Carta, J. J. (1997). *Together we can! Classwide peer tutoring to improve basic academic skills.* Longmont, CO: Sopris West.

Greenwood, C. R., Delquadri, J. C., & Hall, R. V. (1984). Opportunity to respond and student academic performance. In W. L. Heward, T. E. Heron, J. Trap-Porter, & D. S. Hill (Eds.), *Focus on behavior analysis in education* (pp. 58-88). Columbus, OH: Charles Merrill.

Harding, J., Wacker, D., Cooper, J., Millard, T., & Kovlan, P. (1994). Brief hierarchical assessment of potential treatment components with children in an outpatient clinic. *Journal of Applied Behavior Analysis, 27*, 291-300.

Herrnstein, R. J. (1961). Relative and absolute strength of response as a function of frequency of reinforcement. *Journal of the Experimental Analysis of Behavior, 4*, 266-267.

Horner, R. H., & Day, H. M. (1991). The effects of response efficiency on functionally equivalent competing behaviors. *Journal of Applied Behavior Analysis, 24*, 719-732.

Horner, R. H., Day, H. M., Sprague, J. R., O'Brien, M., & Heathfield, L. T. (1991). Interspersed requests: A non-aversive procedure for reducing aggression and self-injury during instruction. *Journal of Applied Behavior Analysis, 24*, 265-278.

Johns, G. A., Skinner, C. H., & Nail, G. L. (in press). Effects of interspersing briefer mathematics problems on assignment choice in students with learning disabilities. *Journal of Behavioral Education.*

Kern, L., Childs, K. E., Dunlap, G., Clarke, S., & Falk, G. D. (1994). Using assessment-based curricular intervention to improve the classroom behavior of a student with emotional and behavioral challenges. *Journal of Applied Behavior Analysis, 27*, 7-19.

Kern, L., Vorndran, C., Hilt, A., Ringdahl, J., Adelman, B., & Dunlap, G. (1998). Choice as an intervention to improve behavior: A review of the literature. *Journal of Behavioral Education, 8*, 151-169.

Killu, K., & Clare, C. (in press). Choice vs. preference: The effects of choice and no choice of preferred and non preferred spelling tasks on the academic behavior of students with disabilities. *Journal of Behavioral Education.*

Lentz, F. E. (1988). On-task behavior, academic performance, and classroom disruptions: Untangling the target selection problem in classroom interventions. *School Psychology Review, 17*, 243-257.

Lindgren, H. C., & Suter, W. N. (1985). *Educational psychology in the classroom* (2nd ed.). Monterey, CA: Brooks/Cole.

Logan, P., & Skinner, C. H. (1998). Improving students' perceptions of a mathematics assignment by increasing problem completion rates: Is problem completion a reinforcing event? *School Psychology Quarterly, 13,* 322-331.

Mace, F. C., McCurdy, B., & Quigley, E. A. (1990). The collateral effect of reward predicted by matching theory. *Journal of Applied Behavior Analysis, 23,* 197-205.

Mace, F. C., Neef, N. A., Shade, D., & Mauro, B. C. (1996). Effects of problem difficulty and reinforcer quality on time allocated to concurrent arithmetic problems. *Journal of Applied Behavior Analysis, 29,* 11 B 24.

Martens, B. K., & Houk, J. L. (1989). The application of Herrnstein's law of effect to disruptive and on-task behavior of a retarded adolescent girl. *Journal of the Experimental Analysis of Behavior, 51,* 17 B 27.

Martens, B. K., Lochner, D. G., & Kelly, S. Q. (1992). The effects of variable-interval reinforcement on academic engagement: A demonstration of matching theory. *Journal of Applied Behavior Analysis, 25,* 143-151.

Martin, J. J., Skinner, C. H., & Neddenriep, C. E. (in press). Extending research on the interspersal procedure to perception of continuous reading assignments: Applied and theoretical implications of a failure to replicate. *Psychology in the Schools.*

McCurdy, M., Skinner, C. H., Grantham, K., Watson, T. S., & Hindman, P. M. (2001). Increasing on-task behavior in an elementary student during mathematics seat-work by interspersing additional brief problems. *School Psychology Review, 30,* 23-32.

Myerson, J., & Hale, S. (1984). Practical implications of the matching law. *Journal of Applied Behavior Analysis, 17,* 367-380.

Neef, N. A., Mace, F. C., & Shade, D. (1993). Impulsivity in students with serious emotional disturbance: The interactive effects of reinforcer rate, delay, and quality. *Journal of Applied Behavior Analysis, 26,* 37-52.

Neef, N. A., Mace, F. C., Shea, M. C., & Shade, D. (1992). Effects of reinforcer rate and reinforcer quality on time allocation: Extension of matching theory to educational settings. *Journal of Applied Behavior Analysis, 25,* 691-699.

Neef, N. A., Shade, D., & Miller, M. S. (1994). Assessing the influential dimensions of reinforcers on choice in students with serious emotional disturbance. *Journal of Applied Behavior Analysis, 27,* 575-583.

Roberts, M. L., & Shapiro, E. S. (1996). Effects of instructional ratios on students' reading performance in a regular education classroom. *Journal of School Psychology, 34,* 73-91.

Roberts, M. L., Turco, T. L., & Shapiro, E. S. (1991). Differential effects of fixed instructional ratios on students' progress in reading. *Journal of Psychoeducational Assessment, 9,* 308-318.

Shapiro, E. S. (1996). *Academic skills problems: Direct assessment and interventions* (2nd ed.). New York: Guilford Press.

Skinner, C. H., (1998). Preventing academic skills deficits. In T. S. Watson & F. Gresham (Eds.), *Handbook of child behavior therapy: Ecological considerations in assessment, treatment, and evaluation* (pp. 61-83). New York: Plenum Press.

Skinner, C. H., Belfiore, P. J., Mace, H. W., Williams, S., & Johns, G. A. (1997). Altering response topography to increase response efficiency and learning rates. *School Psychology Quarterly, 12,* 54-64.

Skinner, C. H., Cashwell, C., & Dunn, M. (1996). Independent and interdependent group contingencies: Smoothing the rough waters. *Special Services in the Schools*, *12*, 61-78.

Skinner, C. H., Fletcher, P. A., Wildmon, M., & Belfiore, P. J. (1996). Improving assignment preference through interspersing additional problems: Brief versus easy problems. *Journal of Behavioral Education*, *6*, 427-437.

Skinner, C. H., Ford, J. M., & Yunker, B. B. (1991). An analysis of instructional response requirements on the multiplication performance of behavior disordered students. *Behavioral Disorders*, *17*, 56-65.

Skinner, C. H., Hall-Johnson, K., Skinner, A. L., Cates, G., Weber, J., & Johns, G. (1999). Enhancing perceptions of mathematics assignments by increasing relative rates of problem completion through the interspersal technique. *Journal of Experimental Education*, *68*, 43-59.

Skinner, C. H., Hurst, K. L., Teeple, D. F., and Meadows, S. O. (manuscript under review). Increasing on-task behavior during mathematics independent seat-work in students with emotional disorders by interspersing brief problems.

Skinner, C. H., Robinson, S. L., Johns, G. A., Logan, P., & Belfiore, P. J. (1996). Applying Herrnstein's matching law to influence students' choice to complete difficult academic tasks. *Journal of Experimental Education*, *65*, 5-17.

Sprague, J., Sugai, G., & Walker, H. (1998). Antisocial behavior in schools. In T. S. Watson & F. Gresham (Eds.), *Handbook of child behavior therapy: Ecological considerations in assessment, treatment, and evaluation* (pp. 451-474). New York: Plenum Press.

Stanovich, K. E. (1986). Mathew effects in reading: Some consequences of individual differences in the acquisition of literacy. *Reading Research Quarterly*, *21*, 360-406.

Vaughn, B., & Horner, R. (1997). Identifying instructional tasks that occasion problem behaviors and assessing the effects of student versus teacher choice among these tasks. *Journal of Applied Behavior Analysis*, *30*, 299-312.

Wildmon, M. E., Skinner, C. H., McCurdy, M., & Sims, S. (1999). Improving secondary students' perceptions of the "dreaded mathematics word problem assignment" by giving them more word problems. *Psychology in the Schools*, *36*, 319-325.

Wildmon, M. E., Skinner, C. H., & McDade, A. (1998). Interspersing additional brief easy problems to increase assignment preference on mathematics reading problems. *Journal of Behavioral Education*, *8*, 337-346.

# Health Promotion Interventions

Leonard A. Jason
Carrie J. Curie
Stephanie M. Townsend
Steven B. Pokorny
Richard B. Katz
Joseph L. Sherk

**SUMMARY.** A large gap exists between research and practice in the development and implementation of validated school health prevention programs. This gap might be narrowed by developments in the emerging field of prevention science, which is making progress in evaluating health promotion and behavioral risk prevention programs. In this paper we review four areas from the prevention science field. They include: (1) promoting healthy behavior and preventing chronic health problems, (2) preventing substance abuse, (3) preventing high-risk sexual behaviors, and (4) preventing child physical and sexual abuse. Promising practices are described for each of these topics. Recommendations are made regarding strategies for implementing empirically validated programs, supplementing school programs with multi-level, ecological prevention

Leonard A. Jason, PhD, is the Director of the Center for Community Research, and Carrie J. Curie, Stephanie M. Townsend, Steven B. Pokorny, Richard B. Katz and Joseph L. Sherk are all affiliated with the Center.

Address correspondence to: Leonard A. Jason, PhD, Center for Community Research, 990 W. Fullerton Ave., DePaul University, Chicago, IL 60614.

The authors appreciate the financial support provided by the Substance Abuse Policy Research Program of the Robert Wood Johnson Foundation, and the National Cancer Institute grant number CA80288.

[Haworth co-indexing entry note]: "Health Promotion Interventions." Jason, Leonard A. et al. Co-published simultaneously in *Child & Family Behavior Therapy* (The Haworth Press, Inc.) Vol. 24, No. 1/2, 2002, pp. 67-82; and: *Behavior Psychology in the Schools: Innovations in Evaluation, Support, and Consultation* (ed: James K. Luiselli, and Charles Diament) The Haworth Press, Inc., 2002, pp. 67-82. Single or multiple copies of this article are available for a fee from The Haworth Document Delivery Service [1-800-HAWORTH, 9:00 a.m. - 5:00 p.m. (EST). E-mail address: getinfo@haworthpressinc.com].

*67*

strategies, and assessing schools' readiness to implement prevention programs. *[Article copies available for a fee from The Haworth Document Delivery Service: 1-800-HAWORTH. E-mail address: <getinfo@haworthpressinc.com> Website: <http://www.HaworthPress.com> © 2002 by The Haworth Press, Inc. All rights reserved.]*

**KEYWORDS.** Prevention, substance abuse, high-risk sexual behaviors, child physical and sexual abuse

Few issues in this area are more important than preventing child and adolescent health problems, particularly those that may be linked to later chronic diseases and mortality. A conceptual model is needed to help guide our efforts in reducing risk factors for our nation's youth. The Centers for Disease Control (CDC) has identified a heuristic template of six behavioral risk factors that cause youth morbidity and mortality. They include:

1. behaviors that may cause intentional or unintentional injuries;
2. substance abuse;
3. early/unprotected sexual activity that contributes to unwanted pregnancies and sexually transmitted diseases;
4. tobacco use;
5. poor nutrition leading to disease; and
6. low levels of physical activity. (CDC, 2000)

A natural setting for developing these types of preventive programs is schools because they are a site where youth are educated about the development of healthy behaviors (Brink, Simons-Morton, Harvey, Parcel, & Tiernan, 1988). Programs that best promote school health strategies involve multi-component interventions, including classroom curricula, parental education, changes in school environment, and community reinforcement (Kelder, Edmundson, & Lytle, 1997). Although schools have the potential to impact youth health behaviors, effective programming is not being implemented by the majority of U.S. schools (Kelder, Edmundson, & Lytle, 1997). Unfortunately, a large gap still exists between research and practice in the development and implementation of validated school health prevention programs.

One way of bridging this gap is through a clearer understanding of the theoretical underpinnings of school-based health education interventions. Principles derived from behavioral and ecological community psychology (Bogat & Jason, 2000) suggest that social, physical, political, and economic factors significantly impact the development of health-related attitudes and behaviors in children, adolescents, and adults (Nation, Wandersman, & Perkins, in press). Based on these principles, for improvements in child and adolescent health to occur, comprehensive changes in health care provisions, improvements in economic conditions, and wide-scale health promotion efforts are needed (Kelder, Edmundson, & Lytle, 1997). Our schools could play key roles in the development of these types of ecologically-sound, comprehensive efforts that might prevent the occurrence of later chronic diseases and mortality.

## SPECIFIC HEALTH ISSUES

The following sections provide brief descriptions of some of the preventive health topics frequently addressed in public schools, including promoting healthy behaviors, and preventing substance use, high-risk sexual behaviors, and child physical and sexual abuse. These issues correspond with the behavioral risk factors identified by the CDC (2000). In each of the sections below, we identify promising interventions, we review research summaries or meta-analyses where available, and we make recommendations for future directions.

### *Promoting Healthy Behaviors/Preventing Chronic Health Problems*

During adolescence, behavior patterns are formed that contribute to the onset of chronic diseases in adulthood (Kelder, Edmundson, & Lytle, 1997). Frequently physical inactivity and unhealthy eating patterns begin during adolescence. These unhealthy behaviors increase with age, and are responsible for at least 300,000 preventable deaths in the United States each year (CDC, 2000). The Youth Risk Behavior Survey (YRBS) found that 16% of youth in grades nine through twelve are at risk for becoming overweight and that 9.9% are currently overweight. The risk of becoming overweight is significantly higher for males and for African-American students (CDC, 2000). Despite the fact that more males are currently overweight, significantly more female students report that they were trying to lose weight. Findings also indicate that 12.6% of all students reported not eating for more than 24 hours to lose weight or to avoid gaining weight, 7.6% of students reported taking diet pills, powders or liquids without a doctor's advice, and 4.8% of students reported vomiting or taking laxatives (CDC, 2000).

Youth who adopt healthy nutrition and exercise patterns during their school years are more likely to maintain those behaviors as adults. In a recent review of youth nutrition and exercise programs, Minden and Jason (in press) identified promising activity and nutrition interventions that included health education, knowledge building, activity-driven competitions with incentives or prizes, self-management and skill development with goal setting, and social marketing. Minden and Jason (in press) suggest that an ecological approach that involves multiple elements in comprehensive interventions will have the greatest chances of leading to lasting beneficial behavioral change.

As one example of a large scale, multiple element intervention, Jason, Greiner, Naylor, Johnson, and Van Egeren (1991) launched a health promotion program during a three week period, on a Chicago TV station. This series featured daily reports on the 12:00 noon and 9:00 p.m. news concerning health nutritional practices and effective exercises. In addition to this media component, the intervention included the distribution of 100,000 self-help manuals on the series throughout Chicago at True Value Hardware stores. One component of this overall study involved a group of viewers who had weight problems. A randomly selected group attended ongoing weight control self-help groups, watched the television show, and read the self-help manuals. This group succeeded in losing more weight than a comparable group, which was only exposed to the media program and manuals and did not attend meetings.

When designing youth oriented nutrition and exercise promotion programs, it is important to take into account the impact of poverty on chronic health conditions. According to the U. S. Bureau of the Census (1992), 46% of African-American, 40% of Hispanic, and 16% of White children are living in poverty, and have limited access to health care services. Those youngsters living in poverty also evidence higher rates of poor nutrition and lower rates of exercise in comparison with those not living in poverty. Consequently, preventive school-based programs must take into account the social context in which youth live. For example, instructing adolescents about the advantages of healthy diets may be more effective if the lessons are accompanied by easy-to-understand strategies for purchasing healthy food on a limited income. Similarly, interventions that advocate for increases in exercise might be accompanied by programs that teach youth to manage their time so that they can exercise amid school, work and family obligations.

### Prevention of Substance Use

Drug, alcohol, and tobacco use are significant risk factors for youth. Since 1975, the Monitoring the Future project has conducted an annual national survey of eighth, tenth and twelfth grade students to assess the prevalence of tobacco, alcohol and other drug use. The most recent survey indicates that 54% of high school seniors surveyed reported having tried an illicit drug, 63% had tried cigarettes, and 80% reported having used alcohol (Johnston, O'Malley, & Bachman, 2000). The reported use of cigarettes and alcohol has remained relatively consistent over the past ten years; however, reported use of illicit drugs has increased from 44% in 1991 to 54% in 2000 (Johnston, O'Malley, & Bachman, 2000).

During the 1960s and 1970s, school-based efforts to prevent the initiation of tobacco, alcohol and other drugs were frequently designed to scare youth, to provide information about drugs and related paraphernalia, to appeal to adolescent morality, and to improve self-esteem (Donaldson, Sussman, MacKinnon, Severson, Glynn, Murray, & Stone, 1996). Smoking prevention programs, for example, used curricula that were mostly aimed at increasing student awareness of the harmful, long-term effects of cigarette smoking (Perry, Killen, Telch, Slinkard, & Danahaer, 1980). In the 1980s, substance use prevention programs shifted toward curricula based on social influences (Donaldson et al., 1996), which emphasized the social environment as a critical factor in tobacco use (Lantz et al., 2000). This model attempted to address environmental, personality and behavioral risk factors (Perry & Kelder, 1992).

In a meta-analysis, Hansen (1992) found that 51% of outcomes from social influence programs were positive, compared with 50% of outcomes from comprehensive life skills programs, 31% of outcomes from information/values clarification programs, and 19% of outcomes from affective education programs. These findings are similar to the weighted effect sizes calculated by Tobler and Stratton (1997) for 56 high quality experimental programs. Among these programs, the weighted effect sizes were significantly greater for the interactive social influences and comprehensive life skills programs than for the non-interactive knowledge only, affective only, and knowledge plus affective programs.

However, one of the better-controlled studies using the social influence approach has recently generated considerable media attention. The Hutchinson Smoking Prevention Project (HSPP) (Peterson, Kealey, Mann, Mark, & Sarason, 2000) was a 15-year randomized, controlled trial of smoking prevention among youth that provided a comprehensive social-influence intervention from grade three through 12 and assessed participants two years after high school graduation. HSPP findings on prevalence of daily smoking for students indicate that there was no significant difference between students in the control and experimental conditions. This study suggests that caution needs to be used when drawing conclusions about the long-term effects of these types of person-oriented interventions.

Preventive interventions that focus exclusively on youth in school settings might overlook pernicious community influences on the initiation and maintenance of tobacco, alcohol, and other drug use. There are problems with relying exclusively on school-based prevention programs, since many programs have relatively small effects on student behavior, and community influences are often ignored (Jason, Biglan, & Katz, 1998). School-based prevention programs might be more effective when coordinated with multi-component, community strategies that attempt to reduce youth substance use.

The problem of youth access to tobacco illustrates the need for a more ecologically-based approach. Most minors can easily purchase cigarettes from retailers (Biglan, Henderson, Humphrey, Yasui, Whisman, Black, & James, 1995; Forster, Komro, & Wolfson, 1996; Johnston, 1995). Jason, Ji, Anes and Birkhead (1991) found that during a baseline condition approximately 70% of tobacco vendors in Woodridge, Illinois sold cigarettes to minors. Subsequently, community antismoking legislation involving licensing vendors and enforcement of those laws was developed. This enforcement procedure directed minors into the stores to make purchase attempts on a regular basis with police issuing citations to merchants who sold cigarettes. In an administrative hearing, fines were imposed on merchants found to have sold to minors. Minors were also fined for tobacco possession.

After enforcement began, illegal cigarette sales to minors dropped to less than 5%. After two years of enforcement using compliance checks and fining minors for tobacco possession, the smoking rate among seventh and eighth graders decreased from 16% to 5% (Jason et al., 1991). These findings were maintained at a follow-up assessment (Jason, Berk, Schnopp-Wyatt, & Talbot, 1999). This study was the first to demonstrate that it is possible to reduce youth access to tobacco through enforcement efforts. The authors are currently testing this model with a randomized community trial intervention designed to examine the effectiveness of both sales and possession enforcement strategies to reduce youth access to tobacco. These types of ecological interventions can be combined with more traditional school-based prevention interventions in order to provide more consistent and high density youth messages both within and outside the school.

Prevention programs that are most effective might involve multiple dimensions including anti-smoking ads in the mass media and various comprehensive school programs (Pechmann, 1997; Kaufman, Jason, Sawlski, & Halpert, 1994). For example, a program developed by Flynn, Worden, Secker-Wlaker, Pirie, Badger, Carpenter, and Geller (1994) found that an intensive mass media campaign combined with a school-based program was more effective than just the school-based program in preventing cigarette smoking. Perry and Kelder's (1992) innovative prevention program used peer leaders who were elected by classmates, who became key trainers of new skills and information within the classroom setting. Children also had access to a multi-year school-based and complimentary community-wide program. Perry et al. (1992) concluded that the absence of environmental and community-wide factors that reinforce individual behavior makes long-term changes more difficult to sustain. Biglan, Ary, Yudelson, Duncan, Hood, James, Koehn, Wright, Black, Levings, Smith, and Gaiser (1996) also found that the prevalence of smoking among adolescents was significantly lower when a community-based intervention (i.e., media advocacy, youth anti-tobacco activities, family communications about tobacco use, reducing youth access to tobacco) was combined with a school-based intervention.

### Prevention of High-Risk Sexual Behaviors

Poor sexual and reproductive health styles among adolescents is a common problem. As evidenced by findings from the Youth Risk Behavior Survey, half of America's adolescents in grades nine through 12 have engaged in sexual intercourse and that 8.3% initiated sexual intercourse before age 13 years (CDC, 2000). In addition to early sexual activity, 16.2% of students reported having sexual intercourse with more than four sex partners and 24.8% had used alcohol or drugs during their latest act of sexual intercourse (CDC, 2000). Of those students who are sexually active, 6.3% reported that their sexual behavior resulted in pregnancy (CDC, 2000). Compared to other developed countries, the United States has one of the highest teen pregnancy rates, with 83.6 pregnancies per 1,000 women aged 15-19 years (Sing & Darroch, 2000). Additionally, the National Institute of Medicine (1997) estimates that 3 million cases of sexually transmitted diseases occur each year among persons 10 to 19 years of age.

Because many adults may feel that educating youth about sex will make young people more sexually active (Friedman, 1993), school-based sex education programs tend to be narrowly focused on risk elimination through abstinence. Campbell and Aggleton (1999) recommend that sexual health promotion programs contain four key components:

1. reliable and factual information educating youth about the risks they may face;
2. age and culturally appropriate choices for risk reduction that correspond with opportunities to examine values, responsibilities, commitments, and personal relationships that can affect motivation and behavior;
3. access to youth friendly services and support networks that will help youth implement what they learn;
4. opportunities to talk with peers and adults about issues related to sex, sexuality, and relationships.

There is a need for more comprehensive sexual education programming that reaches a broader and more heterogeneous group within the community (Robinson, Watkins-Ferrell, Scott-Davis, & Ruch-Ross, 1993).

Barring abstinence, most school-based pregnancy and STD/HIV prevention programs emphasize the use of contraception by youth. Byrne (1983) proposed that the use of contraception involves five behavioral steps:

1. acquiring, processing, and retaining accurate information about contraception;
2. acknowledging the likelihood of engaging in sexual activity;
3. obtaining a contraceptive;
4. communicating with one's partner about contraception;
5. using the chosen contraceptive method.

Successful school-based sex education prevention programs must help youth acquire the skills to complete each of these steps.

The challenge for successful sexual health promotion programs lies in community frameworks that support and enable healthy behaviors (Campbell & Aggleton, 1999). One ecological approach that schools can use is that of multimedia strategies involving students and their families. Crawford, Jason, Riordan, Kaufman, Salina, Sawalski, Ho, and Zolik (1990) provided an innovative example of using telecasts on local television news broadcasts, newspaper supplements that included factual information and interactive communication exercises for families, problem solving, decision making, and values clarification. This preventive intervention was effective in increasing participants' knowledge about AIDS and family discussions regarding sexual topics and AIDS.

Broader contextual factors also influence health related behaviors and can play a central role in the choices that youth make (Campbell & Aggleton, 1999). Such factors include the many facets of adolescent culture, including music, television, film, and advertising; family dynamics; peer influences; and psychosocial stressors. Regarding teen pregnancy, the direct role of adults must also be considered. National data indicate that only 29% of babies born to teenage mothers are fathered by teenage males and that 71% of teen pregnancies are fathered by men over 20 years of age (National Center for Health Statistics, 1988).

### Prevention of Child Physical and Sexual Abuse

Child abuse is classified into two types: physical abuse, where perpetrators are more likely to be female, and sexual abuse, where perpetrators are more likely to be male (Wurtele, 1993). Due to the variety of data collection methods and their concomitant biases it is difficult to determine precisely how many children suffer from abuse each year. Estimates of child maltreatment (physical abuse and neglect) range from 12.9 children per 1,000 (U. S. Department of Health and Human Services, 2000) to 22.6 children per 1,000 (Lung & Daro, 1995). Estimates of child sexual abuse range from 1.4 children per 1,000 (U. S. Department of Health and Human Services, 2000) to a surprisingly high 220 children per 1,000 (Finkelhor, Hotaling, Lewis, & Smith, 1990).

Wurtele (1998) suggests that most sexual abuse prevention programs share these common objectives:

1. teaching children to recognize abusive situations,
2. teaching children to resist and remove themselves from potential perpetrators,
3. encouraging children to report abuse, and
4. reassuring children that abuse is never their fault.

Additionally, due to the time-bound and culture-bound definitions of child sexual abuse, as well as individual values, a rule-based approach rather than a feelings-based approach can better help children recognize abuse, and active-learning programs that provide multiple opportunities for children to practice resistance skills can achieve greater development of those skills (Wurtele, 1998). Examples of validated programs that employ these objectives include Project 12-Ways (Lutzker, 1984), which uses an ecobehavioral approach that addresses both school and home settings; the Behavioral Skills Training Program that addresses sexual abuse in kindergarten, first, fifth, and sixth grades (Wurtele, Saslawsky, Miller, Marrs, & Britcher, 1986); and the teacher directed Safe Child Program which includes role-playing, discussion, and activities to help children master prevention skills (Kraizer, Witte, & Fryer, 1989).

A wide array of primary and secondary prevention programs, such as those implemented in schools, are designed to decrease child maltreatment (Wurtele, 1993). The prevention of child abuse, both physical and sexual, requires external support and reinforcement. For prevention programs to be effective, preventionists must attend to individual, family, community, and societal contexts. Lutzker and Boyle (in press) provide a contemporary view of child abuse that includes child and parent factors, the social ecology of the family, variables relating to culture, and biological variables that may influence behavior. Given the multifaceted nature of child maltreatment, the continued evaluation of an ecobehavioral approach that provides multiple services in multiple settings is certainly warranted (Wurtele, 1993).

One aspect of maltreatment prevention that is often overlooked is child neglect. In 1998, neglect accounted for 53.5% of all reported cases of abuse. Neglect encompasses inadequate nutrition, clothing, heat, or shelter and exposure to environmental hazards (U. S. Department of Health and Human Services, 2000). The high rates of neglect and/or fatalities resulting from neglect warrant greater attention to neglect in child abuse prevention efforts and underscore the need for ecological approaches with target audiences that include parents, children and other adults in the community who are in positions to identify and intervene in cases of both child physical abuse and child neglect.

## CONCLUSION

The implementation of school-based programs that address multiple health issues is both imperative for students' healthy development and challenging when the many mandates that schools are charged with are considered. The scope of the issues described above, the high prevalence of unhealthy student behaviors, and the influences of factors at the personal, familial, peer, cultural, and societal levels can overwhelm school personnel and overshadow the basic mandate of schools to teach general academic skills and specific subjects. What is needed are effective and affordable prevention programs that have significant effects on multiple health issues and that are integrated with the academic lessons and environment of the school setting. For prevention scientists, this next generation of prevention programs requires the development of interventions that have the following characteristics: significant effect sizes; randomized, controlled trials that include long-term follow-up and the use of meta-analytic techniques; generalizability across time, people, behaviors, and places; measurement of and attendance to side effects; use of multiple, integrated theories; and cost-effectiveness (Embry, 2001). Additionally, prevention scientists need to find more effective ways to disseminate their findings to the public so that school personnel are able to use empirical findings in their selection and implementation of programs.

The first step for school personnel responsible for selecting and implementing risk prevention and health programs is to choose empirically validated programs. Such selection will require the use of objective evaluation of programs rather than sole reliance upon publishers' promotional literature. Easily accessible sources that can be used to identify validated programs include online lists of best and promising practices as identified by the Center for Substance Abuse Prevention (2001) and the Western Regional Center for the Application of Prevention Technologies (2000).

Second, school personnel must carefully consider implementation issues since an empirically effective program that is not implemented with fidelity or with sufficient intensity may have little or no effect. Aspects of implementation to consider include program intensity as measured by the number of instruction hours per year; program breadth as measured by instruction across grade levels; integration with academic subjects; widespread involvement and training of staff, use of peer leaders and collaboration with community agencies and experts; school policies, including discipline policies that reinforce the objectives of prevention programs; family involvement in support of the objectives of prevention programs; and regularly scheduled, behaviorally-based evaluation of program effects. Decisions should also be based on local trends that can impact program effects, such as student mobility. Schools with high rates of student mobility will need to implement programs so that students receive the full effect of main components, even if they are not enrolled in the school during all grade levels. Trends such as mobility also underscore the need for implementing prevention programs as public health strategies within large regions such as cities and states rather than solely at the local level of the individual school (Embry, 2001).

Even when schools obtain empirically validated prevention programs to address behavioral risk factors that cause youth morbidity and mortality, they may be unable to implement the programs successfully. These problems could be related to attitudes, resources, and political climate within the school system as well as among the parents and community members. The Tri-Ethnic Center for Prevention Research at Colorado State University developed a useful theoretical model to assess community readiness for prevention (Edwards, Jumper-Thurman, Plested, Oetting, & Swanson, 2000), and such a model could be adapted to assess a school's readiness for prevention programs. The classification of a school within this framework can help identify where efforts should be directed in order to establish and sustain an effective prevention program. For example, a school that is classified in the No Awareness stage will need to begin by obtaining information about the nature and extent of the problem and then use this information to increase awareness and build support for prevention efforts. This classification can also help schools and communities set goals and evaluate change as they initiate or modify existing prevention programs.

Effective school prevention programming should utilize an ecological approach which provides overlapping and consistent messages within school and community environments. Interventions with this type of redundant posturing have more power and permanence (Jason, Engstrom, Pokorny, Tegart, & Curie, 2000). Collaboration between schools, local media and local government may increase the efficacy of health promotion programming (Jason, Biglan, & Katz, 1998). Preventive interventions that involve community-wide efforts to increase behavioral change might include local organizations, local medical programs, school personnel and even police. Communications between such personnel would ensure that new programs both within and outside the schools are sending consistent messages about health promotion throughout the community.

In summary, school-based health promotion and behavioral risk prevention programs need to be developed with a clear understanding of the emerging field of prevention science (Tebes, Kaufman, & Chinman, in press). In developing these types of prevention programs, it might be helpful to involve teachers and school administrators in decisions about the goals and strategies of the interventions. Ultimately, the most promising interventions will be those that empower students with skills and resources and provide relevant scientifically-based evidence to school-officials, parents and decision makers (Biglan & James, in press).

# REFERENCES

Biglan, A., Ary, D.V., Yudelson, H., Duncan, T.E., Hood, D., James, L., Koehn, V., Wright, Z., Black, C., Levings, D., Smith, S., & Gaiser, E. (1996). Experimental evaluation of a modular approach to mobilizing antitobacco influences of peers and parents. *American Journal of Community Psychology, 24,* 311-339.

Biglan, A., Henderson, J., Humphrey, D., Yasui, M., Whisman, R., Black, C., & James, L. (1995). Mobilizing positive reinforcement to reduce youth access to tobacco. *Tobacco Control, 4,* 42-48.

Biglan, A., & James, L. (in press). Making effective use of science to prevent problems of human behavior. In D. S. Glenwick & L.A. Jason (Eds.), *Innovative strategies for preventing psychosocial problems.* New York: Springer Publishing Company.

Bogat, G. A., & Jason, L. A. (2000). Toward an integration of behaviorism and community psychology. In J. Rappaport & E. Seidman (Eds.), *Handbook of community psychology* (pp. 101-114). New York: Kluwer Academic/Plenum Press.

Brink, S. G., Simons-Morton, D. G., Harvey, C. M., Parcel, G. S., & Tiernan, K. M. (1988). Developing comprehensive smoking control program in schools. *Journal of School Health, 58,* 177-180.

Byrne, D. (1983). Sex without contraception. In D. Byrne & W.S. Fisher (eds.), *Adolescents sex and contraception.* (pp. 3-31). Hillsdale, NJ: Erlbaum Associates.

Campbell, C., & Aggleton, P. (1999). Young people's sexual health: A framework for policy debate. *Canadian Journal of Human Sexuality, 8,* 249-262.

Center for Substance Abuse Prevention. (2001). CSAP's Prevention Portal: Model Programs [On-line]. Available: www.samhsa.gov/centers/csap/modelprograms.

Centers for Disease Control and Prevention (2000). Youth risk behavior surveillance–United States, 1999. *Morbidity and Mortality Weekly Report, 49,* 1-96.

Crawford, I., Jason, L. A., Riordan, N., Kaufman, J., Salina, D., Sawalski, L., Ho, F. C., & Zolik, E. (1990). A multimedia-based approach to increasing communication and the level of AIDS knowledge within families. *Journal of Community Psychology, 18,* 361–373.

Donaldson, S. I., Sussman, S. M., MacKinnon, D. P., Severson, H. H., Glynn, T., Murray, D. M., & Stone, E. J. (1996). Drug abuse prevention programming. *American Behavioral Scientist, 39,* 868-883.

Edwards, R. W., Jumper Thurman, P., Plested, B. A., Oetting, E. R., & Swanson, L. (2000). Community readiness theory: Research to practice. *Journal of Community Psychology, 28* (3), 291-307.

Embry, D. (2001, February). *The next generation multi-problem prevention: A comprehensive science-based, practical approach.* Paper presented at the meeting of California Association for Behavior Analysis, Redondo Beach, CA.

Finkelhor, D., Hotaling, G., Lewis, I. A., & Smith, C. (1990). Sexual abuse in a national survey of adult men and women: Prevalence, characteristics, and risk factors. *Child Abuse and Neglect, 14,* 19-28.

Flynn, B.S., Worden, J.K., Secker-Wlaker, R.H., Pirie, P.L., Badger, G.J., Carpenter, J.H., & Geller, B.M. (1994). Mass media and school interventions for cigarette smoking prevention: Effects 2 years after completion. *American Journal of Public Health, 84,* 1148-1150.

Forster, J. L., Komro, K. A., & Wolfson, M. (1996). Survey of city ordinances and local enforcement regarding commercial availability of tobacco to minors in Minnesota, United States. *Tobacco Control, 5*, 46-51.

Friedman, H.L. (1993). Overcoming obstacles to good adolescent health. *Network, 14*
(2), 4-5.

Hansen, W. B. (1992). School-based substance abuse prevention: A review of the state
of the art in curriculum, 1980-1990. *Health Education Research, 7*, 403-430.

Institute of Medicine. (1997). The hidden epidemic: Confronting sexually transmitted
diseases [On-line]. Available: www.nap.edu/books/0309054958/html/.

Jason, L. A., Berk, M., Schnopp-Wyatt, D. L., & Talbot, B. (1999). Effects of enforcement of youth access laws on smoking prevalence. *American Journal of Community
Psychology, 27*, 143-160.

Jason, L. A., Biglan, A., & Katz, R. (1998). Implications of the tobacco settlement for
the prevention of teenage smoking. *Children's Services: Social Policy, Research,
and Practice, 1*, 63-82.

Jason, L.A., Engstrom, M. D., Pokorny, S.B., Tegart, G., & Curie, C.J. (2000). Putting
the community back into prevention: Think locally, act globally. *The Journal of
Primary Prevention, 21*, 25-29.

Jason, L. A., Greiner, B., Naylor, K., Johnson, S., & Van Egeren, L. (1991). A
large-scale short-term, media-based weight loss program. *American Journal of
Health Promotion, 5*, 432-437.

Jason, L. A., Ji, P. Y., Anes, M., & Birkhead, S. H. (1991). Active enforcement of cigarette control laws in the prevention of cigarette sales to minors. *Journal of American
Medical Association, 266* (22), 3159-3161.

Johnston, L. D. (1995). *Smoking rates climb among American teenagers, who find
smoking increasingly acceptable and seriously underestimate the risks.* Ann Arbor:
The University of Michigan News and Information Service.

Johnston, L.D., O'Malley, P.M., & Bachman, J.G. (2000). *Monitoring the Future: National results on adolescent drug use.* Bethesda, MD: U.S. Department of Health
and Human Services.

Kaufman, J.S., Jason, L.A., Sawlski, L.M., & Halpert, J.A. (1994). A comprehensive
multi-media program to prevent smoking among black students. *Journal of Drug
Education, 24*, 95-108.

Kelder, S.H., Edmundson, E.W., & Lytle, L.A. (1997). Health behavior research and
school and youth health for the future. In David S. Gochman (ed.), *Handbook of
health behavior research IV: Relevance for professionals and issues for the future*
(pp. 263-284). New York: Plenum Press.

Kraizer, S., Witte, S.S., & Fryer, G.E. Jr. (1989). Child sexual abuse prevention programs: What makes them effective in protecting children? *Children Today, 18*,
23-27.

Lantz, P. M., Jacobson, P. D., Warner, K. E., Wasserman, J., Pollack, H. A., Berson, J., &
Ahlstrom, A. (2000). Investing in youth tobacco control: A review of smoking prevention and control strategies. *Tobacco Control, 9*, 47-63.

Lung, C., & Daro, D. (1996). *Current trends in child abuse reporting and fatalities:
The results of the 1995 annual fifty state survey.* Chicago: National Committee to
Prevent Child Abuse.

Lutzker, J.R. (1984). Project 12-Ways: Treating child abuse and neglect from an ecobehavioral perspective. In R.F. Dangel & R.A. Polster (eds.), *Parent Training: Foundations of Research and Practice* (pp. 260-297). New York: Guilford Press.

Lutzker, J.R., & Boyle, C.M. (in press). Preventing physical and sexual abuse. In D. S. Glenwick & L.A. Jason (Eds.), *Innovative strategies for preventing psychosocial problems*. New York: Springer Publishing Company.

Minden, J., & Jason, L. A. (in press). Preventing chronic health problems. In D. S. Glenwick & L. A. Jason (Eds.), *Innovative strategies for preventing psychosocial problems*. New York: Springer Publishing Company.

Nation, M., Wandersman, A., & Perkins, D.D. (in press). Promoting healthy communities through community development. In D. S. Glenwick & L. A. Jason (Eds.), *Innovative strategies for preventing psychosocial problems*. New York: Springer Publishing Company.

National Center for Health Statistics. (1988). *Vital Statistics of the United States, Volume 1, Natality*. Hyattsville, MD: Public Health Services.

Pechmann, C. (1997). Do anti-smoking ads combat underage smoking? A review of past practices and research. In M.G. Goldberg, M. Fishbein, & S. Middlestadt (Eds.), *Social marketing: Theoretical and practical perspectives* (pp. 189-216). Hillsdale, NJ: Lawrence Erlbaum Associates.

Perry, C. L., & Kelder, S. H. (1992). Models for effective prevention. *Journal of Adolescent Health, 13*, 355-363.

Perry, C.L., Killen, J., Telch, M., Slinkard, L.A., & Danahaer, B.G. (1980). Modifying smoking behavior of teenagers: School-based interventions. *American Journal of Public Health, 70*, 722-725.

Peterson, A.V., Kealey, K.A., Mann, S.L., Marke, P.M., & Sarason, I.G. (2000). Hutchinson smoking prevention project: Long-term randomized trial in school-based tobacco use prevention–results on smoking. *Journal of the National Cancer Institute, 92*, 1979-1991.

Robinson, W.L., Watkins-Ferrell, P., Scott-Davis, P., & Ruch-Ross, H. S. (1993). Preventing teenage pregnancy. In D. S. Glenwick & L.A. Jason (Eds.), *Promoting health and mental health in children, youth and families* (pp.75-97). New York: Springer Publishing Company.

Sing, S., & Darroch, J. (2000). Adolescent pregnancy and childbearing: Levels and trends in developed countries. *Family Planning Perspective, 32*, 14-23.

Tebes, J. K., Kaufman, J. S., & Chinman, M. (in press). Teaching about prevention to mental health professionals. D. S. Glenwick & L. A. Jason (Eds.), *Innovative strategies for preventing psychosocial problems*. New York: Springer Publishing Company.

Tobler, N. S., & Stratton, H. H. (1997). Effectiveness of school-based drug prevention programs: A meta-analysis of the research. *Journal of Primary Prevention, 18*, 71-128.

U. S. Bureau of the Census. (1992). *Poverty in the United States: 1991. Current Population Reports* (Series P-60, No. 181). Washington DC Government Printing Office.

U. S. Department of Health and Human Services. (2000). *Child maltreatment 1998: Reports from the states to the national child abuse and neglect data system*. Washington, DC: Children's Bureau, U. S. Department of Health and Human Services.

Western Regional Center for the Application of Prevention Technologies. (2000). Alphabetical listing of Best Practices [On-line]. Available: www.open.org/~westcapt/balpha.htm.

Wurtele, S. K. (1993). Prevention of child physical and sexual abuse. In D. S. Glenwick & L.A. Jason (Eds.), *Promoting health and mental health in children, youth and families* (pp. 33-47). New York, NY: Springer Publishing Company.

Wurtele, S. K. (1998). School-based child sexual abuse prevention programs: Questions, answers, and more questions. In J. R. Lutzker (Ed.), *Handbook of child abuse research and treatment* (pp. 501-516). New York: Plenum Press.

Wurtele, S. K., Saslawsky, D.A., Miller, C.L., Marrs, S.R., & Britcher, J.C. (1986). Teaching personal safety skills for potential prevention of sexual abuse: A comparison of treatments. *Journal of Consulting and Clinical Psychology, 54*, 688-692.

# Behavioral Strategies
# to Reduce School Violence

## G. Roy Mayer

**SUMMARY.** Public schools that use punitive approaches toward student discipline can unwittingly promote violence and other antisocial behavior. This article reviews constructive and preventive methods to reduce school violence and vandalism. Various strategies are presented and discussed. *[Article copies available for a fee from The Haworth Document Delivery Service: 1-800-HAWORTH. E-mail address: <getinfo@haworthpressinc.com> Website: <http://www.HaworthPress.com> © 2002 by The Haworth Press, Inc. All rights reserved.]*

**KEYWORDS.** School violence, setting events, contextual factors, violence prevention, school discipline, school vandalism

Antisocial behavior, including school violence, is a complex area of extreme social importance. It is a continual problem affecting all areas of the United States and all socioeconomic levels. Though rates of crime were dropping overall during 1992-1999, reports show that about 2.5 million children under age 18 were arrested (Snyder, 2000), and more juveniles were locked up in secure detention centers, training schools, jails, and prisons than ever before (partially because many

---

G. Roy Mayer, EdD, BCBA, is affiliated with the Charter College of Education, California State University, Los Angeles.

Address correspondence to: G. Roy Mayer, 10600 Pinyon Ave., Tujunga, CA 91042.

[Haworth co-indexing entry note]: "Behavioral Strategies to Reduce School Violence." Mayer, G. Roy. Co-published simultaneously in *Child & Family Behavior Therapy* (The Haworth Press, Inc.) Vol. 24, No. 1/2, 2002, pp. 83-100; and: *Behavior Psychology in the Schools: Innovations in Evaluation, Support, and Consultation* (ed: James K. Luiselli, and Charles Diament) The Haworth Press, Inc., 2002, pp. 83-100. Single or multiple copies of this article are available for a fee from The Haworth Document Delivery Service [1-800-HAWORTH, 9:00 a.m. - 5:00 p.m. (EST). E-mail address: getinfo@haworthpressinc.com].

*83*

states are emphasizing longer and more punitive sanctions rather than treatment or prevention) (Puritz & Shang, 1998).

Related to the current emphasis on more punitive sanctions, Ingersoll and LeBoeuf (1997) have noted that there have been increases in student suspensions and expulsions within our public schools. It is of interest that the major reasons for being suspended are not dangerous or violent acts but minor infractions, such as non-compliance and being tardy or truant (Brooks, Schiraldi, & Ziedenberg, 1999; Skiba, Peterson, & Williams, 1997). Other investigators also have pointed out how school personnel spend more time and energy in implementing punitive rather than positive or preventive measures (Brodinsky, 1980; Greenberg, 1974; Mayer & Leone, 1999). Yet, punitive discipline strategies and a reliance on heavy security arrangements (security guards, metal detectors, locked doors, high fences, etc.) appear to aggravate rather than reduce vandalism, aggression, and disorder (Greenberg, 1974; Mayer & Leone, 1999). In fact, "creating an unwelcoming, almost jail-like, heavily scrutinized environment, may foster the violence and disorder school administers hope to avoid" (Mayer & Leone, 1999). In other words, students resent punitive school environments and react against them. Perhaps this increased emphasis on punitive measures in our schools and society is why, according to Attorney General Bill Lockyer, serious crime has increased 3.5% during the year 2000 in cities with populations of more than 100,000 (Moultrie, 2001). In Los Angeles, for example, homicides jumped 27.5%; rape, 13.3%; robbery, 7.7%; aggravated assault, 6.5%; burglary, 13.5%, and motor vehicle theft, 20.1% (Moultrie, 2001). We also now are experiencing shootings on our school campuses. And what has been the reaction by educators? It has been more security guards and more punitive measures.

Mayer (2001) posited that "security arrangements and punitive measures, when [their implementation is] necessary, must be viewed as temporary, reactive expedients to help gain control in the situation *while* contextual factors are addressed." Security arrangements and punitive discipline measures must not be viewed as *the solution* because, in the long run, they can contribute to increases in violence and disruptions.

## FACTORS WITHIN THE SCHOOL ENVIRONMENT THAT CONTRIBUTE TO VIOLENCE

Research has taught us that aversive or punitive environments predictably promote antisocial behaviors, such as aggression, violence, vandalism, and escape (Azrin, Hake, Holz, & Hutchinson, 1965;

Berkowitz, 1983; Mayer, 1995). Mayer (2001) has pointed out that the school environment is aversive for many students. Not only do many educators emphasize punitive measures to manage student behavior, some do not attend positively to their students' social or academic behavior. Such extinction conditions for positive, pro-social and academic behaviors also are likely to promote additional student aggression (Wehby, Symons, & Shores, 1995).

Research by Mayer and his colleagues (1987, 1995, 2001) has identified a number of contextual factors within the school that appear to contribute to punitive school environments that promote antisocial behavior. These include:

1. an over-reliance on punitive methods of control;
2. unclear rules for student deportment;
3. lack of administrative support for staff, little staff support of one another, and a lack of staff agreement with policies;
4. academic failure experiences;
5. students lacking critical social skills that form the basis of doing well academically and relating positively to others, such as persistence on task, complying with requests, paying attention, negotiating differences, handling criticism and teasing;
6. a misuse of behavior management procedures;
7. lack of student involvement;
8. lack of understanding or appropriate responding to student differences.

The importance of these factors is highlighted by the fact that many are similar to those identified that promote antisocial behavior in the home (e.g., reliance on coercive or punitive discipline, lack of positive consequences, inconsistent rule setting and delivery of consequences) (Loeber, Stouthammer-Loeber, & Green, 1987; Reid & Patterson, 1991). Also, these identified contextual factors within the school have been found to relate significantly to both school vandalism frequency and its resultant cost (Mayer, Nafpaktitis, Butterworth, & Hollingsworth, 1987). Thus, it should come as no surprise that a recent Federal publication stated: *"Studies indicate that approximately four of every five disruptive students can be traced to some dysfunction in the way schools are organized, staff members are trained, or schools are run"* (U.S. Dept. of Education, 2000b, p.10). In addition, research evidence (Mayer & colleagues, 1979, 1981, 1983b, 1991, 1993; Metzler, Biglan, Rusby, & Sprague, in press; Sprague et al., in press) suggests that when these school-related environmental, or contextual, factors are considered and incorporated into a plan that focuses on making school environments more reinforcing for students and staff, a variety of benefits occur. Antisocial behaviors (including vandalism costs) occur less frequently, discipline referrals decrease, attendance improves, dropouts and suspensions decrease, more students spend increased time on assigned tasks, teachers increase their use of praise and decrease their use of disapproval, perceptions of school safety improve, and cooperation and positive feelings among students and staff increase. In other words, it appears that *changing these identified contextual factors within the school not only can help prevent violence and other antisocial behavior, but also can help to create an environment more conducive to learning.* These results are important because most incarcerated adults develop from youths who engage in antisocial behavior and drop out of school (Henggeler, Melton, & Smith, 1992; Hodgkinson, 1991). In addition, more than 80% of the incarcerated individuals in the United States are high school dropouts, and the states with the highest dropout rates tend to have the highest rates of prisoners per 100,000 people (Hodgkinson, 1991).

## STRATEGIES FOR REDUCING/PREVENTING SCHOOL VIOLENCE

The major strategy that educators need to use for creating safe, constructive school environments is to address the contextual factors located within schools that appear to promote antisocial behavior. Several investigators have implemented approaches that have addressed many of these factors. These include the Constructive Discipline Approach described by Mayer and his colleagues (1983c, 1999, 2000), the PEACE POWER! strategy (Mattaini, in press), the Behavior Support program (Metzler et al., in press; Sugai, Horner, & Sprague, 1999) and the Multi-Problem Prevention Approach (Embry, personal communication, February 2, 2001). These approaches do not treat students as though they are the sources of the problems. Rather, they advocate for students by helping teachers and administrators identify and correct factors within the school environment that promote antisocial behavior. As Ysseldyke et al. (1997) point out, problem behaviors, rather than being located within the student, are often due to a "mismatch between the characteristics of the learner and those of the instructional environment or the broader home/school context" (p. 5). Accepting this approach, as pointed out by Ysseldyke et al., will require a paradigm shift for many educators, as well as parents who, for years, have been told that behavior problems originate from within their children, or that the child is at fault and must be punished. Thus, suggestions are offered as to how educators might address each of the identified contextual factors.

## Reduce Punitive Methods of Control

Clovin and Sugai (1988) point out that while proactive strategies are generally used to remediate academic problems, reactive, punitive strategies tend to be used by educators for behavior problems. However, both academic and behavior problems are learned and respond to similar teaching strategies.

Educators can usually use positive behavioral interventions in place of punitive methods, particularly for minor infractions. Positive interventions include modeling and various differential reinforcement strategies. Such strategies are described and illustrated in many resources (e.g., Koegel, Koegel, & Dunlap, 1996; LaVigna & Donnellan, 1986; Mayer, 1999; Mayer, Ybarra, Pegadiotes, Fogliatti, & Pines, 2000; Sulzer-Azaroff & Mayer, 1991, 1994a). Their emphasis, like social skills training, is on teaching youngsters how to behave, not on how not to behave (as are punitive procedures). Thus, an instructional approach that teaches youngsters how to behave is recommended in place of reactive, punitive approaches. Similarly, educators need to spend more time on developing motivational systems for appropriate behavior and less time on designing punitive systems.

## Provide Clear Rules for Student Conduct and Discipline

One often hears the phrase that "youngsters should know how to behave." Yet the reality is that many youngsters do not know what is expected of them unless the expectations are clearly delineated. Expectations and demands vary from teacher to teacher as well as from parent to parent. Unclear discipline policies or rules result in a lack of compliance and an increase in problem behavior, because students are unclear as to what behaviors are acceptable and unacceptable. Unfortunately, the lack of compliance is likely to promote an increase in the use of more punitive sanctions in the classroom and school. In contrast, less discipline problems occur when students know and understand the rules for conduct (Mayer & Leone, 1999). Thus, clearly communicating the rules for student conduct is a major step in setting up effective classroom and schoolwide discipline programs.

Several actions are taken to increase the likelihood that rules will be communicated clearly throughout the school and in the classroom. First, *all relevant parties*–including administrators, counselors, psychologists, teachers, parents, and students–*should be represented when schoolwide rules are being developed*. Rules tend to be better accepted, understood, supported, and enforced when all concerned parties have been included in drawing up a conduct code. Once an initial draft of the schoolwide rules and consequences has been developed, it should be shared as a mechanism for broadly-based community input. A draft, including formulated consequences, can be circulated to *all* staff, students, and parents for additional comments. A legal review of the document also is often necessary before a final draft is drawn up by the committee for administrative approval.

As with schoolwide rules, students should be involved in the development of classroom rules. Mayer (1999) presented seven major guidelines for clearly communicating classroom rules for acceptable student conduct. Each is reviewed below.

*Involve students in the development of the rules.* When students are involved in the development of the rules they tend to become more aware of and understand the rules better, and they are more likely to adopt and adhere to them. Students can be asked for their suggestions about rules that will help promote a positive learning environment and/or a possible set of rules can be presented to the class for discussion and suggestions.

*State the rules positively.* Once the rules have been listed, review them and state them positively. For example, "Don't be late to class" does not clearly communicate what is expected of the students. Are students not late as long as at least one foot is in the classroom by the time the tardy bell rings, or must students be in their seats? The rule, "Be in your seat before the tardy bell rings," more clearly communicates the desired or expected behavior. Similarly, "Don't blurt out" does not communicate what a student must do to answer a question or attain help. Stating the rule as, "Raise your hand and wait to be called on before asking or answering a question," explains what students must do in order to obtain positive teacher attention or assistance. Again, positively stated rules more clearly communicate what is expected. The focus also now has moved from teaching students "what not to do" to "how to behave": An approach that is more positive and educational vs. less suppressive.

*Keep the rules simple and short.* Students, as well as educators, tend not to remember a long list of rules. Thus, once the list has been stated positively, help the students combine the suggested rules into a total of about six to eight. Here is a sample list of eight classroom rules:

- Bring books, pencil, and paper
- Be in your seat when tardy bell rings
- Listen carefully
- Follow directions
- Complete assignments
- Show courtesy and respect to other
- We will help others who are being bullied by getting adult help and/or speaking out
- We will try to include ALL students in activities

Some schools, particularly middle and high schools, often prefer to come up with as set of rules that will apply to all classrooms. Such an approach helps to avoid confusion for students who have more than one teacher. Thus, one high school developed the following set of five common rules:

- Be in your seat in the assigned classroom before the tardy bell rings
- Bring proper books, pencil and other needed materials to class
- Keep your hands, feet and objects to yourself
- Listen carefully to your teacher's instruction
- Treat others, students and staff with respect

Individual teachers could add a rule or two if needed (as determined by the teacher and class).

*Review school policies and make sure the rules do not conflict with them.* Once the rules have been developed, the classroom rules, such as the schoolwide rules, should be shared with and approved by the responsible administrator(s).

*Teach the rules to the students.* It is helpful to present classroom rules both visually and orally to promote communication and reduce misunderstandings. The rules can be displayed prominently on a poster, printed in handout form, and copied by the students in their notebooks. For preschool and primary pupils, and for students with cognitive handicaps, it is helpful to role-play each rule as part of the explanatory process.

*Rules alone do not bring about appropriate behavior.* Classroom rules are part of the management plan that also includes frequent reinforcement for appropriate behavior (in addition to predictable routines, frequent monitoring, etc.). Reinforcement must be delivered for rule following and not for rule violations. As Mayer and Sulzer-Azaroff (1991) have pointed out, *rules will be followed only when differential consequences are applied for compliance and noncompliance.* When rule following is reinforced consistently, where as infractions are not, the environment will soon cue the students to behave in accordance with the rules.

*Inform parents and solicit their support.* Parental support helps classroom rules to be effective. Therefore, share the final draft with parents. A letter home detailing the rules can help to avoid misunderstandings and solicit increased parental support.

*Review the rules periodically and revise as necessary.* Rules should be reviewed orally as needed, and are never written in cement. They are working drafts that will need to be modified as needs arise and the student body changes.

In summary, Mayer et al. (2000) point out, "Students need meaningful interactions with the rules to learn the code of conduct. Do not just give the students a paper or booklet about the rules."

### Assure Support for Educators

Weak or inconsistent administrative support tends to cause staff *not* to receive reinforcement for their teaching or classroom management programs (Mayer, Butterworth, Komoto, & Benoit, 1983a). A lack of support can be aversive for staff, fostering a greater reliance on punitive methods of control in managing student behavior (Mayer, Nafpaktitis, Butterworth, & Hollingsworth, 1987) and more teacher absenteeism (Manlove & Elliott, 1979). Thus, as Mayer (2001) points out, "A lack of support for the teacher is likely to result in an increase in student problem behavior, because of the escalation of punitive methods of control."

Support for staff is a necessary component of violence prevention programs. In the same way that social support from a spouse or family member increases the effectiveness of the interventions used in the home, support from other teachers and administrators appears critical for effective program implementation by a teacher at school. Good teaching needs to be recognized and faculty requests for curriculum or discipline assistance acted upon promptly.

Support is particularly important for implementing discipline codes because it is everyone's mutual responsibility to apply and enforce them. In particular, teachers and administrators depend on one another's support. Administrators need to know what steps a teacher took before he or she decided to send a student to the office if they are going to feel supported by the staff. Similarly, teachers must know that appropriate action will be taken consistently by the administration when a student is sent to the office if they are to feel supported. Thus, classroom and schoolwide discipline programs must be mutually coordinated.

To develop additional support for staff, use programs designed to improve staff morale, communication, and cohesiveness. Many of these programs–such as "secret pals" for staff members, "extra thanks board," and "hot messages" to teachers–have been illustrated elsewhere (Mayer et al., 1983b, Sulzer-Azaroff & Mayer, 1991, 1994c). Briefly, their purpose is to decrease aversiveness and increase the reinforcement for teachers and administrators. For example, administrators and other support staff are asked to comment positively on the constructive programs that their teachers are implementing in their classes. Similarly, other teachers and parents are encouraged to make positive comments and demonstrate their appreciation for what others in the school do to assist students and one another. For example, colleagues write one another positive notes on a "Fuzzy Gram" or "Thank-U-Board" located in the faculty lounge. Individual staff might also be assigned "secret pals" to whom they are responsible for writing positive notes. A principal may send "hot messages" to teachers congratulating them for the successful programs implemented in their classrooms. Part of the rationale for implementing such activities is to help the school environment become a discriminative stimulus, or prompt, for implementing constructive discipline programs.

### Minimize Academic Failure Experiences

We now know there is a strong negative relationship between delinquency and literacy. Failure level academic tasks produce significant increases in problem behavior for some students, and "poor scholastic experiences are significant causes of delinquent and disruptive behavior" (Gold & Mann, 1982, p. 313). Berlin and Sum (1988) reported that poor basic skills are evident in 69% of all those arrested, 79% of welfare dependents, 85% of unwed mothers, 85% of dropouts, and 72% of the unemployed.

Repeated academic failure experiences are punishing to students and result in more behavior problems. For example, several instructions followed by several errors can provide a context in which the next instruction can result in an aggressive response by the student (Munk & Repp, 1994). Moreover, it is common to discover mismatches between a student's assignment and his or her level of academic functioning. For example, a group of high school students may be asked to read and comprehend material at the eleventh grade level when their reading skill is at the third grade level. Thus, *academic failure situations result in punitive/aversive experiences for students that promote increases in problem behavior both in and out of the classroom.*

Academic assignments need to be appropriate for each student's functional level to minimize failure. It also would be beneficial to program frequent success into the academic experiences by interspersing tasks that have a high probability of success (Munk & Repp, 1994; Sulzer-Azaroff & Mayer 1994b). Such an activity could serve as review and help develop fluency.

### Teach Critical Social Skills

Many students lack the social skills necessary to do well academically and to relate positively to peers. For example, most youngsters learn to pay attention when they are read to and when they participate in family discussions. Others, however, do not have these experiences and do not learn to pay attention effectively. Similarly, some students might not have learned to persist on a task, comply with requests, negotiate differences, handle criticism from adults nor teasing from peers, or make appropriate decisions. To illustrate, one youngster, who came from a home environment featuring many threats that were seldom followed through upon, was told by a school principal that he had to leave the lunch area because it was time for the staff to clean it. He refused because he was not done with his lunch. The principal told him that, if he continued to refuse, she would have to suspend him for the rest of the day. He refused and was suspended. When asked why, his honest response was "I didn't believe her." Accustomed to receiving threats that were not "backed up," he had learned to ignore them.

Too often youngsters who lack critical social skills are punished by educators for their "misbehavior" (e.g., not paying attention, noncompliance) rather than taught the necessary social skill(s). As a result, they continue not to learn the necessary social skills and to receive punishment. This results in an unnecessarily punitive classroom environment that fosters student misbehavior.

Similarly, some youngsters have not learned the appropriate social skills that will help them to be accepted by their peers. These youngsters are often rejected and/or bullied by others, making the school a very punitive place for them. Bullying is now recognized as a dangerous, abusive, behavior that often leads to violent behavior by the bully and sometimes the victim (Mayer et al., 2000). Alternative social skills should be taught to bullies while the victims need to be taught appropriate responses (e.g., leave situation, rebuff in a firm manner, etc.), and other appropriate peer relationship skills as needed (e.g., assisting others, sharing, caring for physical appearance, etc.). Bullying needs to be addressed in the classroom and schoolwide rules, and not tolerated (see Mayer et al., 2000; and U.S. Dept. of Education, 2000a for possible interventions for bullying).

Social skills training must be addressed in our schools, and several training strategies and programs are available (e.g., Mayer et al., 2000; McGinnes, & Goldstein, 1997; Panayan, 1998; Sheridan, 1995; Sulzer-Azaroff & Mayer, 1994c).

## *Use Appropriate Behavior Management Procedures*

Behavioral assessment can help teachers avoid misusing behavior management procedures. Functional assessments are defined (Neef & Iwata, 1994) as "an attempt to identify the environmental determinants of specific responses that currently exist in an individual's repertoire" (p. 211). According to Horner (1994), the purpose of a functional assessment is to provide information that will improve the effectiveness and efficiency of treatment, and it includes the following four basic requirements:

a. problem behaviors are operationally defined,
b. antecedent events that predict the occurrence and nonoccurrence of the problem behaviors are identified,
c. hypotheses are developed concerning the consequent variables that maintain problem behaviors,
d. direct observation data are collected to provide at least correlational confirmation of hypotheses associated with antecedent and consequent events. (p. 402)

In addition it is useful, in determining function and selecting relevant interventions, to collect the same information on the replacement behavior (if it has occurred).

Functional assessments have also been used with groups of students to improve behaviors in the lunch area, lavatory, on the school grounds, and on the school bus. For illustrations, see Sulzer-Azaroff and Mayer (1994a) and Mayer et al. (1983b). Interventions based on the behavior's function usually are more effective, and can reduce the need to use punitive approaches (Iwata et al., 1994; Mayer, 1996, 1993; Sulzer-Azaroff &

Mayer, 1991, 1994a). Of course, it would be most difficult to conduct functional assessments on every student. However, teachers can often do informal functional assessments based on their knowledge and observations of their students, particularly when they have been taught for what to look (See Mayer et al., 2000). Some teachers can do more elaborate functional assessments on one or two of their students when the student is not responding as anticipated to the implemented program. In more difficult or complex cases the school psychologist can often be of help in that many, particularly the more recently trained school psychologists, have training in conducting functional assessments, and are Board Certified Behavior Analysts.

Frequently identified behavioral functions include escape/avoidance; attention seeking; access to materials, activities, or food; and sensory stimulation. Treatment approaches based on such behavioral function, then, can result in major reductions in (a) the misuse of behavior procedures and (b) the use of punishment by educators, which in turn can provide a more reinforcing environment conducive to learning. For example, teachers learn not to place a child in time-out when the student is misbehaving to escape from an activity, request, assignment, or demand. The use of time-out in this situation (when the student is misbehaving) would be teaching the student to misbehave. Why? Because if the student misbehaves, he or she will be able to escape from the request or difficult task by being placed in time-out. Similarly, teachers learn not to redirect students who are misbehaving into another activity in order to obtain attention. Redirection would give them some of the attention they are seeking; therefore the misbehavior works, proving functional for the youngsters. Any behavior that proves functional, or gets the student what he or she wants, is likely to be repeated. It follows that consequences that reinforce the function of the student's misbehavior can result in an increase, rather than a decrease, in the misbehavior. Thus, *the use of inappropriate consequences can result in teaching misbehavior.* And, as we have seen, the resultant increase in misbehavior often results in the administration of more punitive consequences that can further increase the occurrence of future problem behaviors. There is a variety of sources on functional assessment that can assist educators in determining what would be the most appropriate behavioral strategy to use (e.g., Durand, 1993; Mayer, 1996; Mayer et al., 2000; O'Neill, Horner, Albin, Storey, & Sprague, 1990; Tilly et al., 1998).

### Support Student Involvement

Low student participation in class work and in after school activities is usually caused by one of the other factors discussed above (e.g., academic failure experiences, or critical social skills are lacking that form the basis of doing well academically and relating positively to others). Often, students become disengaged and "hate" school because they are rejected by their peers, and/or because of a history of failure and frequent punishment in the classroom. Thus, by addressing the above contextual factors, student involvement can be enhanced. Also, sometimes it is helpful to provide incentives and/or motivational programs for involvement (see Mayer et al., 2000, for illustrations).

### Respect, Value, and Understand Student Differences

Some behavior problems result from a lack of understanding and sensitivity by students, teachers, and others towards students who present behavior and learning challenges, or are from different cultures. It is important to recognize that "what teachers consider to be 'discipline problems' are determined by their own culture, personal values, and teaching styles" (Kea, 1998). Research clearly shows that punishment occurs disproportionately with males, minorities, students from low-income homes, and those with learning disabilities and emotional problems (McFadden, Marsh, Price, & Hwang, 1992; Shaw & Braden, 1990; Shores et al., 1993). These students are disciplined, suspended, and expelled more often than other students. For example, Larson (1994) reported that students with learning disabilities and emotional problems experience a more aversive punitive environment in public schools than when they are incarcerated in youth prisons. Similarly, minority students experience a more aversive punitive environment in our schools than White students (Brooks et al., 1999).

A body of literature is now developing describing ethnic and cultural differences. Teachers who are aware of this information are in better positions to avoid inequitable discipline, and to understand and work more effectively with students who are culturally and linguistically different from their own cultures. A number of researchers (e.g., Kea, 1998; Steinberg, Brown, & Dornbusch, 1996) have summarized ethnic/cultural differences in the literature. However, findings from one study or report may not be representative of the ethnic or cultural group in a particular community, and therefore may not apply. There also is a wide variety of values and beliefs within any ethnic or cultural group. *Caution*: Do not assume that findings from one report are necessarily true for every student within a particular ethnic or cultural group. Also remember that individual differences are incorporated throughout the application of behavioral procedures that are based on functional assessments.

## *CONCLUSIONS*

School environments within the United States are punitive for a number of students. The increased emphasis on the use of punitive measures within our schools, as well as our society, may well be contributing to school violence and other antisocial behaviors.

As Mayer (1999) has pointed out in his approach to school discipline, punitive measures need to be reserved for major infractions. Positive behavioral interventions often work very effectively upon minor infractions. When punishment is chosen for most infractions, it is being overused and becomes less effective. In addition, the overuse of punitive measures results in lowered self-concepts, negative attitudes towards school, escape reactions (being tardy, truant, and/or dropping out), and aggression/violence against property and people.

Reactive solutions that rely on security (e.g., alarm systems, security personnel) and punitive measures appear to aggravate, not reduce, antisocial behavior over time. Thus, security arrangements and punitive measures, when necessary, must be viewed as temporary, reactive expedients to help gain control in the situation while contextual factors that appear to contribute to violence and other antisocial behaviors are addressed within the school. In addressing these factors, an over-reliance on punitive methods of control must be reduced and replaced with constructive alternatives or positive behavioral interventions. Schoolwide and classroom rules must be clearly communicated. Staff must be supported. Assignments and instruction must address each student's level of academic functioning. Similarly, because many youngsters do not have the social skills needed to do well academically (e.g., persistence on task, paying attention) or to relate positively to others (e.g., compliments others, handles criticism and teasing), educators need to teach these skills, rather than punishing students because they do not engage in the skills. Teachers also need to understand why misbehavior is occurring in order to prevent the misuse of behavior management procedures that can result in teaching students to misbehave. Students need to be encouraged to become involved in school activities, and individual differences (e.g., cultural and linguistic) need to be respected and valued, not punished.

Punitive measures are not *the* solution for eliminating violence and other antisocial behaviors. We will not be able to *prevent* violence durably and other antisocial behavior until we address the identified contextual factors. We cannot afford to fail a large percentage of our human resources by continuing to place the emphasis in school discipline on the reactive measures of security arrangements, punishment, suspensions/expulsions, or incarceration.

# REFERENCES

Azrin, N. H., Hake, D. G., Holz, W. C., & Hutchinson, R. R. (1965). Motivational aspects of escape from punishment. *Journal of the Experimental Analysis of Behavior*, *8*, 31-34.

Berkowitz, L. (1983). Aversively stimulated aggression: Some parallels and difference in research with animals and humans. *American Psychologist*, *38*, 1135-1144.

Berlin, J. A., & Sum, A. (1988). *Toward more perfect union: Basic skills, poor families, and our economic future*. New York: The Ford Foundation.

Brodinsky, B. (1980). *AASA critical issues report: Student discipline, problems, and solutions* (Report No. 021 00334). Arlington, VA: American Association of School Administrators.

Brooks, K., Schiraldi, V., & Ziedenberg, J. (1999). *School house hype: Two years later*. San Francisco, CA: Center of Juvenile and Criminal Justice (www.cjcj.org).

Colvin, G., & Sugai, G. (1988). Proactive strategies for managing social behavior problems: An instructional approach. *Education and Treatment of Children*, *11*, 341-348.

Durand, V. M. (1993). Functional assessment and functional analysis. In *Behavior modification for exceptional children and youth* (pp. 38-60). Edited by M. D. Smith. Stoneham, Mass: Andover Medical Publishers.

Gold, M., & Mann, D. W. (1982). Alternative schools for troublesome secondary students. *Urban Review*, *14*, 305-316.

Greenberg, B. (1974). School vandalism: Its effects and paradoxical solutions. *Crime Prevention Review*, *1*, 105.

Henggeler, S. W., Melton, G. B., & Smith, L. A. (1992). Family preservation using multisystemic therapy: An effective alternative to incarcerating serious juvenile offenders. *Journal of Consulting and Clinical Psychology*, *60*, 1-9.

Hodgkinson, H. (1991). Reform versus reality. *Phi Delta Kappan*, *73*, 8-16.

Horner, R. H. (1994). Functional assessment: Contributions and future directions. *Journal of Applied Behavior Analysis*, *27*, 401-404.

Ingersoll, S., & LeBoeuf, K. (1997, February). Reaching out to youth out of the education mainstream. *Juvenile Justice Bulletin*, 1-11. U.S. Department of Justice, Office of Juvenile Justice and Delinquency Prevention.

Iwata, B. A., Pace, G. M., Dorsey, M. F., Zarcone, J. R., Vollmer, T. R., Smith, R.G., Rodgers, T. A., Lerman, D. C., Shore, B. A., Mazaleski, J. L., Goh, H., Cowdery, G. E., Kalsher, M. J., McCosh, K. D., & Willis, K. D. (1994). The functions of self-injurious behavior: An experimental-epidemiological analysis. *Journal of Applied Behavior Analysis*, *27*, 215-240.

Kea, C. (1998, June). Focus on ethnic and minority concerns. *Newsletter, Council for Children with Behavioral Disorders*, *11*(6), 4-5.

Koegel, L.K., Koegel, R. L., & Dunlap, G. (1966). *Positive behavioral support including people with difficult behavior in the community*. Baltimore: P. Brooks Publishing Co.

Larson, K. (1994). *Negative school culture*. Office of Special Education Programs, Spring Leadership Conference Executive Report, May, 9-12, p. 8. Available from the Mountain Plains Regional Resource Center, Utah State University, Logan, Utah 84341.

La Vigna, G. D., & Donnellan, A. (1986). *Alternatives to punishment: Solving behavior problems with non-aversive strategies*. New York: Irvington.

Loeber, R., Stouthamer-Loeber, M., & Green, F. (1987). Prediction. In H. C. Quay (Ed.). *Handbook of juvenile delinquency* (pp. 325-382). New York: Wiley.

Manlove, D. C., & Elliott, P. (1979). Absent teachers. Another handicap for students? *The Practitioner, 5*, 2-3.

Mattaini, M. A. (in press). Constructing cultures of non-violence: The PEACE POWER! strategy. *Education and Treatment of Children, 24*.

Mayer, G. R. (1995). Preventing antisocial behavior in the schools. *Journal of Applied Behavior Analysis, 28*, 467-478.

Mayer, G. R. (1996). Conducting a functional assessment and its relevance to intervention. *California School Psychologist, 1*, 29-34.

Mayer, G. R. (1999). Constructive discipline for school personnel. *Education and Treatment of Children, 22*, 36-54.

Mayer, G. R. (2001). Antisocial behavior: Its causes and prevention within our schools. *Education and Treatment of Children, 24*, 414-429.

Mayer, G. R., & Butterworth, T. (1979). A preventive approach to school violence and vandalism: An experimental study. *Personnel and Guidance Journal, 57*, 436-441.

Mayer, G. R., & Butterworth, T. (1981). Evaluating a preventive approach to reducing school vandalism. *Phi Delta Kappan, 62*, 498-499.

Mayer, G. R., Butterworth, T., Komoto, T., & Benoit, R. (1983a). The influence of the school principal on the consultant's effectiveness. *Elementary School Guidance & Counseling, 17*, 274-279.

Mayer, G. R., Butterworth, T., Nafpaktitis, M., & Sulzer-Azaroff, B. (1983a). Preventing school vandalism and improving discipline: A three-year study. *Journal of Applied Behavior Analysis, 16*, 355-369.

Mayer, G. R., Butterworth, T., Spaulding, H. L., Hollingsworth, P., Amorim, M., Caldwell-McElroy, C., Nafpaktitis, M., & Perez-Osorio, X. (1983b). *Constructive discipline: Building a climate for learning. A Resource manual of programs and strategies*. Downey, CA: Office of the Los Angeles County Superintendent of Schools.

Mayer, G. R., Mitchell, L., Clementi, T., Clement-Robertson, E., Myatt, R., & Bullara, D. T. (1993). A dropout prevention program for at-risk high school students: Emphasizing consulting to promote positive classroom climates. *Education and Treatment of Children, 16*, 135-146.

Mayer, G. R., Nafpaktitis, M., Butterworth, T., & Hollingsworth, P. (1987). A search for the elusive setting events of school vandalism: A correlational study. *Education and Treatment of Children, 10*, 259-270.

Mayer, G. R., & Sulzer-Azaroff, B. (1991). Interventions for vandalism. In G. Stoner, M. K. Shinn, & H. M. Walker (Eds.), *Interventions for achievement and behavior problems*. Washington, DC: National Association of School Psychologists Monograph.

Mayer, G. R., Ybarra, W. J., Pegadiotes, D., Fogliatti, H., & Pines, M. (2000). *Classroom management: A California resource guide*. CA Dept. of Education and LA County Office of Education, Safe Schools Center.

Mayer, M. J., & Leone, P. E. (1999). A structural analysis of school violence and disruption: Implications for creating safer schools. *Education and Treatment of Children, 22*, 333-356.

McFadden, A. C., Marsh, G. E., Price, B. J., & Hwang, Y. (1992). A study of race and gender bias in the punishment of school children. *Education and Treatment of Children, 15*, 140-146.

McGinnis, E., & Goldstein, A. P. (1997). *Skillstreaming the elementary school child: A guide for teaching prosocial skills*. Champaign IL.: Research Press.

Metzler, C. W., Biglan, A., Rusby, J. C., & Sprague, J. R. (in press). Evaluation of a comprehensive behavior management program to improve school-wide positive behavior support. *Education and Treatment of Children, 24*.

Moultrie, D. (2001, March 21). Violent crime rises in state's large cities. *Los Angeles Times*, A3.

Munk, D. D., & Repp, A. C. (1994). The relationship between instructional variables and problem behavior: A review. *Exceptional Children, 60*, 390-401.

Neff, N. A., & Iwata, B. A. (1994). Current research on functional analysis methodologies: An introduction. *Journal of Applied Behavior Analysis, 27*, 211-214.

O'Neill, R. E., Horner, R. H., Albin, R. W., Storey, K., & Sprague, J. R. (1990). *Functional analysis of problem behavior: A practical assessment guide*. Pacific Grove, CA: Brooks/Cole.

Panayan, M. V. (1998). *How to teach social skills*. Austin: Pro-ed.

Puritz, P., & Shang, W. W. L. (1998, Dec.) Innovative approaches to juvenile indigent defense. *OJJDP Juvenile Justice Bulletin, December*, 1-8.

Reid, J. B., & Patterson, G. R. (1989). The development of antisocial behavior patterns in childhood and adolescence. *European Journal of Personality, 3*, 107-119.

Shaw, S. R., & Braden, J. P. (1990). Race and gender bias in the administration of corporal punishment. *School Psychology Review, 19*, 378-383.

Sheridan, S. M. (1995). *The tough kid social skills book*. Longmont, CO: Sopris West.

Shores, R. E., Jack, S. L., Gunter, P. L., Ellis, D. N., DeBriere, J. J., & Wehby, J. H. (1993). Classroom interactions of children with behavior disorders. *Journal of Emotional and Behavioral Disorders, 1*, 27-29.

Skiba, R. J., Peterson, R. L., & Williams, T. (1997). Office referrals and suspension: Disciplinary intervention in middle schools. *Education and Treatment of Children, 20*, 295-315.

Snyder, H. N. (2000, December). Juvenile Arrests 1999. *Juvenile Justice Bulletin*, 1-11, U. S. Department of Justice, Office of Juvenile Justice and Delinquency Prevention.

Sprague, J., Walker, H., Golly, A., White, K., Myers, D., & Shannon, T. (in press). Translating research into effective practice: The effects of a universal staff and student intervention on indicators of discipline and school safety. *Education and Treatment of Children, 24*.

Steinberg, S., Brown, B. B., & Dornbusch, S. M. (1996). Ethnicity and adolescent achievement. *American Educator, 20*(2), 28-35, 44-48.

Sugai, G., Horner, R. H., & Sprague, J. (1999). Functional assessment-based behavior support planning: Research-to-practice-to-research. *Behavior Disorders, 24,* 223-227.

Sulzer-Azaroff, B., & Mayer, G.R. (1991). *Behavior analysis for lasting change.* Fort Worth: Harcourt, Brace & Jovanovich.

Sulzer-Azaroff, B., & Mayer, G. R. (1994a). *Achieving educational excellence: Behavior analysis for school personnel.* P.O. Box 427, San Marcos, CA: Western Image.

Sulzer-Azaroff, B., & Mayer, G. R. (1994b). *Achieving educational excellence: Behavior analysis for improving instruction.* P.O. Box 427, San Marcos, CA: Western Image.

Sulzer-Azaroff, B., & Mayer, G. R. (1994c). *Achieving educational excellence: Behavior analysis for achieving classroom and schoolwide behavior change.* P.O. Box 427, San Marcos, CA: Western Image.

Tilly, W. D., Kovaleski, J., Dunlap, G., Knoster, T. P., Bambara, L., & Kincaid, D. (1998). *Functional behavioral assessment: Policy development in light of emerging research and practice.* Alexandria, VA: National Association of State Directors of Special Education (NASDSE).

U.S. Department of Education. (2000a). *Preventing bullying: A manual for schools and communities.* Washington, DC.

U.S. Department of Education. (2000b). *Effective alternative strategies: Grant competition to reduce student suspensions and expulsions and ensure educational progress of suspended and expelled students.* Washington, DC: Safe and drug-free schools program. OMB# 1810-0551.

Wehby, J. H., Symons, F. J., & Shores, R. E. (1995). A descriptive analysis of aggressive behavior in classrooms for children with emotional and behavioral disorders. *Behavioral Disorders, 20,* 87-105.

Ysseldyke, J., Dawson, P., Lehr, C., Reschly, D., Reynolds, M., & Telzrow, C. (1997). *School psychology: A blueprint for training and practice II.* Bethesda, MD: National Association of School Psychologists.

# Using Curriculum-Based Measurement to Evaluate Intervention Efficacy

Gary Stoner
Stanley E. Scarpati
Robin L. Phaneuf
John M. Hintze

**SUMMARY.** The use of Curriculum-Based Measurement for evaluating treatment efficacy is described and discussed. The basic methods and applications of Curriculum-Based Measurement are described, followed by examples of its application in two intervention program evaluation projects. The first project involved one individual student experiencing academic difficulties. The second project focused on evaluating a reading instruction program for a group of students. In both examples, the use of Curriculum-Based Measurement contributed significantly to monitoring student progress in response to educational program variables and making treatment evaluation decisions. *[Article copies available for a fee from The Haworth Document Delivery Service: 1-800-HAWORTH. E-mail address: <getinfo@haworthpressinc.com> Website: <http://www.HaworthPress.com> © 2002 by The Haworth Press, Inc. All rights reserved.]*

**KEYWORDS.** CBM, academic instruction, educational intervention

Gary Stoner, Stanley E. Scarpati, Robin L. Phaneuf, and John M. Hintze are affiliated with the University of Massachusetts at Amherst.

Address correspondence to: Gary Stoner, PhD, School Psychology Program, School of Education, University of Massachusetts at Amherst, Amherst, MA 01003-4150.

[Haworth co-indexing entry note]: "Using Curriculum-Based Measurement to Evaluate Intervention Efficacy." Stoner, Gary et al. Co-published simultaneously in *Child & Family Behavior Therapy* (The Haworth Press, Inc.) Vol. 24, No. 1/2, 2002, pp. 101-112; and: *Behavior Psychology in the Schools: Innovations in Evaluation, Support, and Consultation* (ed: James K. Luiselli, and Charles Diament) The Haworth Press, Inc., 2002, pp. 101-112. Single or multiple copies of this article are available for a fee from The Haworth Document Delivery Service [1-800-HAWORTH, 9:00 a.m. - 5:00 p.m. (EST). E-mail address: getinfo@haworthpressinc.com].

The environment for professional practice in today's public schools increasingly is one characterized, and sometimes dominated, by discussion of accountability, data-based decision making, and program effectiveness. Administrators, educators, parents, students, and other community members all are interested in a positive return on their varying forms of educational investment. Professional organizations across areas of education and psychology also emphasize these themes. For example, the National Association of School Psychologists has endorsed among its top priorities for professional training and practice, data-based decision making and accountability, effective instruction, prevention, wellness promotion, and program evaluation (Ysseldyke et al., 1997). Similarly, the American Psychological Association emphasizes evidence-based intervention strategies in professional training and practice (Kratochwill & Stoiber, 2000; Stoiber & Kratochwill, 2000), and the National Council for the Accreditation of Teacher Education (National Council for the Accreditation of Teacher Education, 2001) standards for personnel preparation emphasize knowledge and skill development with a focus on student learning. As such, instructional and curricular programs of all types are the focus of increasing scrutiny, with an eye toward the provision of continued support for what works to improve child/student outcomes and the discontinuation of support for what does not work.

Evaluations of what does and does not work are particularly important for students experiencing behavior and achievement problems, and who may be characterized as difficult-to-manage and/or difficult-to-teach. Continuation of ineffective interventions places these students further behind their typically developing peers, and at increasingly greater risk for adjustment problems, school dropout, referral to special education, and a host of problematic life outcomes (Patterson, Reid, & Dishion, 1992). Conversely, the promotion of positive educational and life outcomes for these students is, at least in part, dependent on the design, implementation, and evaluation of effective interventions. As Ikeda, Tilly, Stumme, Volmer, and Allison (1996) have discussed with regard to district-wide innovations in school-based problem solving, one critical foundation of such efforts is a commitment to measuring student performance frequently and changing programs when students are not progressing.

One important tool useful for systematically evaluating interventions through measurement of student performance is Curriculum-Based Measurement (CBM). Developed over the past two decades (Deno, 1992; Shinn, 1998), CBM is user friendly (Shinn, 1989), has foundations in behavioral assessment (Shinn, 1998), is grounded in a problem solving approach to educational practice (Deno, 1995), and is useful for making program evaluation decisions both for individual students as well as groups of students (Deno, 1986).

In the following sections we provide a basic description of CBM, followed by two examples of its use in consultation to evaluate intervention efficacy. The first example focuses on interventions for an individual student achievement problem. The second example describes a program evaluation project examining a reading instruction program for a group of students identified as at risk for or having reading problems.

## WHAT IS CURRICULUM-BASED MEASUREMENT?

Grounded in behavioral assessment, Curriculum-Based Measurement (CBM) was developed to both provide a technology for systematic, formative evaluation of student academic outcomes in the basic skill areas of reading, spelling, writing, and math, and to support intervention effectiveness evaluations using single-case study designs (Deno, Mirkin, & Chiang, 1982). Primary CBM data are derived from brief (1- to 3-min) *fluency* measures of student performance. These measures are content valid in that the materials used to evaluate outcomes are sampled directly from the student's curriculum. Also, the measures assess important and socially valid terminal behaviors, such as the number of words read correctly, number of correct letter sequences written, number of correct math problems or correct digits written.

A goal of CBM is to provide teachers with assessment information that can be used to plan instructional programs and to evaluate overall student growth. This goal is facilitated by CBM yielding rate-based measures of student performance, such as words read correct per minute (WRC). WRC then often is translated into slope of progress over time, such as 2 WRC gain per week over a 4-week time frame. Another distinctive feature of CBM is that an extensive body of research has accumulated to support the technical adequacy of the principal measures from both behavioral and traditional psychometric perspectives (Fuchs & Deno, 1991; Good & Jefferson, 1998). Further, the standardized procedures for conducting CBM probes are designed for simple, low-cost, repeated administration (Knutson & Shinn, 1991).

A systematic program of research was initiated in the late 1970s to investigate the technical adequacy of the standardized academic tasks used in CBM (Marston, 1989). Since then, an extensive body of empirical evidence has been accumulated that supports the reliability and validity of CBM procedures for educational decision-making. For example, in the CBM reading task, the number of words read correctly has been validated as a reliable and accurate measure of students' general reading skills, including reading comprehension (Shinn, Good, Knutson, Tilly, & Collins, 1992). A summary of the standardized tasks and scoring procedures along with references to several studies documenting the technical adequacy of CBM reading, math, spelling and written expression measures are presented in Table 1. A number of researchers have demonstrated that CBM data are sensitive to changes in student performance as a result of various instructional interventions (Deno, Mirkin, & Chiang, 1982; Marston, Fuchs, & Deno, 1986), and as a result of interventions to address social behavior problems in classrooms. For example, CBM measures have been used to evaluate the effects of computer-assisted instruction (Fuchs, 1988), classwide peer-tutoring (DuPaul & Henningson, 1993), goal-setting strategies on students' academic achievement (Fuchs, Fuchs, & Hamlett, 1989), and stimulant medication on the academic performance of children presenting with disruptive behavior disorders (Stoner, Carey, Ikeda, & Shinn, 1994).

TABLE 1. CBM measures of reading, math, spelling and written expression: Standardized tasks, scoring procedures and technical adequacy research

| Academic Area | Task | Scoring | Technical Adequacy Evidence |
|---|---|---|---|
| Reading | Students read passages aloud for 1 minute. | Number of words read correctly. Number of errors. | Deno, Mirkin, & Chiang (1982); Fuchs, Fuchs, & Maxwell (1988) |
| Spelling | Students write words dictated orally for 2 minutes. | Number of correct letter sequences. Number of words spelled correctly. | Deno, Marston, Mirkin, Lowry, Sindelar, & Jenkins (1982); Marston, Lowry, Deno, & Mirkin (1981) |
| Written Expression | After being given a story starter or topic sentence, students write a story for 3 minutes. | Number of words written. Number of words spelled correctly. Number of correct word sequences. | Deno, Marston, & Mirkin (1982) |
| Math | Students write answers to written computation problems for 2-5 minutes. | Number of correct digits. | Fuchs & Fuchs (1987); Marston, Fuchs, & Deno (1986) |

## USING CBM TO EVALUATE A READING INTERVENTION PROGRAM FOR ONE STUDENT

Michael was a first-grade student referred by his teacher with concerns centering around his lack of progress in reading. As reported by the teacher, while typical students in the class were being instructed in the Grade-1 reader, Michael was being taught in Primer Level books (e.g., kindergarten level picture books) and still was experiencing frustration with respect to word recognition and reading fluency.

Upon initial assessment, Michael was asked to read isolated words presented on individual flash cards. From a pool of approximately 500 words, Michael was able to accurately read only 75 of the words presented. In addition to individual words, Michael also was asked to read selected passages from the material in which he was being instructed (i.e., Primer Level). When asked to do so, Michael on average was able to read only about 12 words correct per minute. School-based CBM norms indicated that typical first-grade students at that time of the year were able to read approximately 37 words correct per minute in Grade-1 material. Overall, results of the reading assessment indicated that, relative to his classmates, Michael was experiencing considerable difficulty in his beginning reading skills and was at risk for further reading problems.

Based on the results of the initial assessment, an intervention strategy was proposed that focused on building and strengthening Michael's word recognition and sight-word vocabulary skills. Specifically, a flash-card drill strategy was designed that contained both words that Michael had mastered and words that he had yet to learn (Gickling & Havertape, 1981). Mastered words were incorporated into the intervention to enhance Michael's sense of competence through success, as well as to foster his motivation to tackle new unlearned words. As presented, the flash-card drill and practice intervention contained all essential elements of effective instruction including modeling of accurate word reading by the teacher, prompting, and frequent opportunities to respond to instructional material. When words were pronounced incorrectly, the teacher provided the correct pronunciation, asked Michael to repeat the correct pronunciation, and then use the word correctly in a sentence. Furthermore, when Michael correctly read a previously unknown word five times in a row the word was considered mastered. When this happened, the newly mastered word was replaced by a new unmastered word in the flash-card drill packet.

The effect of the flash-card drill strategy on CBM oral reading fluency skills is presented in Figure 1. As can be seen, prior to any intervention Michael read on average about 12 words correct per minute in Grade-1 Level material. Initiation of the flash-card drill strategy improved Michael's oral reading fluency to about 19 words read correct per minute. This amounted to a gain of 7 words correct per minute over a two-week period, or about 3.5 words correct gain per week. Examination of the trend line during this first phase of intervention suggests, however, that although Michael was improving in his oral reading fluency skills at a rate of improvement that was normally expected of first-grade students, continued growth at this rate would not ameliorate the discrepancy between his current level of performance and that of his same age peers. Figure 1 data also indicate that after some initial improvement from days 5 to 11 in Michael's oral reading fluency skills, the slope of progress tapered off with negligible improvement observed over the following two weeks. Left unattended, the discrepancy between Michael's oral reading fluency skills and those of his peers would continue to grow. This prediction led to a decision to change the nature of the intervention and incorporate strategies that explicitly targeted oral reading fluency skills in connected text. In doing so, two intervention strategies were combined: (a) listening passage preview (LPP), and (b) repeated readings (RR) (Daly, Martens, Hamler, Dool, & Eckert, 1999). During this phase of intervention, the teacher first read a selected reading passage at a comfortable reading pace, and instructed Michael to follow along with his finger and read the words to himself (i.e., LPP).

FIGURE 1. Curriculum-based measurement oral reading fluency data for Michael as a function of baseline and intervention conditions.

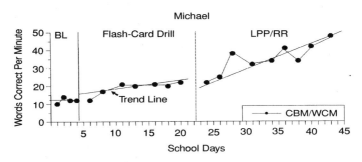

Note. BL = Baseline; LPP/RR = Listening Passage Preview/Repeated Reading. Portions of this figure are reproduced from Daly, Hintze, and Hamler (2000) with permission from John Wiley & Sons, Inc.

After this, Michael was asked to read the same passage three times in succession with the total amount of time required to finish the passage noted each time. The time it took to read the passage each time was graphed and combined with verbal praise and reinforcement for lowering the time it took to read the passage with each successive attempt. The results of this second phase of the intervention on CBM oral reading fluency skills can also be seen on Figure 1. With the initiation of LPP/RR, Michael's rate of improvement increased significantly. On average, Michael's overall reading rate increased from 19 words correct per minute during the first phase of intervention to 35 words read correct during the second phase of intervention. More importantly, however, the slope of Michael's growth was substantially greater as a result of LPP/RR. Specifically, Michael's rate of growth increased from about 3.5 words correct per week during the first intervention phase, to about 7 words correct per week during the second intervention phase. Such growth is nearly triple that of what can otherwise be normally expected of typically developing first-grade students. In comparing the trend lines across the two phases it is easy to see that the fluency based intervention was demonstrably better than the flash-card drill alone and served Michael well in helping to close the gap between his reading performance and that of his peers. Indeed, at the ninth week of intervention Michael was reading upwards of 50 words correct per minute in the Grade-1 level reader, a level commensurate with typical peer performance at that time of the school year in his school.

## USING CBM TO EVALUATE A GROUP READING INTERVENTION PROGRAM

Educators often are faced with the need to determine the effectiveness of instruction, that is, to simply answer questions about the efficacy of a particular curriculum or teaching strategy for a group of students, for example, at the program, classroom, or building level. The purpose of the project presented here was to evaluate a experimental reading instruction program (i.e., one with unproven efficacy) aimed at improving the reading skills of students with reading disabilities and/or students at risk for developing such problems. The program had been in place for a number of years, yet few data had been collected to speak to its effectiveness. Our primary goal was to determine the efficacy of the instruction and the progress of the students receiving instruction. The focus of the evaluation was on the progress in reading skills made by ten grade 3, 4, and 5 student participants, randomly selected from the total of twenty students in the experimental program. The same outcome measures were used for all children, and consisted of repeated curriculum-based measures of reading–specifically oral reading fluency. For each student in the evaluation, three oral reading fluency probes were administered at one sitting, on a weekly basis throughout the course of the evaluation, and the median score was taken as representative of that week's student performance.

CBM was selected as the tool for evaluating three aspects of student performance. First, CBM was used to determine the growth trajectories of students in the specialized reading group as indicated by rates of oral reading fluency. CBM data were used to determine the individual rates of progress as measured using time-series slopes of progress over a 10-12 week period of time. The slopes were described as words per week gain over time. Using both professionally agreed upon criterion for expected progress (i.e., 2-3 words per week gain in progress monitoring materials; see Fuchs et al., 1993), and projections of rates of gain necessary to approximate typical peer achievement, CBM data were used to determine how many children in the sample could be characterized as being successful or not successful in reading. Second, CBM was used to compare growth trajectories of students in the experimental group to students receiving instruction in general education (Shinn, 1988). The majority of children in an effective remedial reading program should experience average to above average gains via program participation. Comparison of experimental group students to students receiving instruction in general education provides a means of evaluating whether students in the experimental group are making gains over and above their peers. Finally, CBM was used to predict achievement trajectories beyond the time frame of the evaluation.

Data for five of the ten children evaluated are summarized in Table 2; the other five all entered the experimental program reading at skill levels above the 25th percentile relative to district norms, and as such were considered inappropriate candidates for continued program participation by our evaluation team. Outcomes of the evaluation generally indicated students in the experimental group most in need of remedial reading instruction typically were making less than average progress. Those participants least in need of remedial reading instruction typically were making average to above average progress. There were two exceptions to these findings in that one student with poor beginning level skills was found to be making above average progress, and one student with reasonably good beginning level skills was found to be making very little progress in reading. In general, the findings suggest a phenomenon of "the rich getting richer, and the poor getting poorer"–certainly not the intent of a specialized reading instruction program for low performing students. In addition, but beyond the scope of this paper, the data called into question the methods for selecting students for participation in the specialized program.

The data in Table 2 for two students, FG and JD, represent two of the major findings of the evaluation. During the course of the evaluation, FG was observed to be making progress in oral reading fluency at the rate of 2.7 words gain per week over the course of eleven weeks. Given this rate of progress and FG's beginning percentile rank, FG should be considered a student who is unsuccessful in reading skill development. FG needs to be making much greater progress in order to improve his relative standing, in the same manner as Michael in our first case study needed an additional intervention. By comparison, JD was observed to be making progress in oral reading fluency at the rate of 0.0 words per week gain. Given this lack of progress over three months time, and JD's beginning percentile rank, JD should be considered a student who is not successful in reading skill development. In order to improve her relative

TABLE 2. Reading achievement and progress data for experimental reading program students whose entry level reading skills were below the 25th percentile of local normative data.

| Student; grade in school | Percentile rank at program entry | Words read correct gain per week | Reading progress relative to expected progress | General conclusion |
|---|---|---|---|---|
| NP; 4th grade boy | 7th | 3.5 | Above average | Making above average progress; should be reintegrated into general education reading instruction |
| FG; 4th grade boy | 1st | 2.7 | Average | Making average progress; needs to make above average gains, given such low entry skills |
| KH; 5th grade girl | 9th | 1.45 | Below average | Making poor progress; needs intensive, more effective instruction |
| TS; 3rd grade girl | 7th | 1.25 | Below average | Making poor progress; needs intensive, more effective instruction |
| JD; 3rd grade girl | 6th | 0.00 | Below average | Making no progress; needs intensive, more effective instruction |

standing, she needs to be making much better progress than she currently is.

The use of CBM in this program evaluation clarified issues of identification of students in need of specialized instruction and accountability procedures to ensure exiting of successful students and additional support for students still struggling despite remedial efforts. Specific design constraints limited the ability of the evaluation to further address the effectiveness of the experimental reading instruction program. The most legitimate evaluation of such a program would include at least the following components:

1. random assignment of identified children to experimental and control groups,
2. blinded, placebo controlled evaluations of treatment outcomes,
3. carefully examined and documented manipulations of the treatment components thought to be salient or powerful,
4. use of outcome measures meeting professional standards for technical adequacy and administered under standardized conditions.

However, despite the methodological limits placed on this evaluation, the CBM based approach yielded valid and useful data about the efficacy of the experimental reading program.

In summary, Curriculum-Based Measurement of basic academic skills represents a technically adequate and useful set of strategies for measuring and monitoring student achievement. Use of these strategies in monitoring student progress can contribute significantly to questions of intervention program efficacy at both the individual and group level, for interventions for achievement and behavior problems.

## REFERENCES

Daly, E. J., III, Hintze, J. M., & Hamler, K. R. (2000). Improving practice by taking steps toward technological improvements in academic intervention in the new millennium. *Psychology in the Schools, 37*, 61-72.

Daly, E. J., III, Martens, B. K., Hamler, K. R., Dool, E. J., & Eckert, T. L. (1999). A brief experimental analysis for identifying instructional components needed to improve oral reading fluency. *Journal of Applied Behavior Analysis, 32*, 83-94.

Deno, S. L. (1986). Formative evaluation of individual student programs: A new role for school psychologists. *School Psychology Review, 15*, 358-374.

Deno, S. L. (1992). The nature and development of curriculum-based measurement. *Preventing School Failure, 36(2)*, 5-10.

Deno, S. L. (1995). School psychologists as problem solvers. In A. Thomas and J. Grimes (Eds.), *Best Practices in School Psychology (3rd Ed.)*, pp. 471-484. Bethesda, MD: National Association of School Psychologists.

Deno, S. L., Marston, D., & Mirkin, P. K. (1982). Valid measurement procedures for continuous evaluation of written expression. *Exceptional Children, 48*, 368-371.

Deno, S. L., Marston, D., Mirkin, P. K., Lowry, L., Sindelar, P., & Jenkins, J. (1982). *The use of standardized tasks to measure achievement in reading, spelling, and written expression: A normative and developmental study.* Minneapolis: University of Minnesota Institute for Research on Learning Disabilities.

Deno, S. L., Mirkin, P. K., & Chiang, B. (1982). Identifying valid measures of reading. *Exceptional Children, 49,* 36-45.

DuPaul, G. J., & Henningson, P. N. (1993). Peer tutoring effects on the classroom performance of children with attention deficit hyperactivity disorder. *School Psychology Review, 22,* 134-143.

Fuchs, L. S. (1988). Effects of computer-managed instruction on teachers' implementation of systematic monitoring programs and student achievement. *Journal of Educational Research, 81,* 294-304.

Fuchs, L. S., & Deno, S. L. (1991). Paradigmatic distinctions between instructionally relevant measurement models. *Exceptional Children, 57,* 488-500.

Fuchs, L. S., Fuchs, D., & Hamlett, C. (1989). Effects of alternative goal structures within curriculum-based measurement. *Exceptional Children, 55,* 429-438.

Fuchs, L. S., Fuchs, D., Hamlett, C. L., Walz, L., & Germann, G. (1993). Formative evaluation of academic progress: How much can we expect? *School Psychology Review, 22,* 27-48.

Fuchs, L. S., Fuchs, D., & Maxwell, L. (1988). The validity of informal reading comprehension measures. *Remedial and Special Education, 9,* 20-28.

Gickling, E. E., & Havertape, S. (1981). *Curriculum-based assessment (CBA).* Minneapolis, MN: School Psychology Inservice Training Network.

Good, III, R. H., & Jefferson, G. (1998). Contemporary perspectives on curriculum-based measurement validity. In M. R. Shinn (Ed.), *Advanced applications of curriculum-based measurement* (pp. 61-88). New York: Guilford.

Ikeda, M. J., Tilly III, W. D., Stumme, J., Volmer, T., & Allison, R. (1996). Agency-wide implementation of problem solving consultation: Foundations, current implementation, and future directions. *School Psychology Quarterly, 12,* 28-39.

Knutson, N., & Shinn, M. R. (1991). Curriculum-based measurement: Conceptual underpinnings and integration into problem-solving assessment. *Journal of School Psychology, 29,* 371-393.

Kratochwill, T. R., & Stoiber, K. C. (2000). Empirically supported interventions and school psychology: Conceptual and practical issues–Part II. *School Psychology Quarterly, 15,* 233-253.

Marston, D. B. (1989). A curriculum-based measurement approach to assessing academic performance: What it is and why do it. In M. R. Shinn (Ed.), *Curriculum-based measurement: Assessing special children.* (pp. 18-78). New York: Guilford.

Marston, D., Fuchs, L. S., & Deno, S. L. (1986). Measuring pupil progress: A comparison of standardized achievement tests and curriculum-related measures. *Diagnostique, 11,* 77-90.

Marston, D., Lowry, L., Deno, S. L., & Mirkin, P. K. (1981). *An analysis of learning trends in simple measures of reading, spelling, and written expression: A longitudinal study* (Research Report No. 49). Minneapolis: University of Minnesota Institute for Research on Learning Disabilities.

National Council for Accreditation of Teacher Education (2001). *A decade of growth 1991-2002.* Washington, DC: Author.

Patterson, G. R., Reid, J. B., & Dishion, T. J. (1992). *Antisocial boys.* Eugene, OR: Castalia Publishing.

Shinn, M. R. (1988). Development of curriculum-based norms for use in special education decision-making. *School Psychology Review, 17,* 61-80.

Shinn, M. R. (1989). *Curriculum-based measurement: Assessing special children.* New York: Guilford Press.

Shinn, M. R. (1998). *Advanced applications of curriculum-based measurement.* New York: Guilford Press.

Shinn, M. R., Good, R. H., Knutson, N., Tilly, W. D., & Collins, V. L. (1992). Curriculum-based measurement of oral reading fluency: A confirmatory analysis of its relation to reading. *School Psychology Review, 21,* 459-479.

Stoiber, K. C., & Kratochwill, T. R. (2000). Empirically supported interventions and school psychology: Rationale and methodological issues, Part I. *School Psychology Quarterly, 15,* 75-105.

Stoner, G., Carey, S. P., Ikeda, M. J., & Shinn, M. R. (1994). The utility of curriculum-based measurement for evaluating the effects of methylphenidate on academic performance. *Journal of Applied Behavior Analysis, 27,* 101-113.

Ysseldyke, J. Dawson, S., Lehr, C., Reschly, D., Reynolds, M., & Telzrow, C. (1997). *School psychology: A blueprint for training and practice II.* Bethesda, MD: National Association of School Psychologists.

# Expanding Technical Assistance Consultation to Public Schools: District-Wide Evaluation of Instructional and Behavior Support Practices for Students with Developmental Disabilities

Robert F. Putnam
James K. Luiselli
Gretchen L. Jefferson

**SUMMARY.** We describe consultation to a public school district in the form of a systems-wide evaluation of instructional and behavior support

---

Robert F. Putnam, PhD, is Vice President of Consultation and School Support Services at The May Institute Inc., Norwood, MA.

James K. Luiselli, EdD, ABPP, BCBA, is Vice President of Applied Research and Peer Review at The May Institute Inc., Norwood, MA.

Gretchen L. Jefferson, MEd, is affiliated with the Department of Counseling, Education, and Developmental Psychology, Eastern Washington University, Cheney, WA.

Address correspondence to: Dr. James K. Luiselli, The May Center for Applied Research, The May Institute Inc., One Commerce Way, Norwood, MA 02062 (E-mail: jluiselli@mayinstitute.org).

The authors acknowledge the support and assistance provided by the Massachusetts Department of Mental Retardation: Jo Anne Bayliss (Child Service Coordinator), Dr. Phyllis Lochiatto (Area Director), Donna Boucher (Regional Systems Manager), Diane Enochs (Regional Director), and Dr. Janet George (Assistant Commissioner of Children's Services).

[Haworth co-indexing entry note]: "Expanding Technical Assistance Consultation to Public Schools: District-Wide Evaluation of Instructional and Behavior Support Practices for Students with Developmental Disabilities." Putnam, Robert F., James K. Luiselli, and Gretchen L. Jefferson. Co-published simultaneously in *Child & Family Behavior Therapy* (The Haworth Press, Inc.) Vol. 24, No. 1/2, 2002, pp. 113-128; and: *Behavior Psychology in the Schools: Innovations in Evaluation, Support, and Consultation* (ed: James K. Luiselli, and Charles Diament) The Haworth Press, Inc., 2002, pp. 113-128. Single or multiple copies of this article are available for a fee from The Haworth Document Delivery Service [1-800-HAWORTH, 9:00 a.m. - 5:00 p.m. (EST). E-mail address: getinfo@haworthpressinc.com].

*113*

practices for students with developmental disabilities. The evaluation targeted (1) the financial costs of educating students out-of-district, (2) an analysis of a representative sample of Individualized Educational Plans, and (3) interviews with and a questionnaire completed by teachers. The primary objective of the evaluation was to determine practice standards in the public school district and to make recommendations to improve service delivery. The format of the evaluative model, respective findings, suggested remedies, and implications for large-scale public school consultation are presented. *[Article copies available for a fee from The Haworth Document Delivery Service: 1-800-HAWORTH. E-mail address: <getinfo@haworthpressinc.com> Website: <http://www.HaworthPress.com> © 2002 by The Haworth Press, Inc. All rights reserved.]*

**KEYWORDS.** Special education expenditures, cost-efficacy analysis, behavioral consultation

Many students with developmental disabilities receive educational services in their neighborhood public schools. Although there are disparate views concerning the practice, rationale, and effectiveness of "inclusive education" (Fuchs & Fuchs, 1994), federal law mandates that children who have "special needs" are entitled to a free and appropriate public education (FAPE). To meet this challenge, a public school system must institute effective instructional methods that are adapted to its special education population. In cases where students also display behaviors that interfere with learning or cause disruption to others, school personnel must provide intervention to ameliorate those problems (Drasgow, Yell, Bradley, & Shriner, 1999).

In response to students who have learning and behavior challenges, many public school systems seek out-of-district placement alternatives such as private day-school or residential-care programs. Although out-of-district placements may be indicated in some cases, they are costly and put a significant financial burden on school districts. Another disadvantage is that when students are enrolled in an out-of-district educational placement, it can be difficult to return them to their local public school. The costs of maintaining out-of-district placements means that financial resources are not utilized to improve and expand the already existing services within the public school system.

Behavioral consultation can provide technical assistance to public schools in designing more effective instructional and behavior supports for students with developmental disabilities (Luiselli, 1997; Northup,

Wacker, Berg et al. 1994). Defined broadly, behavioral consultation is a problem-solving approach that is implemented through consultant-consultee interviews, formulated on principles of applied behavior analysis, and focused on objective outcome evaluation (Bergan & Kratochwill, 1990). With regard to public school systems, the recipients of consultation would be students, teachers, principals, or ancillary educational personnel.

Most research on school-based behavioral consultation has been "case centered," by which individual students are referred for intervention to address academic difficulties and classroom behavior problems. More recently, consultation services have included whole-school and district-wide interventions (Lewis, Sugai, & Colvin, 1998; Mayer, 1995; Walker, Sugai, Bullis, Sprague, Bricker, & Kaufman, 1996). This orientation targets entire school populations and multiple schools in a system through:

1. early identification assessment,
2. preventive approaches to behavior support,
3. teacher training,
4. comprehensive curriculum design,
5. leadership building,
6. multi-source efficacy evaluation.

In particular, this "systems" approach to public school behavioral consultation incorporates "best practice" and empirically validated procedures (Luiselli, Putnam, & Handler, 2001; Sugai, Horner, Dunlap et al. 2000).

For district-wide behavioral consultation to be maximally effective, there must be comprehensive evaluation of a public school system's service delivery, resource allocation, and standards of practice. The information gathered from evaluation should be used to identify relative strengths and weaknesses of the system, which, in turn, can be translated into action plans to improve educational programming. Broad-scale evaluations of this type include multiple foci that should define the recipients of service delivery, intended outcomes, process variables, and cost-efficiency (Doucette-Gates, 2000).

This report illustrates a district-wide approach to public school consultation in the form of an evaluation of instructional and behavior support practices for students with developmental disabilities. We describe a multi-purpose evaluation of one public school district to exemplify the type of methodology that behavioral consultants might employ to assess and analyze the delivery of special education services. The findings produced from this evaluation are presented, along with the recommendations that were made to the school district.

## METHOD

### Overview

The public school district that was evaluated included two suburban communities located in north central Massachusetts. The evaluation addressed the provision of educational services during the 1998-1999 school year. The two communities were comprised of 5,433 and 6,191 citizens of predominantly Caucasian background, with representation from African-American, Native American, Eskimo, Aleut, Asian, and Hispanic cultures. The school district had three elementary schools (kindergarten through fifth grade), one middle school (sixth through eighth grade), and one high school (ninth through twelfth grade) serving approximately 2,411 students. Average class size for these five schools was 16.8 students. From data presented in the Massachusetts Department of Education FY1998 per Pupil Expenditure Report (1998), the average per pupil expenditure cost (excluding special education) was $4,605 yearly (state average = $5,221).

With regard to special education, approximately 14% of the student population received services during the 1998-1999 school year. Using the FY1998 statistics provided by the Massachusetts Department of Education, the average per pupil expenditure cost for students receiving in-district special education services was $8,714 (state average = $9,873).

This evaluation, initiated by the special education director of the school district, was funded by a grant from the Massachusetts Department of Mental Retardation. The primary purpose of the evaluation was to assess current behavior support and instructional practices in the public school district. A second purpose was to provide recommendations to improve these practices.

### Evaluation Measures

The district-wide evaluation targeted students who received special education services within existing school programs and those who were enrolled in out-of-district placements (day-school and residential-care). The following information sources comprised the evaluation:

*Out-of-District Placement Expenditures.* This evaluative measure targeted the financial costs of enrolling students in out-of-district placements. The database compiled by the Massachusetts Department of Education was accessed to determine the total out-of-district tuition costs expended by the school district during FY1998. In addition, these same data were gathered for the preceding four academic years to examine placement trends.

*Individual Educational Plan Analysis.* All students receiving special education services in Massachusetts must have an Individualized Educational Plan (IEP) written each year. The IEP designates the goals of a student's school program, the staff responsible for delivering services, and a listing of measurable learning objectives. For this evaluation, IEPs were analyzed in two ways. First, we examined the instructional components of plans according to the criteria listed in Table 1. These criteria were applied to the IEPs of randomly selected students during the academic year that preceded their enrollment in an out-of-district placement (PRE-IEP) and during the first year they attended the out-of-district placement (POST-IEP). Thus, this analysis compared the content of IEPs developed by the school district and by the staff providing services outside of the school district.

*Teacher Questionnaire.* A questionnaire was prepared by the authors to sample the opinions of special education teachers in the school district. Several sections of the questionnaire had teachers indicate how many of their students during the preceding year demonstrated specific social skills deficits and challenging behaviors (all students, half of students, less than half of students, none of students). Respondents also indicated the percentage of time each week students participated in whole class instruction, small group instruction, individual seatwork, and cooperative group activities (0%, 25%, 50%, 75%, and 100%). With re-

TABLE 1. IEP Analysis: Criteria for Best Practice Instructional Procedures

| Component | Criteria |
|---|---|
| *Functional Skills* | |
| Basic Skills | Focus on communication, daily living, social, motor, preacademic, and vocational skills. |
| Critical Activity | Activities that require another individual to perform if the student did not possess the relevant skill. |
| Interaction Activity | Activities that require reciprocal interaction with one or more peers. |
| *Age Appropriate* | Materials and activities are appropriate to the developmental age of the student. |
| *Documentation* | Learning objectives for identified skills are written in measurable terms that include a timeline for acquisition. |

gard to instructional and behavioral objectives, the questionnaire requested information about how assessments were conducted, the types of intervention procedures that were implemented, and the positive outcomes that were achieved. Finally, the questionnaire allowed teachers to make recommendations about how the school district could improve special education services.

*Teacher Interviews.* Using a format prepared by the authors, teachers were interviewed to determine their perceptions of how students were referred for out-of-district placements by the school system. The interview form captured information about the types of educational and behavioral concerns that led to out-of-district placement considerations, how such referrals were initiated, and what steps were taken to maintain a student within the school system as an alternative to out-placement.

The second type of analysis concerned the specification of behavioral components found in the IEP. Similar to the identification of instructional supports, we sampled the IEPs of students for the year that preceded enrollment in an out-of-district placement (PRE-IEP) and during the first year that they attended that setting (POST-IEP). The IEPs were reviewed according to the criteria presented in Table 2.

### Evaluation Methodology and Procedures

The teacher questionnaire was distributed to a total of 21 special education teachers across the three elementary schools, middle school, and high school within the district. Teachers were informed that the purpose of the questionnaire was to evaluate special education services. Completed questionnaires were returned to the special education director and subsequently forwarded to the authors.

The authors evaluated out-of-district expenditure costs by locating these data directly from the Massachusetts Department of Education FY1998 per Pupil Expenditure Report.

The analyses of IEPs were completed by the third author. The IEPs of four students were selected randomly for the evaluation of instructional support components, and the IEPs of five students were randomly selected for the evaluation of behavior support components.

## RESULTS

All teachers (100%) completed and returned the questionnaire. The majority of teachers indicated that less than half of their students had

TABLE 2. IEP Analysis: Criteria for Best Practice Behavior Support Procedures

| Component | Criteria |
|---|---|
| Problem Behavior Identification | Behavior stated and defined such that it could be observed and measured. |
| Alternative Positive Behavior | A behavior identified and defined that can serve as a functional replacement for the problem behavior. |
| Quantified Goal | Goals state the criteria for attainment. |
| Intervention Plan | A set of procedures is described to effect change in the problem behavior. |
| Progress Monitoring System | Procedures described to assess the effectiveness of the intervention plan. |
| Progress Monitoring Plan | Description of the type and schedule of monitoring plan. |
| Functional Behavior Assessment | Statement of the type of functional assessment completed with the student. |
| Positive Behavior Support | Statement indicating the preparation of a written positive behavior support plan. |
| Written Protocol | Inclusion of a written protocol that describes implementation of a positive behavior support plan. |

negative social interactions with peers and adults in the school setting. Instructional approaches varied little across classrooms, with most teachers reporting use of a combination of small group, individual seatwork, and whole class methods. Eighty percent of teachers indicated that their students had made measurable gains in academic skills within the past year. The types of assessment included informal methods, standardized instruments, observations, narrative records, and work samples.

All teachers encountered students with behavior challenges. Classroom disruptions, "disrespect," and defiance were the highest rated problems. Based on teacher report, functional behavioral assessments were conducted with very few students. Referrals for special education services on the basis of challenging behaviors occurred for less than half of the students in 10 classrooms, none of the students in three classrooms, and all of the students in one classroom. Redirection when challenging behaviors occurred and earning privileges contingent upon assignment completion were the most prevalent interventions. Other strategies included loss of privileges, social skills training, time-out, and self-management protocols. Behavioral gains were measured predominantly by teacher reports, daily, weekly, or monthly data collection, and administration of standardized measurement. A summary of recommendations made by the teachers to improve educational services is presented in Table 3.

Ten teachers participated in interviews. The information gathered revealed that out-of-district placement recommendations typically were made by the school district during educational team meetings and were based primarily on the severity of presenting challenging behaviors. Although behavioral issues were a dominant concern, teachers verified

TABLE 3. Teacher Recommendations to Improve Educational Services

| Category | Recommendations |
| --- | --- |
| Staff Development | -Train counselors to make long-range IEP goals. |
| | -Increase special education teachers' familiarity with general education classroom curriculum. |
| | -Provide general education teachers with knowledge about developmental disabilities. |
| | -Offer training in assessment methodologies. |
| Instruction | -Build in more community-based instruction. |
| | -Allow more planning time between teachers and assistants. |
| | -Schedule more involvement between regular and special education teachers. |
| | -Make available a reading specialist for classroom consultation. |
| Behavior Support | -Increase social skills training for students. |
| | -Ensure that written behavior support plans are prepared and "follow" students who transition to new schools. |
| | -Schedule ongoing behavioral consultation to teachers. |
| Organizational | -Build closer alignment between general education and special education instructional practices. |
| | -Improve communication between general education and special education teachers. |
| | -Make fewer changes to daily classroom schedules. |
| | -Increase training to parents. |
| | -Increase staff so that there is a lower teacher-to-student ratio in the schools. |
| | -Do not place multiple students with challenging behaviors in the same classroom. |

that most students with such problems did not have a written intervention plan. Another issue raised by the teachers was a difficulty with the transition of students from elementary school to middle school to high school programs. One cause for concern was the absence of a continuous curriculum of academic, social, and life skills domains for students with developmental disabilities. A related concern was the informal nature by which school transitions were implemented, as opposed to a more systematic and strategic approach to better prepare students for enrollment in the new school.

The assessment of out-of-district placement expenditures found that these costs consumed 32% of the public school system's special education budget (state average = 28%). Table 4 shows the trend in the number of students enrolled in out-of-district programs and respective tuition costs according to the type of placement (collaborative program, day-school, residential-care facility, specialized home-based services) for five consecutive school years. For the five-year period, students in residential settings remained relatively stable, students enrolled in collaborative programs decreased, and only one student was served in a private day-school. The most significant trend was the increase in home-based services (intensive applied behavior analysis) for students during 1997-1998 and 1998-1999. Total tuition costs were relatively stable with the exception of the increase reported for the 1998-1999 school year. This outcome was attributable to the increase in costs for supporting the intensive home-based services. Table 5 shows the percent of annual tuition costs that were devoted to the type of out-of-district placement over the five-year period.

An analysis by grade level of students in out-of-district placements during the preceding 5 years found that 38% were at the middle

TABLE 4. Number of Students Enrolled in Out-Of-District Programs and Respective Tuition Costs

| Program | 1994-1995 | 1995-1996 | 1996-1997 | 1997-1998 | 1998-1999 |
|---|---|---|---|---|---|
| Collaborative | 14 | 6 | 4 | 5 | 5 |
| Private Day-School | 0 | 0 | 0 | 0 | 1 |
| Residential Facility | 3 | 2 | 3 | 4 | 3 |
| Specialized Home-Based Services | 0 | 0 | 0 | 5 | 4 |
| Tuition Costs | $281,685 | $197,922 | $244,969 | $235,830 | $417,826 |

school/junior high school levels and 42% were at the high school level. These proportions were reported to be due to significant social skills deficits and difficulty managing challenging behaviors posed by older students in the district.

In the IEP analysis of instructional components, 55 objectives were examined. In total, the number of daily living, academic, and communication goals for each PRE-IEP varied from 2-5. The number of objectives for each student ranged from 8-18 (objectives are sub-classified under goals in the IEP). Table 6 reports the percent of PRE-IEP and POST-IEP objectives that met best practice criteria. These data reveal that 100% of the PRE-IEP objectives achieved the criteria for basic and critical skills. However, only 5% of these skills were taught by having students interact with each other and only 18% were taught using age-appropriate materials although 100% of the tasks selected for instruction were age-appropriate. None of the objectives that were evalu-

TABLE 5. Percent of Annual Tuition Costs Per Out-Of-District Program

| Program | 1994-1995 | 1995-1996 | 1996-1997 | 1997-1998 | 1998-1999 |
|---|---|---|---|---|---|
| Collaborative | 61% | 50% | 33% | 36% | 20% |
| Private Day-School | 0% | 0% | 0% | 0% | 4% |
| Residential Facility | 38% | 50% | 67% | 43% | 26% |
| Specialized Home-Based Services | 0% | 0% | 0% | 20% | 50% |

TABLE 6. Percent of PRE-IEP and POST-IEP Objectives Meeting Best Practice Criteria for Instructional Procedures

| Criteria | PRE | POST |
|---|---|---|
| *Functional Skills* | | |
| Basic Skills | 100% | 93% |
| Critical Activity | 100% | 93% |
| Interaction Activity | 5% | 6% |
| *Age Appropriate* | | |
| Materials | 18% | 6% |
| Activities | 100% | 93% |
| *Documentation* | 0% | 8% |

ated had measurable referents. The POST-IEP analysis showed that, with the exception of the documentation criteria, no appreciable difference in best practice procedures was identified.

Table 7 shows that for the behavior support component of the PRE-IEP analysis, none of the plans identified and defined challenging behaviors, included a quantified goal, specified a system of progress monitoring, used functional assessment methods, or contained a positive behavior support plan. These data virtually were identical for the POST-IEP analysis.

## *DISCUSSION*

This report illustrates an approach toward district-wide evaluation of public school instructional and behavior support practices for students with developmental disabilities. As noted previously, the focus and breadth of behavioral consultation to school settings has expanded greatly in recent years, moving beyond technical assistance with individual students to whole school and systems applications. Such large-scale consultation must address multiple features of service delivery in order to understand better how school districts can improve special education practices. Accordingly, our model incorporated the opinions of stakeholders (teachers), school district policies, implementation parameters (e.g., the formulation of IEPs), and costs associated with serving students outside of the school system. Through this evalua-

TABLE 7. Percent of PRE-IEP and POST-IEP Objectives Meeting Best Practice Criteria for Behavior Support Procedures

| Criteria | PRE-IEP | POST-IEP |
|---|---|---|
| Problem Behavior Identification | 0% | 0% |
| Alternative Positive Behavior | 4% | 5% |
| Quantified Goal | 0% | 0% |
| Intervention Plan | 3% | 4% |
| Progress Monitoring System | 0% | 0% |
| Progress Monitoring Plan | 5% | 5% |
| Functional Behavior Assessment | 0% | 0% |
| Positive Behavior Support | 0% | 0% |
| Written Protocol | 0% | 0% |

tion we were able to synthesize several findings that produced a number of recommendations to the school district administration (reviewed below).

Our evaluation found that when compared to a state-wide average, the school system used more of its special education budget to fund out-of-district placements. Therefore, a critical aspect of the evaluation was to identify factors that might account for this finding and to propose possible solutions. One observation was that the large majority of students who were placed in out-of-district programs left the school system during their middle and high school years. This placement pattern may have been the result of ineffective practices for teaching prosocial skills to students at the elementary school level, as well as inadequate preparation of transitions to middle and high school grades. For example, the school district did not have a continuous curriculum that covered the entire school year or a standardized method of social skills instruction. Also, the analysis of IEPs identified many deficiencies in behavior support practices relative to the identification, definition, functional assessment, and progress monitoring of challenging behaviors. It would be expected that these omissions would result in fewer inclusionary activities, reduced skill acquisition, and persistent behavioral difficulties among students, thereby increasing the likelihood of referral to an out-of-district program.

In line with the preceding discussion, and as an outcome from the district-wide evaluation, the following recommendations were presented:

1. The public school district should initiate a system to identify systematically students "at risk" for out-of-district placements. Early detection of students who present challenging behaviors and other risk factors would be used to design interventions that have the objective of preventing referral to an out-of-district educational setting.

2. Assessment practices in the school system did not include an evaluation of social skills for students referred for special education services. Adoption of a norm-referenced instrument such as the Walker-McConnell Scale of Social Skills and School Adjustment (Walker & McConnell, 1988) would be one approach to screen students who had interpersonal skills deficits, determine intervention alternatives, and monitor behavior change in response to those interventions.

3. The school district should select one or more social skills training curricula that would be applicable and could be adapted to different grade levels (e.g., Begun, 1995a, 1995b, 1995c, 1995d; McGinnis &

Goldstein, 1997). Those students most "at risk" for outside services would be involved actively in social skills training as an objective in their IEP. All school staff, but particularly those responsible for teaching students who have developmental disabilities, would be taught how to implement the social skills curriculum. In addition, there should be greater opportunities for students with developmental disabilities to interact with typical peers during organized and naturally occurring social contexts.

4. Student tracking systems should be established at each school, combined with a centralized reporting format, to document empirically the acquisition of social skills by "at-risk" students. Other behavior indices such as office discipline referrals, detentions, and school suspensions should be quantified and aggregated at individual schools and district-wide level (Putnam, Luiselli, Handler, & Jefferson, 2001; Sugai, Sprague, Horner, & Walker, 2000). These data sources would be used to measure the effectiveness of already existing interventions and to identify students in need of more intensive behavior support.

5. The school district was advised to increase the frequency and variety of community-based instruction dedicated to daily living, recreational, and vocational activities. Ideally, a functionally-based model such as the Syracuse Community-Referenced Curriculum Guide should be considered (Ford, Schnorr, Meyer, Davern, Black, & Dempsey, 1989).

6. The evaluation of behavior support components within the IEPs of students placed in out-of-district programs revealed that these documents did not include functional behavioral assessments, written support plans, or data-based measures. Therefore, the school system must acquire competencies in applying best practice approaches toward positive behavior support and functional behavioral assessment as outlined by Sugai, Horner, Dunlap et al. (2000). A clear implication from our evaluation is that the public school system could reduce its out-of-district placements by embracing contemporary and community-referenced guidelines for the behavior support of students with developmental disabilities (Hieneman & Dunlap, 2000).

7. Another factor that can lead to out-of-district placements is parents' dissatisfaction with educational services in the home school. In addition to improving parent perceptions by building better instructional and behavior supports, it was recommended that the school district create structured opportunities for parents of stu-

dents with developmental disabilities to communicate with school personnel. This objective could be addressed by having parents

a. share in the preparation of their child's IEP,
b. serve as an information source when assessing academic, social, and behavioral domains,
c. receive timely and accurate appraisals of school progress.

The preceding recommendations focused on strategic and coordinated procedures to strengthen preventive, instructional, and behavior support practices in the public school district. In our opinion, the capacity to achieve these goals was dependent on a combination of staff training initiatives and expert consultation. Although many teachers had expertise in a number of areas, as a whole they were not well-versed in principles of behavior analysis, functional behavioral assessment, and contemporary methods of positive behavior support. In effect, the school district required competency-based staff training on these topics so that teachers would be better able to serve students with serious behavior disorders. As proposed by Dunlap, Hieneman, Knoster et al. (2000), inservice training on behavior support should be provided by the school district and include a case study format emphasizing assessment-derived support plans, contextually relevant intervention, and comprehensive staff involvement.

Staff training and consultation also would be integral to improve instructional services within the school district. Earlier, we discussed the IEP analysis which revealed that 100% of learning objectives did not have a methodology to measure skill acquisition outcomes. A second focus of staff training then would be the integration of simple data collection procedures within IEPs. Learning objectives would be written with reference to what the student must do, at a predetermined criterion, during a designated time frame (e.g., "When given the first 10 letters of the alphabet in random order, the student will identify the letters at 100% accuracy, 8 out of 10 trials over four consecutive weeks"). Ensuring that teachers write behavior-specific objectives, record data properly, and use the information to guide decision-making would be another direction of training and consultation.

In summary, we have described a model of district-wide evaluation of special education services in a public school district. Large-scale systems analyses have become the purview of technical assistance consultation to public schools and reflect a new direction for specialists in applied behavior analysis. The foundation of such consultation should be the empirical evaluation of educational practices which, as illustrated in this report, address multiple and inter-related dependent measures.

# REFERENCES

Begun, R. W. (1995a). *Social skills lessons and activities for grades preK-K.* West Nyak, NY: The Center for Applied Research in Education.

Begun, R. W. (1995b). *Social skills lessons and activities for grades 1-3.* West Nyak, NY: The Center for Applied Research in Education.

Begun, R. W. (1995c). *Social skills lessons and activities for grades 4-6.* West Nyak, NY: The Center for Applied Research in Education.

Begun, R. W. (1995d). *Social skills lessons and activities for grades 7-12.* West Nyak, NY: The Center for Applied Research in Education.

Bergan, J. R., & Kratochwill, T. R. (1990). *Behavioral consultation and therapy.* New York, NY: Plenum Press.

Doucette-Gates, A. (2000). Capturing data: Negotiating cross-agency systems. *Education and Treatment of Children, 23,* 5-19.

Drasgow, E., Yell, M. L., Bradley, R., & Shriner, J. G. (1999). The IDEA amendments of 1997: A school-wide model for conducting functional behavioral assessments and developing behavior intervention plans. *Education and Treatment of Children, 22,* 244-266.

Dunlap, G., Hieneman, M., Knoster, T., Fox, L., Anderson, J., & Albin, R. W. (2000). Essential elements of inservice training in positive behavior support. *Journal of Positive Behavior Interventions, 2,* 22-32.

Fuchs, D., & Fuchs, L. S. (1994). Inclusive schools movement and the radicalization of special education reform. *Exceptional Children, 60,* 294-309.

Hieneman, M., & Dunlap, G. (2000). Factors affecting the outcomes of community-based behavioral support: I. Identification and description of factor categories. *Journal of Positive Behavior Interventions, 2,* 161-169.

Lewis, T. J., Sugai, G., & Colvin, G. (1998). Reducing problem behavior through a school-wide system of effective behavior support: Investigation of a school-wide social skills training program and contextual interventions. *School Psychology Review, 27,* 446-459.

Luiselli, J. K. (1997). Behavioral intervention in school-based consultation for children with developmental disabilities. *The Habilitative Mental Healthcare Newsletter, 16,* 22-26.

Luiselli, J. K., Putnam, R. F., & Handler, M. W. (2001). Improving discipline practices in public schools: Description of a whole-school and district-wide model of behavior analysis consultation. *The Behavior Analyst Today, 2,* 18-27.

Massachusetts Department of Education FY1998 per Pupil Expenditure Report (1998). [On-line]. Available: http://finance1.doc.mass.edu.

Mayer, R. (1995). Preventing antisocial behavior in the schools. *Journal of Applied Behavior Analysis, 28,* 467-478.

McGinnis, E., & Goldstein, A. P. (1997). *Skillstreaming the elementary school child-revised.* Champaign, IL: Research Press.

Northrup, J., Wacker, D. P., Berg, W. K., Kelly, L., Sasso, G., & DeRaad, A. (1994). The treatment of severe behavior problems in school settings using a technical assistance model. *Journal of Applied Behavior Analysis, 27,* 33-47.

Putnam, R. F., Luiselli, J. K., Handler, M. W., & Jefferson, G. L. (2001). *Behavioral assessment of office discipline referrals and intervention efficacy in a public school setting.* Manuscript submitted for publication.

Sugai, G., Horner, R. H., Dunlap, G., Hieneman, M., Lewis, T. J., Nelson, C. M., Scott, T., Liaupsin, C., Sailor, W., Turnbull, A. P., Turnbull, H. R., Wickham, D., Wilcox, B., & Ruef, M. (2000). Applying positive behavior support and functional behavioral assessment in schools. *Journal of Positive Behavior Interventions, 2,* 131-143.

Sugai, G., Sprague, J. R., Horner, R. H., & Walker, H. M. (2000). Preventing school violence: The use of office discipline referrals to assess and monitor school-wide discipline interventions. *Journal of Emotional and Behavioral Disorders, 8,* 94-101.

Walker, H. M., Horner, R. H., Sugai, G., Bullis, M., Sprague, J. R., Bricker, D., & Kaufman, M. J. (1996). Integrated approaches to preventing antisocial behavior patterns among school-age children and youth. *Journal of Behavioral and Emotional Disorders, 4,* 193-256.

Walker, H. M., & McConnell, S. R. (1988). *The Walker-McConnell scale of social competence and school adjustment.* Austin, TX: PRO-ED.

# School-Wide Behavior Support:
# Legal Implications and Requirements

Erik Drasgow
Mitchell L. Yell

**SUMMARY.** Administrators and teachers have long been challenged by student discipline problems. In the last few years more efforts have been aimed at the prevention of both disruptive and violent behavior through school-wide discipline programs. These programs have great promise as effective ways to address disruptive behavior. In this article we examine laws and policies that support the use of school-wide discipline programs. To do this, first we present a brief overview of the primary components of these policies. Next, we examine laws and court cases that address school-wide discipline policies and procedures. Finally, we discuss the legal implications when developing school-wide discipline policies and procedures. *[Article copies available for a fee from The Haworth Document Delivery Service: 1-800-HAWORTH. E-mail address: <getinfo@haworthpressinc.com> Website: <http://www.HaworthPress.com> © 2002 by The Haworth Press, Inc. All rights reserved.]*

**KEYWORDS.** Legal concerns, legislation, IDEA

## SCHOOL-WIDE BEHAVIOR SUPPORT:
## LEGAL IMPLICATIONS

Administrators and teachers have been challenged by student discipline problems since the beginning of public education in the United

---

Erik Drasgow and Mitchell L. Yell are affiliated with the University of South Carolina.

[Haworth co-indexing entry note]: "School-Wide Behavior Support: Legal Implications and Requirements." Drasgow, Erik, and Mitchell L. Yell. Co-published simultaneously in *Child & Family Behavior Therapy* (The Haworth Press, Inc.) Vol. 24, No. 1/2, 2002, pp. 129-145; and: *Behavior Psychology in the Schools: Innovations in Evaluation, Support, and Consultation* (ed: James K. Luiselli, and Charles Diament) The Haworth Press, Inc., 2002, pp. 129-145. Single or multiple copies of this article are available for a fee from The Haworth Document Delivery Service [1-800-HAWORTH, 9:00 a.m. - 5:00 p.m. (EST). E-mail address: getinfo@haworthpressinc.com].

*129*

States. In fact, one of the earliest education textbooks was on classroom management (Bagley, 1907). Recently, efforts to address the problem of student discipline in schools have taken on a greater sense of urgency because of the increases in aggressive and violent behavior. The recent schoolyard murders in Mississippi, Kentucky, California, Pennsylvania, Oregon, and Colorado have focused the nation's attention on the severity of discipline problems.

Solutions to these problems often include targeted and random searches of students and their property, "get tough" policies, and rapid responding to aggression or violence (Yell & Rozalski, 2000). Get tough policies refer to laws in local (e.g., school districts) and state educational agencies that are designed to remove students from schools as a consequence for serious behavior problems.

One approach to reducing school violence has included ways that educators can recognize warning signs so that problems could be stopped before they occurred. In late 1998, every school administrator in the United States received "Early Warning, Timely Response: A Guide to Safe Schools" (Dwyer, Osher, & Warger, 1998). The purpose of this U.S. Department of Education report was to help school districts develop comprehensive violence prevention plans. The guide summarized the research on violence prevention, interventions, and crisis response in schools. According to the guide, well-functioning schools had a strong focus on learning and achievement, safety, and socially appropriate behaviors (Dwyer, Osher, & Warger, 1998). Additionally, Horner and Sugai (in press) noted that if schools are to be safe and effective environments, proactive behavior support must become a priority.

In the last few years, therefore, efforts have been aimed at the prevention of both disruptive (e.g., noncompliance) and violent behavior (e.g., physical assault) through school-wide discipline programs rather than through just reacting to discipline problems after they have occurred (Horner, Sugai, & Horner, 2000; Walker & Epstein, 2001). School-wide discipline programs refer to strategies that schools develop both to prevent and to respond to problem behavior. Such programs have been shown to have great promise as an effective way to define, teach, and support appropriate behaviors and to address disruptive behavior in the schools. In this article we examine laws and policies that support the use of school-wide discipline programs. To do this, first we present a brief overview of the primary components of these policies. Next, we examine laws and court cases that address school-wide discipline policies and procedures. Finally, we discuss the legal implications when developing school-wide discipline policies.

We also discuss the implications of school discipline policies from a federal perspective. Readers should note that their individual states might mandate procedures that schools must adhere to when fashioning discipline policies and procedures. An examination of pertinent state laws is beyond the scope of this paper. However, failing to observe state mandates would be legal grounds to overturn school district policy. For a thorough understanding of federal and state laws affecting school-wide discipline, readers should become familiar with the laws in their respective states.

## SCHOOL-WIDE DISCIPLINE

Although there is no one model of school-wide discipline, three basic practices often are followed in effective disciplinary systems (Horner, Sugai, & Horner, 2000; Walker et al., 1996). First, schools with effective policies invest in preventing problem behavior by defining, teaching, and supporting desirable student behavior. This means that school personnel develop important rules about expected behavior and clearly communicate these expectations to students. Moreover, school officials recognize students who adhere to these expectations, and respond effectively when students do not. Second, effective school-wide discipline systems have rapid, effective support systems for identifying and addressing needs of students who are at risk of developing problem behavior. According to Lewis and Sugai (1999), these procedures often involve increased adult monitoring and group behavior support. Third, schools using effective discipline systems have support for high-intensity problem behavior. Such systems focus on a small number of students who display high rates of disruptive behavior and include specialized individual behavior programs (e.g., functional behavioral assessment and behavior intervention plans).

We previously noted that school-wide discipline procedures show great promise as ways that schools can effectively address problem behavior. In this paper we propose that these procedures not only have empirical support but legal support as well. In the next sections we review laws and court cases that have addressed issues regarding schools and problem behavior. Before we review these laws, however, it is important that readers have an understanding of the legal traditions that have developed in the U.S.A. with respect to a school's rights and responsibilities when disciplining students.

### In Loco Parentis

Court decisions over the years have established court-made or case law regarding the mutual responsibilities and obligations of educators and students in our public schools (Alexander & Alexander, 2001). In this case law, courts have granted school authorities the power to establish and conduct educational programs. The courts' recognition of the importance of school authority over student behavior originates from the English common law concept of *in loco parentis* (i.e., in place of the parent). According to this concept, parents implicitly consent to school control over their children when their children are placed in the charge of school personnel (Alexander & Alexander, 2001). Thus, principals and teachers have the authority not only to teach but also to guide, correct, and discipline a child to accomplish educational objectives. *In loco parentis* does not mean that the teacher stands fully in the place of parents in controlling their child during the school day. Rather, it means that school officials, acting in concert with appropriate laws and regulations, have a legal duty to maintain an orderly and effective learning environment through reasonable and prudent control of students (Yell, 1998). Although this concept no longer has the importance it once did it remains an active legal concept that helps to define the school-student relationship.

### Reasonableness

From a legal standpoint, reasonableness refers to actions that are proper, rational, and fair (Alexander & Alexander, 2001; Valente & Valente, 2001). Actions are not reasonable when they are excessive, cruel, or unsuited to circumstances. Reasonableness applies primarily to the nature of rules and discipline regarding school-wide discipline policies. The authority of school administrators and teachers must be applied in sometimes unique and unusual circumstances (Alexander & Alexander, 2001). Therefore state law and local regulations must be very flexible. Moreover, courts have tended to use similar flexibility when determining what reasonable behavior is in a school setting. This flexibility means that the courts recognize that school officials must have wide latitude in disciplinary matters; nevertheless, the rules they develop and the procedures they use to achieve school-wide discipline must be reasonable and humane (Valente & Valente, 2001).

*In loco parentis* and reasonableness related to disciplinary procedures imply that schools have a duty to maintain order by requiring students to obey reasonable rules and commands, and to respect the rights of others. This duty includes the power to regulate and control student conduct through the development of rules, procedures, and disciplinary sanctions. School officials' powers in this regard are broad, but they are not absolute. It is important that school officials understand these court-made requirements and adhere to them, particularly with respect to (a) developing school-wide discipline rules and procedures and (b) applying disciplinary sanctions. Next we review legal requirements and how schools may fashion school-wide discipline policies according to these requirements.

## *Developing School-Wide Discipline Policies*

According to Sugai, Sprague, Horner, and Walker (2001), 85% to 90% of students begin school having already learned the social skills necessary to be effective learners. That is, they pay attention, are actively engaged in learning, and follow school rules and procedures. The most important aspect of any school-wide discipline procedure is to ensure that these skills become part of the school's culture (Horner, Sugai, & Horner, 2000). One way for schools to guarantee that such behaviors become ingrained in a school's culture is through the development and use of universal interventions. Universal interventions are systemic interventions in which school personnel develop rules and consequences that focus on improving the overall level of appropriate behavior of most students in a school (Sugai et al., 1999). The most important components of universal interventions are that (a) behavioral expectations in the form of rules are defined and taught to all students and (b) inappropriate behaviors are corrected through the systematic application of consequences. Next we review legal guidelines for developing school-wide rules and consequences.

## *Rules and Consequences*

When developing universal interventions, schools must define, teach, and support expected student behaviors. To maintain discipline, and to operate efficiently and effectively, schools must have rules that regulate student conduct. This means that students should clearly know which behaviors are acceptable and which behaviors are prohibited. Schools recognize and reinforce students who follow the rules regarding acceptable behaviors. Additionally, if students violate reasonable school rules by behaving in ways that are prohibited they should be held accountable.

Student accountability to rules implies that violators will be subject to disciplinary sanctions or consequences. School officials have long known that students are more likely to conduct themselves appropriately when they understand

a. the types of behavior that are expected of them when they are in school,
b. the positive consequences of engaging in behaviors that meet these expectations,
c. the consequences of engaging in prohibited behavior.

A number of courts have addressed the issue of school-wide discipline policies and have tended to give great authority to teachers and school officials to write rules that govern student behavior (Yell, Katsiyannis, Bradley, & Rozalski, 2000).

When developing school policies regulating student conduct, rules and consequences should have a carefully considered rationale and school-related purposes. The rules should be clear enough to allow students to distinguish permissible from prohibited behavior. Appropriate school rules are specific and definitive. School rules that are too vague or general may result in the violation of students' rights because students will not have a clear understanding of them. In fact, if a court finds that a school rule is so vague that students may not understand what behavior is prohibited it is likely that that rule would be legally invalid (Gorn, 1999). Thus, teachers and administrators must take care that their school rules are sufficiently clear and are communicated to students. Furthermore, school officials may not prohibit or punish conduct that is not related to their school's educational purposes.

As previously noted, an important legal requirement for developing school-wide discipline policies is that rules and consequences must be reasonable. From a legal perspective, rules should be rational and fair. Rules that are vague and consequences that are excessive or unsuitable to the particular circumstances may be legally invalid. Additionally, disciplinary procedures that are harsh or excessive are also likely to be ruled legally invalid if they are challenged in court. Therefore, school officials must use reasonable means to achieve compliance with a school's rules.

When schools focus on improving the overall level of appropriate behavior by developing school-wide rules and consequences they can expect that problem behavior will be prevented in 80% to 90% of all students (Sugai et al., 2001). However, there are 10% to 20% of students who will not respond to such interventions. For these students more intensive interventions are required. Next we briefly examine programming for students with serious problem behavior.

### *Programming for Students with Serious Behavior Problems*

Lewis and Sugai (1999) found that the level and intensity of interventions must be increased for students at risk for developing serious problem behavior (5% to 15% of the student population) and for students who already have chronic and intense problem behavior (1% to 7% of the student population). Unfortunately, for many students who may fall in these categories there are no legal guidelines to direct school districts in developing these more intensive and individualized interventions to cope with problem behavior. Although there are federal laws and programs that fund the development of violence prevention programs in schools (e.g., the Safe and Drug Free Schools and Communities Act of 1994), unless students have a disability, laws address only reactive and exclusionary practices (e.g., zero tolerance policies, searches of students and their property; for a review of these laws see Yell & Rozalski, 2000). For students with disabilities, however, the Individuals with Disabilities Act (hereafter IDEA) is specific when directing schools to address problem behavior. We now turn to a discussion of the IDEA's requirements for addressing student problem behavior.

### *The Individuals with Disabilities Education Act*

President Gerald Ford signed The Education for All Handicapped Children Act (EAHCA) into law on November 29th, 1975. In 1990, the name of the law was changed to the Individuals with Disabilities Education Act (IDEA). Since the EAHCA became law 25 years ago, there have been numerous changes and accomplishments in the ways that students with disabilities are educated. Perhaps the most significant of these changes was the addition to the law that addresses the discipline of students with disabilities when the law was amended and reauthorized in 1997. In the IDEA Amendments of 1997 (hereafter IDEA '97), Congress expanded the authority of school officials to protect the safety of all children by maintaining orderly, drug-free, and disciplined school environments, while ensuring that the essential rights of students with disabilities were protected (*Letter to Anonymous,* 1999). Congress sought to help school officials and IEP teams to respond appropriately when students with disabilities exhibit serious problem behavior and to address problem behavior appropriately in the IEP process.

When a student with disabilities is in the 10% to 20% of students who require more intensive interventions to address their behavior problem, the IDEA is specific about how schools should address the behavior. Perhaps the most important implications of the discipline provisions of the IDEA is the section that requires IEP teams to take a proactive, problem-solving approach toward problem behaviors of students with disabilities.

*Addressing Problem Behavior in the IEP Process.* IDEA '97 requires that, if a student with disabilities exhibits problem behaviors that impede his or her learning or the learning of others, then the student's IEP team shall consider "strategies, including positive behavioral interventions, strategies, and supports to address that behavior" (IDEA, 20 U.S.C.§ 1414 [d][3][B][i]). Comments to the federal regulations indicate that if a student has a history of problem behavior, or if such behaviors can be readily anticipated, then the student's IEP must address that behavior (IDEA Regulations, 34 C.F.R§ 300 Appendix A question 39). This requirement applies to all students in special education regardless of their disability category.

Student problem behaviors should be addressed in the following manner. First, when a student exhibits problem behavior, the IEP team must determine if the behavior impedes his or her learning or other students' learning. Second, if the team decides that the problem behavior does interfere with the student's learning, then they must conduct an assessment of the behavior. Third, the IEP team must develop a plan based on the information gained from the assessment that reduces problem behaviors and increases socially acceptable behaviors.

The results of the team's decisions must be included in the IEP. This means that the IEP of a student with serious problem behaviors must include the information from the assessment in the "Present Levels of Performance" section of the IEP. Because educational needs must be addressed by developing appropriate special education programming, the IEP must also include (a) measurable goals and objectives and (b) special education and related services that address the problem behavior. Moreover, if the student's behavioral program involves modifications to the general education classroom, these modifications must be included in the IEP. When an IEP team addresses a student's problem behavior, "the needs of the individual child are of paramount importance in determining the behavior strategies that are appropriate for inclusion in the child's IEP" (OSEP Analysis of Comments and Changes, 1999).

If an IEP team fails to address a student's problem behaviors in the IEP, then that failure would deprive the student of a free appropriate public education (FAPE). This could result in application of the law's sanctions against the school district. To underscore the importance of including positive programming that addresses significant problem behavior in students' IEPs, Thomas Hehir, former director of the U.S. Department of Education's Office of Special Education Programs, stated that "the key provision in IDEA '97 is using positive behavioral interventions and supports" in the IEPs of students who exhibit significant problem behaviors (*Letter to Anonymous*, 1998, p. 708). Failure to do so "would constitute a denial of the free appropriate public education (mandate of the IDEA)" (IDEA Regulations, Appendix B, Question 38, p. 115).

IDEA '97 encourages, and sometimes demands, that IEP teams address problem behaviors by conducting functional behavioral assessments (FBAs) and by developing education programming based on the results of the assessment (Drasgow & Yell, 2001). In the following section we examine the law's requirements regarding FBAs.

*Conducting Functional Behavioral Assessments.* An FBA is a process that searches for an explanation of the purpose behind a problem behavior (OSEP Questions and Answers, 1999). Although the U.S. Department of Education does not directly define an FBA, it is a reasonable to assume that Congress intended that the term be consistent with the meaning in the professional literature (Drasgow, Yell, Bradley, & Shriner, 1999; Gorn, 1999). FBA is a process to gather information about factors that reliably predict and maintain problem behavior in order to develop more effective intervention plans (Horner & Carr, 1997; O'Neill et al., 1997). In essence, an FBA is used to identify the "cause" and purpose of problem behavior (Drasgow et al., 1999).

The law's intent is that an FBA should be part of the process of addressing problem behavior. Moreover, the purpose of an FBA, or any special education assessment, is not merely to determine eligibility. Rather, its purpose is to determine the educational needs of students with disabilities and then to develop effective programming to meet those needs.

IDEA '97 does not detail the components of a FBA, nor did the U.S. Department of Education include additional information on FBAs in their final regulations. This means that the composition of FBAs will be left to states, school districts, and IEP teams. According to OSEP, a definition was not offered in the IDEA '97 regulations because IEP teams need to address the various situational, environmental, and behavioral circumstances occurring in individual cases (OSEP Questions and Answers, 1999). The decision to conduct an FBA is therefore left to the professional judgment of the IEP team. Nonetheless, there are certain situations, in which an IEP team *must* conduct an FBA. These situations are when a student in special education is suspended for over 10 cumulative days in a school year or placed in an interim alternative educational setting (IAES) for a similar period of time.

In summary, the FBA is a dynamic problem-solving process in which information is gathered that leads to goal identification, hypothesis development, support plan design, implementation, and monitoring (Sugai et al., 1999). The purpose of the FBA process is to give the IEP team the information needed to develop individualized, positive, proactive behavioral programming for a student. The information gathered in this process helps the IEP team to develop behavior support plans that are effective, relevant, and efficient (Carr et al., 1999; O'Neill et al., 1997). This information then becomes part of the IEP as a BIP. Next we review this requirement of the IDEA.

*Developing Behavior Intervention Plans.* The IEP team develops a BIP based on the FBA. As was the case with FBAs, IDEA '97 does not provide details about the composition of the BIP beyond indicating that the plan has to be individualized to meet the needs of different students in different educational environments. The U.S. Department of Education also refused to define a BIP: Congress and the Department of Education apparently expected that the term "behavioral intervention plan" had a commonly understood meaning in the special education field (Gorn, 1999).

Behavior intervention plans need to be proactive and multidimensional. This means that IEP teams should implement multiple BIP strategies aimed at preventing problem behavior before it becomes severe enough to warrant such sanctions as suspension or expulsion, and teaching prosocial behavior to replace a student's inappropriate behavior (Drasgow et al., 1999; Gorn, 1999; Yell et al., 2000). In fact, behavioral plans that merely describe acts of prohibited misconduct and then specific consequences for misbehavior are almost certainly illegal because they are reactive and not proactive (Gorn, 1999).

The BIP is a behavior change program that emphasizes a thorough assessment prior to programming and developing multiple strategies that include teaching prosocial behaviors. The key component of the BIP is the use of multiple positive behavioral interventions that do not rely on coercion or punishment for behavior change (Dunlap & Koegel,

1999). Teaching and environmental redesign are the central behavior change tools in the system (Sugai et al., 1999). BIPs include strategies to:

a. alter the environment to eliminate events that trigger problem behavior,
b. teach new skills that replace problem behavior,
c. eliminate reinforcement for problem behavior,
d. maximize reinforcement for appropriate behavior. (Carr et al., 1999)

The purpose of the BIP, therefore, is multicomponent proactive programming that emphasizes skill-building, rather than reactive programming that relies on crisis management techniques (e.g., time-out, restraint) following the occurrence of problem behavior (Drasgow & Yell, 2001).

To ensure that our behavioral programs lead to meaningful results requires that IEP teams use ongoing evaluations to monitor a student's progress and to make the appropriate changes when data indicate that a program is not effective. This approach promotes the collection of meaningful data and analysis of these data to inform educators about the effectiveness of their behavior change interventions. The purpose of data collection is to provide objective evidence of student performance that can be used to guide instructional decisions (e.g., Deno, 1992; Fuchs & Fuchs, 1990; Snell & Brown, 2000). The IDEA now emphasizes measurable annual goals and frequent monitoring and reporting of a student's progress toward meeting these goals (Yell & Drasgow, 2000).

## Summary of the IDEA and School-Wide Discipline

Perhaps the most important implications of the discipline provisions of IDEA '97 are those that require IEP teams to take a proactive, problem-solving approach toward addressing the problem behaviors of students with disabilities. According to Sugai et al. (1999), the IDEA's emphasis on proactive approaches to problem behavior represented an important effort to improve the quality of behavioral interventions and behavior support planning and thus achieve socially important behavior change. Rather than relying on traditional methods of punishing inappropriate behavior, the IDEA now focuses on developing positive programming that will lead to meaningful improvements in students' lives.

To ensure that these goals are realized, IEP teams must become competent in conducting appropriate assessments and evaluations. Furthermore, the IEP team must design and deliver appropriate programming based on positive behavioral interventions and supports to meet these students' needs. School districts will have to employ people who are competent in conducting functional behavioral assessments and in developing positive behavior intervention plans to include in students' IEPs. Finally, IEP teams must become proficient at developing data collection systems to determine students' progress toward their behavioral goals. Moreover, instructional decisions should be based on the data collected. As Smith (2000) aptly states, if we cannot acquire these skills "the legal and financial repercussions of our inability to consistently deliver in the behavioral domain may be high" (p. 411).

## LEGAL GUIDELINES

Problem behavior in schools is a significant issue that administrators and teachers must address. Responses to these problems should begin with establishing discipline policies and procedures as a school-wide priority. In this section we offer important considerations for developing legally sound school district plans to address school discipline problems.

### Know the Law

Prior to developing school-wide discipline policies and procedures, school district personnel should understand federal laws, state laws, and regulations addressing these issues. The development of a school policy that is in line with state laws and regulations is essential. As reviewed previously, discipline policies should be reasonable, rationale, and fair and communicated to all school personnel, parents, and students. Additionally, staff, students, and parents should clearly know which behaviors are acceptable and which behaviors are prohibited. Disciplinary procedures and consequences should be commensurate with the offense, reasonable, humane, and applied equally and fairly.

It is critical that administrative personnel and general and special education teachers understand their responsibilities under the IDEA, especially for students in special education who exhibit serious behavioral challenges. These responsibilities are that

    a. IEP teams must address a student's problem behavior in his or her IEP,

   b. FBAs must be conducted and multidimensional and proactive BIPS should be developed in a timely manner,

   c. general educators should be informed about their roles in a student's IEP.

### *Include the Entire School Community When Developing Discipline Policies*

School-wide discipline policies and procedures will be more meaningful if the entire school community (e.g., school personnel, parents, students) is involved in developing and implementing the plan (Dwyer, Osher, & Warger, 1998). This strategy will help ensure involvement in and understanding of the school's policies. Similarly, staff, students, and parents should understand and support the discipline procedures.

### *Conduct District-Wide Training of All Staff*

Administrators, teachers, school staff, and other members of the district and school teams should receive ongoing professional development in school-wide discipline policies and procedures. Training should provide information about:

   a. the school-wide discipline plan,

   b. classroom management and discipline,

   c. the implementation of safe and effective intervention procedures with students who exhibit severe problem behaviors,

   d. the FBA and BIP process for students in special education.

Schools districts should ensure that well-trained faculty are on the IEP teams because these teams are responsible for implementing the FBA and BIP requirements in the IDEA. Training is especially important for:

   a. conducting assessments that lead to educational programming,

   b. developing IEPs that contain measurable goals and result in meaningful educational benefits,

   c. addressing problem behavior in positive and proactive ways.

It is the responsibility of school districts to ensure that IEP team members are properly prepared to carry out these tasks in accordance with best practices.

Appropriate training is especially important for school personnel who conduct FBAs and develop BIPs because failure of IEP teams to translate the law's requirements into students' educational programs will likely result in inappropriate IEPs and, thus, the denial of a FAPE.

The denial of a FAPE may, in turn, lead to due process hearings, litigation, and application of the law's sanctions against the offending school districts. Therefore, preservice and inservice educational opportunities should be provided so that members of IEP teams thoroughly understand their responsibilities under IDEA '97 and have the skills to carry them out. Public schools must ensure that personnel involved in implementing FBAs and BIPs have the necessary training and expertise. Public schools will be well served if this technology is implemented in a proactive manner to address serious and chronic maladaptive behaviors.

### Collecting Meaningful Data on Program and Student Progress

If school-wide discipline plans are to be effective, school personnel should develop and implement a set of procedures for monitoring program effectiveness. The collection of meaningful data will allow school officials to determine the efficacy of the school-wide policies and to maintain effective components of the program while eliminating the ineffective components. Data collection may include analysis of discipline referrals, behavior incident reports, and records of attendance, truancy, and tardiness (Lewis & Sugai, 1999).

Similarly, when students with serious problem behaviors are in special education their IEP teams must continuously collect meaningful data to document student progress toward their goals and, thus, to document the program's efficacy. Data should be collected during behavioral programming so that student progress is continually monitored. The purpose of data collection is to provide objective evidence of program efficacy, assess student performance, and guide programming decisions (e.g., Deno, 1992; Fuchs & Fuchs, 1990, Yell & Drasgow, 2000). IEP teams can ensure that they provide effective programming by collecting meaningful numerical data and by demonstrating that these data guided sound instructional decisions.

IEP teams also must make decisions about the nature of the data that will be collected to monitor student progress and to make program adjustments when necessary (Heflin & Simpson, 1998). Anecdotal data and other subjective procedures are not appropriate for monitoring student progress, and should never be the basis of a data collection system (Yell & Drasgow, 2000). The most appropriate data collection systems are those from applied behavior analysis (e.g., Alberto & Troutman, 1999; Wolery, Bailey, & Sugai, 1988) in which target behaviors are defined in observable and measurable ways so that the resulting data are numerical. Numerical data then can be graphed and visually inspected to evaluate progress toward goals and objectives.

## CONCLUSIONS

School districts have legal rights and responsibilities to ensure that their students attend safe and orderly environments where they can receive a meaningful education. To do this, educational personnel need to develop school-wide discipline plans and behavior support programs that define, teach, and reinforce appropriate behaviors while discouraging and reducing inappropriate behaviors. School-wide discipline programs eschew traditional methods of reducing inappropriate behaviors through punishment and exclusion, and, instead, focus on a positive, proactive, problem-solving model for promoting appropriate behavior and discouraging inappropriate behavior. For students with the most serious problem behaviors, the IDEA now requires adoption of a similar problem-solving approach using FBAs and BIPs to address these students' problems. FBAs and BIPs, properly conducted and developed, will result in educational programming that does not rely on punitive reductive procedures to change behavior but, rather, develops skill-based programming designed to improve the lives of these students.

## REFERENCES

Alberto, P. A., & Troutman, A. C. (1999). *Applied behavior analysis for teachers (5th edition)*. Upper Saddle River, NJ: Prentice Hall/Merrill.

Alexander, K., & Alexander, M.D. (2001). *American public school law* (4th ed.). St. Paul, MN: West Publishing Company.

Bagley, W.C. (1907). *Classroom management*. Norwood, MA: MacMillan.

Carr, E.G., Horner, R.H., Turnbull, A.P., Marquis, J.G., Magito-McLaughlin, D., McAtee, M.L., Smith, C.E., Ryan K.A., Ruef, M.B., & Doolah, A. (1999). *Positive behavior support as an approach for dealing with problem behavior in people with developmental disabilities: A research synthesis*. Washington, DC: American Association on Mental Retardation Monograph Series.

Deno, S.L. (1992). The nature and development of curriculum-based measurement. *Preventing School Failure, 36*, 5-11.

Drasgow, E., & Yell, M.L. (2001). Functional behavioral assessment: Legal requirements and challenges. *School Psychology Review, 30*, 239-251.

Drasgow, E., Yell, M.L., Bradley, R., & Shriner, J.G. (1999). The IDEA Amendments of 1997: A school-wide model for conducting functional behavioral assessments and developing behavior intervention plans. *Education and Treatment of Children*, *22*, 244-266.

Dunlap, G., & Koegel, R. L. (1999). Welcoming introduction. *Journal of Positive Behavior Interventions*, *1*, 2-3.

Dwyer, K.P., Osher, D., & Warger, W. (1998). *Early warning, timely response: A guide to safe schools*. Washington, DC: U.S. Department of Education.

Fuchs, D., & Fuchs, L.S. (1990). Making educational research more important. *Exceptional Children*, *57*, 102-107.

Gorn, D. (1999). *What do I do when . . . The answer book on discipline*. Horsham, PA: LRP Publications.

Heflin, L. J., Simpson, R.L., & Simpson, R. (1998). Interventions for children and youth with autism: Prudent choices in a world of exaggerated claims and empty promises. Part 11: Legal/policy analysis and recommendations for selecting interventions and treatments. *Focus on Autism and Other Developmental Disabilities*, *13*, 212-220.

Horner, R., & Carr, E.G. (1997). Behavioral support for students with severe disabilities: Functional assessment and comprehensive intervention. *Journal of Special Education*, *31*, 84-104.

Horner, R., & Sugai, G. (in press). School-wide behavior support: An emerging initiative. *Journal of Positive Behavior Support* (available at www.pbis.org).

Horner, R.H., Sugai, G., & Horner, H.F. (2000). A school-wide approach to student discipline. *The School Administrator*, *24*, 20-23.

Individuals with Disabilities Education Act, 20 U.S.C. § 1401-1485.

Individuals with Disabilities Education Act Regulations, 34 C.F.R. § 300 et. seq.

*Letter to Anonymous*, 1998. 30 IDELR 707.

Lewis, T.J., & Sugai, G. (1999). Effective behavior support: A systems approach to proactive school-wide management. *Focus on Exceptional Children*, *31(6)*, 1-24.

Office of Special Education Programs (OSEP) Analysis of comments and changes (1999, March 12), 64 *Federal Register* 12, 620. Volume 64, No. 48.

Office of Special Education Programs (OSEP) Questions and answers (1999, March 12). *Federal Register*, *64*, 12617-12632. Volume 64, No. 48.

O'Neill, R.E., Horner, R.H., Albin, R.W., Sprague, J.R., Storey, K., & Newton, J.S., (1997). *Functional assessment and program development for problem behavior*. Pacific Grove, CA: Brooks/Cole Publishing Company.

Safe and Drug Free Schools and Communities Act of 1994, 20 U.S.C.§ 7107 et seq.

Smith, C. R. (2000). Behavioral and discipline provisions of IDEA '97: Implicit competencies yet to be confirmed. *Exceptional Children*, *66*, 403-412.

Snell, M. E., & Brown, F. (2000). *Instruction of students with severe disabilities (5th edition)*. Upper Saddle River, NJ: Merrill/Prentice Hall.

Sugai, G., Horner, R.H., Dunlap, G., Hieneman, M., Lewis, T.J., Nelson, C.M., Scott, T., Liapsin, C., Sailor, W., Turnbull, A., Turnbull, H.R., Wickham, D., Ruef, M., & Wilcox, B. (1999). Applying positive behavioral support and functional behavioral assessment in schools. Eugene, OR: OSEP Center on Positive Behavioral Interventions and Supports.

Sugai, G., Sprague, J.R., Horner, R.H., & Walker, H.M. (2001). Preventing school violence: The use of office discipline referrals to assess and monitor school-wide discipline interventions. In H. M. Walker & M. H. Epstein (Eds.), *Making schools safer and violence free: Critical issues, solutions, and recommended practices* (pp. 50-57). Austin, TX: PRO-ED.

Valente, W.D., & Valente, C.M. (2000). *Law in the schools* (4th ed.). Upper Saddle River, NJ: Merrill/Prentice Hall.

Walker, H.M., & Epstein, M.H. (2001). *Making schools safer and violence free: Critical issues, solutions, and recommended practices*. Austin, TX: PRO-ED

Walker. H.M., Horner, R.H., Sugai, G., Bullis, M., Sprague, J.R., Bricker, D., & Kaufman, M.J. (1996). Integrated approaches to preventing antisocial behavior patterns among school-age children and youth. *Journal of Emotional and Behavioral Disorders, 4,* 193-209.

Wolery, M., Bailey, D.B., & Sugai, G. M. (1988). *Effective teaching: Principles and procedures of applied behavior analysis with exceptional students*. Boston: Allyn and Bacon.

Yell, M.L. (1998). *The law and special education*. Upper Saddle River, NJ: Merrill/Prentice Hall.

Yell, M.L., & Drasgow, E. (2000). Litigating a free appropriate public education: The Lovaas hearings and cases. *Journal of Special Education, 33,* 206-215.

Yell, M.L., Katsiyannis, A., Bradley, R., & Rozalski, M. (2000). Ensuring compliance with the disciplinary provisions of IDEA '97: Challenges and opportunities. *Journal of Special Education Leadership, 13,* 3-18.

Yell, M.L., & Rozalski, M.E. (2000). Searching for safe schools: Legal issues in the prevention of school violence. *Journal of Emotional and Behavioral Disorders, 8,* 146-180.

# Training School Psychologists in Behavior Support Consultation

Brian K. Martens

Scott P. Ardoin

**SUMMARY.** Although school consultation began as a means of providing assistance to individual teachers on a voluntary basis, it has evolved into a stand-alone service regulated by state and federal law. In order to meet the demand for increased accountability in the services they provide, school psychologists and other prereferral intervention team members have expressed a need to develop skills in two key areas: (a) selecting interventions that are conceptually relevant and therefore likely to be effective in responding to children's behavior problems, and (b) providing teachers with the resources and support needed to ensure successful plan implementation. In this paper, we describe various strategies that have been shown to be effective at addressing each of these issues by drawing on recent research in school consultation and applied behavior analysis. Considerations surrounding the use of these strategies by school consultants are discussed, as are implications for increasing the effectiveness and accountability of school consultation services. *[Article copies available for a fee from The Haworth Document Delivery Service: 1-800-HAWORTH. E-mail address: <getinfo@haworthpressinc.com> Website: <http://www.HaworthPress.com> © 2002 by The Haworth Press, Inc. All rights reserved.]*

---

Brian K. Martens, PhD, is Professor and Director of Training for the School Psychology Program at Syracuse University.

Scott P. Ardoin, PhD, is Director of the Center for Equitable Educational Placement and is affiliated with the School Psychology Program at Louisiana State University.

Address correspondence to: Brian K. Martens, Department of Psychology, Syracuse University, 430 Huntington Hall, Syracuse, NY 13244-2340.

[Haworth co-indexing entry note]: "Training School Psychologists in Behavior Support Consultation." Martens, Brian K., and Scott P. Ardoin. Co-published simultaneously in *Child & Family Behavior Therapy* (The Haworth Press, Inc.) Vol. 24, No. 1/2, 2002, pp. 147-163; and: *Behavior Psychology in the Schools: Innovations in Evaluation, Support, and Consultation* (ed: James K. Luiselli, and Charles Diament) The Haworth Press, Inc., 2002, pp. 147-163. Single or multiple copies of this article are available for a fee from The Haworth Document Delivery Service [1-800-HAWORTH, 9:00 a.m. - 5:00 p.m. (EST). E-mail address: getinfo@haworthpressinc.com].

**KEYWORDS.** School consultation, functional assessment, implementation support

School consultation emerged in the 1970s and early 1980s as a cost-effective means of helping regular education teachers accommodate children with special needs (Bergan, 1977; Reschly, 1988). Consultation was viewed as a voluntary, collaborative relationship between co-equal professionals, the goals of which were to address children's problems and increase the ability of teachers to respond to similar problems in the future (Gutkin & Curtis, 1982). During this time, school psychologists who attempted to provide consultation services often did so outside the boundaries of their normal job description (Piersel & Gutkin, 1983). As consultees, teachers were responsible for implementing plans developed during the consultative process and therefore had the right to reject or modify consultants' suggestions.

Early reviews of consultation research showed it to be an effective professional practice with the potential to decrease significantly the number of children referred for special education placement (Graden, Casey, & Bonstrom, 1985; Gutkin, Henning-Stout, & Piersel, 1988; Mannino & Shore, 1975; Medway, 1979; Ritter, 1978). As a result, consultation became increasingly popular during the 1980s and 1990s as a basis for prereferral intervention programs (Erchul & Martens, 1997). As early as 1987, almost 70% of all states mandated prereferral intervention services in their schools and this number has since increased (Carter & Sugai, 1989; Zins, Kratochwill, & Elliott, 1993). Following passage of the 1997 amendments to the Individuals with Disabilities Education Act (IDEA '97), consultation has also become a vehicle through which positive behavioral supports are put in place for students with handicaps (Telzrow, 1999). Although once delivered informally to teachers on a voluntary basis, consultation has grown into a stand-alone educational service regulated by state and federal law. This situation has raised the accountability of school consultation services by increasing the demand to demonstrate beneficial outcomes for children (Witt, 1997).

To what extent are school consultants prepared for increased accountability in the services they provide? The available data suggest that we may already possess many of the skills required to deliver effective consultation services. For example, in a survey of practicing school psychologists, Costenbader, Swartz, and Petrix (1992) found that participants gave themselves high marks when it came to maintaining collaborative relationships with consultees and defining children's problems. More recently, McDougall, Clonan, and Martens (2000) found that members of prereferral intervention teams judged themselves to be effective at creating a collaborative atmosphere, defining target problems, and designing interventions that teachers found acceptable.

Despite favorable self-ratings for relationship-building and problem-definition, participants in these studies perceived their consultation skills to be inadequate or lacking in several areas:

a. identifying antecedents and consequences for problem behavior,
b. designing effective interventions,
c. supporting teachers in their implementation efforts, and
d. monitoring intervention integrity and outcome. (Costenbader et al., 1992; McDougall et al., 2000)

With respect to the first two points (identifying conditions and designing interventions), school consultants are typically faced with a variety of interventions from which to choose, particularly when working as part of a multidisciplinary team. Their choices, however, are often driven by considerations such as familiarity, practicality, and perceived ease of use rather than insight into potential causes for students' problems (e.g., Ysseldyke, Pianta, Christenson, Wang, & Algozzine, 1983; Martens, Peterson, Witt, & Cirone, 1986). Selecting interventions that have theoretical relationships to variables believed to cause or maintain problem behavior has been referred to as *conceptual relevance* (Yeaton & Sechrest, 1981). Within the past 10 years, a considerable amount of research has shown that behavioral interventions are more likely to be effective if they are conceptually relevant (e.g., Martens, Witt, Daly, & Vollmer, 1999).

With respect to the latter two points (intervention and outcome monitoring), research has suggested that without ongoing support, teachers are likely to stop using an intervention after meetings with the consultant have ended. For example, Happe (1982) found that approximately 80% of consultees agreed verbally to implement an intervention plan, but only half of these individuals carried the plan through to conclusion. Noell, Witt, Gilbertson, Ranier, and Freeland (1997) monitored the number of intervention steps completed by three teachers each day after the procedure was explained and necessary materials were provided. All of the teachers implemented 100% of the treatment steps initially, but within two weeks this level had dropped to 0% for two teachers and 40% for the third teacher. Witt, Noell, LaFleur, and Mortenson (1997) found similar drops in the number of treatment steps completed even after teachers had received one session of coaching and feedback.

The goal of this paper is to provide school consultants with information and strategies for addressing two critical steps in the consultation process:

    a. selecting conceptually relevant interventions, and
    b. giving teachers enough support to ensure their successful implementation.

These strategies are considered "best practices" in satisfying the IDEA '97 mandate for functional assessment, are derived from recent consultation research and our experiences in the schools, and have the potential to increase the effectiveness and accountability of school consultation services (Drasgow & Yell, 2001; Erchul & Martens, 1997).

## *SELECTING CONCEPTUALLY RELEVANT INTERVENTIONS*

The first step in selecting conceptually relevant school-based interventions is to evaluate teachers' concerns and collect enough information to generate educated guesses about why students are behaving inappropriately. There are many reasons why students might engage in inappropriate behavior, and consultants must identify those reasons that are pertinent to each case (Martens, Eckert, Bradley, & Ardoin, 1999). In the absence of such information, one may be forced to select an intervention plan from a standard battery or one based on trial-and-error, options which are likely to prove ineffective or waste precious time and resources. To develop hypotheses regarding the causes of problem behavior, consultants must typically rely on information obtained through teacher interview, direct observation, assessment of the instructional environment, and/or direct assessment of the child's behavioral and academic skills (e.g., Ervin, DuPaul, Kern, & Friman, 1998). Once hypotheses are made based on the obtained information the second step is to develop an intervention that counteracts, eliminates, or weakens the variables believed to be maintaining problem behavior (Martens et al., 1999). As a third step, school consultants must monitor whether the intervention was implemented as planned and whether it produced the desired results.

### *Why Do Children Misbehave?*

One reason why children engage in appropriate behavior is that they may *lack the necessary skills or understanding for how to behave ap-*

*propriately.* Students may lack certain skills because appropriate behavior was never modeled for them or they had insufficient opportunities to practice it, thereby making problem behavior an easier, or more efficient, way to obtain what they desire (Erchul & Martens, 1997). In such cases, posting classroom rules alone may be insufficient to promote behavior change. Due to neurological (e.g., Attention Deficit Hyperactivity) or other disorders, some children may require more intensive guidance to engage in appropriate behavior (e.g., behavioral or pharmacological intervention). Other students may have the skills necessary to engage in appropriate behavior, but are not able to differentiate times when rules are in place or suspended (e.g., Gresham & Elliott, 1984). For instance, hand raising is not generally required across settings. Therefore, a student may be praised for calling out an answer during a small group session but reprimanded during large-group instruction.

Children may also engage in inappropriate behavior because it *leads to rewards that are presented more frequently or consistently, more immediately, or that are more highly valued than those for desired behavior.* Inappropriate behavior may provide students with more frequent or immediate access to reinforcers such as peer or teacher attention, desired objects, or activities (Martens, Witt et al., 1999; Taylor & Romanczyk, 1994). For example, engaging in appropriate behavior may result in positive teacher attention on average every 20 minutes, but engaging in inappropriate behavior, which requires less effort, may result in teacher attention on average every 5 minutes plus nearly constant peer attention. Children may also learn that if they engage in appropriate behavior they are forced to wait for rewards, but by engaging in inappropriate behavior they can obtain the same attention immediately. Inappropriate behavior may also be more reinforcing if what teachers consider to be negative consequences are actually seen as positive from the child's perspective. For example, teachers often use time out as a means of decreasing disruptive classroom behavior. In some instances, however, time out is more stimulating and may even allow the student to escape work (e.g., going to the office) (Watson, Ray, Turner, & Logan, 1999). If students do not value the reinforcers that are available for desired behavior or have not had the opportunity to earn them, then "time-in" is not likely to encourage desired behavior. It is therefore important that reinforcers used by teachers are valued by students and that students have the opportunity to earn them, even if teachers have to initially decrease the requirements for doing so.

Another reason students may engage in inappropriate behavior is to *escape teacher demands, difficult or boring schoolwork, or other unde-*

*sirable situations.* Engaging in disruptive behavior often results in a student being taken out of the situation he/she is in, and thus the student may successfully avoid having to complete a difficult task, be near a peer, or sit through a difficult or boring class period. In such cases, allowing students to earn breaks for completing specified amounts of schoolwork can be a potent incentive (Martens, Witt et al., 1999).

## Developing Hypotheses

Several methods of gathering information can be used to develop hypotheses about why inappropriate behavior is occurring. Of these methods, perhaps the most widely used is to conduct an interview to assess the scope of teacher's concerns, determine which behavior the intervention should target, and define the target behavior in terms that will allow adults consistently to record its occurrence (Bergan & Kratochwill, 1990). Other questions that must be answered to develop hypotheses are provided in Table 1.

Though teachers can often provide a considerable amount of information during the interview, this will depend on the interviewing skills of the consultant, the teacher's ability to recall prior events, and the extent to which the teacher is aware of, or has had the opportunity to ob-

TABLE 1. Questions for Developing Hypotheses About Potential Causes of Problem Behavior

---

1) When does the behavior occur? Does it occur more often during certain times of the day, academic periods, following specific commands, settings, when specific adults/peers are present/not present?

2) Is there anything that usually occurs before the behavior (e.g., an assignment is given, teacher walks away from the student, teacher announces that it is time for math class)?

3) What is the child typically doing before he/she engages in the behavior?

4) How does the teacher respond when the child engages in the behavior?

5) How do the child's peers respond when he/she engages in the behavior?

6) What are the consequences of the behavior?

7) What other, more appropriate behaviors are expected of the child?

8) How is appropriate behavior rewarded?

9) Does the student know how to engage in appropriate behavior?

10) Can the student do the work that is assigned?

11) What interventions have already been attempted?

12) What does the child like that could be used to reward appropriate behavior?

---

serve, conditions surrounding student behavior. When additional information is needed, school consultants may have to rely on other, more direct forms of assessment (Martens & Kelly, 1993). One such method is to have teachers complete the Motivation Assessment Scale or MAS (Durand & Crimmins, 1988). The MAS is a 16-item questionnaire that asks teachers to rate the frequency with which, for various reasons, problem behavior seems to occur using a seven-point scale (0 = never, 6 = Always; Sample item: Does the behavior occur following a request to perform a difficult task?). Items on the MAS are combined into four subscales representing possible sources of reinforcement (sensory stimulation, escape, attention, access to tangibles).

Another assessment method is to ask teachers to record occurrences of the target behavior across different times of the day (e.g., morning, after lunch), different content areas (e.g., math, reading, social studies), or different instructional arrangements (e.g., independent seatwork, small-group instruction, large-group lecture) (e.g., Axelrod, 1987). These data can help pinpoint when problem behavior is most likely to occur and lead to the development of hypotheses concerning aspects of these situations that are problematic (e.g., a difficult curriculum, presence or absence of an adult/peer, different rules, less assistance, less structure, fewer available reinforcers) (Touchette, MacDonald, & Langer, 1985). These data can also be used as a baseline to gauge the effectiveness of interventions that are implemented at these times or in these situations.

The type of information that teachers record during these observations will depend on the nature of the target behavior. For behavior that occurs frequently, it may be sufficient for the teacher to obtain a simple frequency count. For behavior that occurs infrequently, it may be best for the teacher to write a brief narrative of events that precede the behavior (antecedents), the behavior itself, and events that occur as a result of the behavior (consequences). This strategy may be necessary with low frequency behavior because the consultant may not have the opportunity to observe events surrounding its occurrence firsthand.

Direct observation by the consultant is a third method of information gathering. This method can help confirm information provided by the teacher and assess whether the child's inappropriate behavior is typically preceded or followed by certain events. One means of collecting this information is to conduct narrative ABC recordings in three columns on a sheet of paper (Bijou, Peterson, & Ault, 1968). The observer records the target student's behavior in the center column, peer or teacher behavior that precedes the student's behavior in the left-hand column, and peer or teacher behavior that occurs as a consequence of the student's behavior in the right-hand column. Once these narratives are collected, consultants can calculate the types and frequencies of various consequences provided by the teacher for appropriate as well as inappropriate behavior. Based on previous teacher interviews or anecdotal observations, the consultant may already have an idea of the consequences available for specific behaviors (e.g., praise, help from the teacher, removal of work, ignoring). In such cases, simply recording the frequency with which each of these events follow occurrences of the behavior can be helpful in identifying what the child might gain from behaving inappropriately (e.g., noncompliance is followed by help from the teacher 80% of the time).

Another method of gathering information is to assess the student's skills. Skill assessment can be conducted by reviewing the student's previous work products and/or having the student complete work from his/her curriculum. To determine if students have the skills necessary to engage in appropriate behavior, they can be asked to describe classroom rules and demonstrate examples of appropriate behavior in accordance with those rules. The student's view of why he/she engages in undesired behavior is one source of information that consultants often fail to consider (Kern, Childs, Dunlap, Clarke, & Falk, 1994). Finally, a reinforcer preference assessment should be conducted to determine whether rewards that are being used in the classroom are valued by students and what rewards might be used as part of the intervention (Berkowitz & Martens, in press; Northup, George, Jones, Broussard, & Vollmer, 1996).

### Selecting an Appropriate Intervention for the Problem

Determining why behavior occurs can enable school consultants to develop interventions that teach new skills or that counteract, eliminate, or weaken events in the classroom that initiate or support problem behavior. Key components that should be included in reinforcement-based interventions are listed in Table 2. Regardless of the hypothesized cause, these interventions must provide students with the same or more highly preferred reinforcers than previously maintained inappropriate behavior (Ringdahl, Vollmer, Marcus, & Roane, 1997). Therefore, if it was hypothesized that peer attention was supporting inappropriate behavior, then peer attention could be made contingent on appropriate behavior. Likewise, the frequency and consistency with which reinforcement is provided for appropriate behavior should be of equal or greater

TABLE 2. Key Elements of Effective Reinforcement-Based Programs

| Problem Behavior Results from a Lack of Knowledge or Skill |
|---|
| - Give the student step-by-step instructions |
| - Model appropriate behavior |
| - Provide opportunities to practice behavior |
| - Provide feedback regarding the correctness of behavior and correct errors as needed |
| - Provide student with reinforcement for engaging in or attempting new behavior |
| - Provide explicit instructions in each setting to enable the student to differentiate when rules are suspended and in force |

| Problem Behavior Is More Rewarding |
|---|
| - Assess the student's preferences for various reinforcing items or activities |
| - Increase the frequency of reinforcement for appropriate behavior |
| - Provide reinforcement for behavior that is incompatible with problem behavior |
| - Eliminate or reduce reinforcement for inappropriate behavior |
| - Implement negative consequences for inappropriate behavior (e.g., punishment) |
| - Teach the student alternative behavior that can replace inappropriate behavior, but allows him/her access to the same reinforcement |

| Problem Behavior Leads to Escape from Task Demands |
|---|
| - Teach the student how to ask for help and reward this behavior |
| - Match the student's curriculum to his/her skills |
| - Guide the student to comply and then reinforce compliance |
| - Give the student breaks for completing specified amounts of work |

value than it was for inappropriate behavior (Martens, 1992). As mentioned before, the level of behavior required of students to earn reinforcement must allow them actually to obtain the rewards.

The effectiveness of school-based interventions can be determined by comparing the frequency, duration, and/or intensity of behavior prior to baseline to the same measure(s) following plan implementation. If there is no difference in behavior, the consultant should attempt to determine the following:

a. Was the student able to obtain reinforcement or were the goals for behavior set too high?
b. Did the student value the reinforcers that were available?
c. Did the student understand the connection between appropriate behavior and how to receive reinforcement?
d. Was reinforcement provided frequently and consistently?
e. Was inappropriate behavior still being supported?

As discussed in the next section, the consultant must also take steps to ensure that the intervention was implemented by the teacher as planned (Gresham, 1989).

## SUPPORTING TEACHERS IN THEIR IMPLEMENTATION EFFORTS

As an indirect service-delivery model, school consultation relies on changes in teacher behavior as a means of providing services to children. These changes typically involve more intensive or direct approaches to academic instruction (e.g., word list training, classwide peer tutoring) or more structured forms of classroom management (e.g., self-monitoring and charting, time-out) (Martens, Witt et al., 1999). As such, intervention programs that are developed during consultation require teachers to learn new skills and make what are often significant changes in the way they interact with students.

Noell, Witt, LaFleur, Mortenson, Ranier, and LeVelle (in press) observed that school consultants rarely have formal administrative authority over teachers whose behavior they are attempting to change. Thus, the extent to which teachers actually follow through in implementing agreed-upon plans may depend largely on the consultant's interpersonal influence and implementation support skills (Erchul & Martens, 1997). Until recently, however, efforts to promote intervention use by teachers have relied primarily on oral instruction from the consultant prior to implementation. For example, Bergan and Kratochwill (1990) described four roles that must be executed in order to implement a consultation plan: implementation director, plan executor, behavior observer, and implementation skill developer. Of these four roles, the consultant was expected to function only as skill developer by conducting training sessions before the intervention began. Our experiences in the schools suggest that, as consultants, we typically *underestimate* the amounts of training and support that teachers require to change their behavior successfully. Consistent with this notion, Joyce and Showers (1981) reviewed effective strategies for in-service training and concluded that didactic instruction alone is not likely to promote maintenance of behavior change unless it is followed by demonstration, practice, feedback, and in vivo application. Goldstein and Martens (2000) identified several strategies that have been shown to be effective in the consultation literature for promoting teachers' use of school-based interventions and these are discussed below.

## Social Influence Strategies

Effective consultation involves a social influence component, yet school consultants typically employ a limited range of influence strategies (Erchul & Martens, 1997). The most common of these strategies include appealing to a teacher's sense of responsibility to help children by doing what the consultant asks (i.e., legitimate power) and promoting the view that the consultant's suggestion is really the best course of action to take (i.e., informational power). We believe that several other social influence strategies that have been discussed in the literature hold particular promise for school consultation. As professionals-in-training who are external to a school building, practicum students in consultation are often cast in a "one-down" position relative to full-time staff members. At the same time, as observed by Sarason (1982), teachers who spend most of the day talking with children often like to connect and interact professionally with other adults. Under these circumstances, our practicum students have realized some success in promoting consultee behavior change by:

a. assuming the bulk of responsibility for material development and plan implementation initially and then gradually reducing their involvement over time (i.e., the legitimate power of reciprocity),
b. praising teachers for participating in meetings and following through with assigned responsibilities (i.e., reward power),
c. highlighting similarities with teachers in terms of educational values or past teaching experiences (i.e., positive referent power),
d. highlighting the successful use of similar interventions by other teaching staff (i.e., invoking the influence of third parties). (Goldstein & Martens, 2000)

## Setting Goals for Teacher Behavior

In behavioral consultation, tentative goals for student behavior change are established during the problem-identification interview to determine if teachers harbor unreasonable expectations, whereas formal goals are set during the problem-analysis interview to assess treatment outcome (Bergan & Kratochwill, 1990). Interestingly, the same level of goal specificity is not required with respect to changes in teacher behavior which ultimately mediate student improvement. Given the demand for increased accountability in consultation service delivery, we believe that setting explicit standards for consultee behavior represents an important but largely untapped method for promoting plan implementation. This potential was illustrated in a study by Martens, Hiralall, and Bradley (1997) in which an intervention was designed to address the disruptive and off-task behavior of two kindergarten-age students diagnosed with emotional disturbances. Baseline observations revealed generally low but variable levels of appropriate student behavior as well as low rates of teacher praise (approximately three times in a 30 min. period). This information was shared with the teacher who was encouraged to set a goal for herself of six praise statements every 30 min. Each morning thereafter, the teacher was given a brief feedback note prompting her as to which behaviors to praise for each student and stating whether or not she had met her goal the previous day. As a function of the goal setting plus feedback intervention, the average number of praise statements delivered by the teacher to each student increased to over 14 in a 30 min. period, and mean levels of appropriate student behavior increased to over 80% of the intervals observed.

### *Modeling, Coaching, and Performance Feedback*

Noell and his colleagues (Noell et al., in press; Noell et al., 1997; Witt et al., 1997) have conducted a series of investigations examining the effectiveness of performance feedback at increasing intervention use by teachers. Each of the studies employed a similar approach to staggering when feedback began for each teacher, sequence of consultation activities, and method for monitoring teacher implementation. The intervention plan was first described to the teacher, materials needed to implement the plan were provided, and use of the plan was modeled by the consultant who coached the teacher through implementation during one classroom session. After this initial training, the teacher implemented the plan independently, received a performance feedback package, and again implemented the plan independently (i.e., a maintenance phase). The performance feedback package consisted of graphs depicting levels of student behavior and teacher implementation (i.e., percentage of steps completed), discussion of implementation errors, and praise for implementing the intervention as planned.

A consistent pattern of findings emerged across the studies. Although teachers initially implemented all intervention steps, implementation dropped considerably within several weeks. Implementation levels increased dramatically with introduction of performance feedback, but maintenance after feedback ended was variable. Because the start of each condition was staggered across teachers, some teachers received performance feedback during a large number of sessions before moving to the maintenance phase. Interestingly, these teachers tended to show greater maintenance, suggesting that performance feedback may have helped them master the skills required for correct implementation and perhaps reinforced their use.

### Implementation Protocols

A primary reason why teachers seek consultative assistance is that their usual methods of responding to students' problems have proven unsuccessful. Together with the observation by Piersel and Gutkin (1983) that consultees have often received little, if any, training in the use of behavioral interventions, skill building becomes an important consultative function. One way to train consultees in the use of an intervention plan and promote its use after training has ended is to provide them with checklists or scripts detailing the steps required to carry out the plan. For example, Ehrhardt, Barnett, Lentz, Stollar, and Reiffin (1996) developed intervention scripts collaboratively with caregivers for use in responding to behavior problems exhibited by four preschoolers. The scripts detailed in step-by-step fashion what each caregiver was supposed to do in order to implement the intervention and contained a place to indicate when each step had been completed. Results suggested that the scripts were effective at increasing implementation integrity and these levels were maintained at follow-up.

In a similar study, Hiralall and Martens (1998) developed a scripted protocol for use by four teachers in implementing a direct instruction sequence. The protocol was used during a structured art activity and required teachers to engage in the six-step instructional sequence depicted in Table 3. The teachers were observed providing instruction with and without use of the protocol and at one month follow-up. Not only did all four teachers increase their use of instructional statements, modeling, and praise with use of the protocol, but two teachers maintained these levels at follow-up. Implementation protocols appear to be effective at promoting intervention use by teachers, are easy to develop, can be used to monitor treatment integrity, and can be used in conjunction with performance feedback (e.g., Witt et al., 1997).

### CONCLUSION

Erchul and Martens (1997) described a number of advances that were made in consultation research and practice during the 1980s and early 1990s. They went on to identify challenges that we would face in the

TABLE 3. Direct Instruction Protocol Used in Hiralall and Martens (1998)

_____Teacher:        _____Date:        Day: M T W Th F

Check off each step as you complete it. Time limits are in parentheses. Remember to circle those steps you were unable to complete today on tomorrow's protocol.

1- ____Begin instruction by calling the children's attention to you by demanding eye contact. Ex: "Look at me and listen. The activity we are going to do today is ..." Next use a "teaser" statement to get the children's interest level up. (1 minute)

2- ____Be sure the children are looking at you while you give clear, oral directions in a step-by-step format. Model each step of the task after each direction is given. Ex: "The first thing you have to do is X, now look at me, watch how I do it ..." Demanded eye contact can be used to signal children who are not paying attention. (4-5 minutes)

3-____Deliver specific verbal praise to each child individually who is behaving appropriately. Ex: "NAME, you are doing a wonderful job cutting out the shapes." Be sure the praise includes their name and the action they are performing. (2 minutes)

4-____Redirect each child individually who is off-task by demanding eye contact and using a single directive statement. Ex: "NAME, look at me, stop playing with X and cut out the circle please." Praise the child once he/she is on-task. (3 minutes)

5-____Praise each child individually who is on-task as specified in Step 3. (2 minutes)

6-____Redirect and praise each child individually who is off-task as specified in Step 4. (3 minutes)

new millennium as likely consequences of the increased bureaucratization of school consultation services. These challenges included:

    a. promoting the use of effective instructional and intervention technologies,
    b. increasing our base of knowledge concerning how to change teacher behavior,
    c. routinely providing teachers with the resources and assistance needed to support their use of interventions.

We believe that recent research in school consultation and applied behavior analysis can inform practitioners in their efforts to meet each of these three challenges. Having said this, however, we also recognize that many of the strategies described in this paper require more intensive or direct consultant involvement. As with many attempts to increase the accountability of school-based service delivery, perhaps the greatest challenge we face in putting these suggestions into practice is that of time.

## REFERENCES

Axelrod, S. (1987). Functional and structural analyses of behavior: Approaches leading to reduced use of punishment procedures? *Research in Developmental Disabilities, 8,* 165-178.

Bergan, J.R. (1977). *Behavioral consultation.* Columbus, OH: Merrill.

Bergan, J.R, & Kratochwill, T.R. (1990). *Behavioral consultation and therapy.* New York, NY: Plenum Press.

Berkowitz, M.J., & Martens, B.K. (in press). Assessing teachers' and students' preferences for school-based reinforcers: Agreement across methods and different effort requirements. *Journal of Developmental and Physical Disabilities.*

Bijou, S.W., Peterson, R.F., & Ault, M.H. (1968). A method to integrate descriptive and experimental field studies at the level of data and empirical concepts. *Journal of Applied Behavior Analysis, 1,* 175-191.

Carter, J., & Sugai, G. (1989). Survey of prereferral practices: Responses from state departments of education. *Exceptional Children, 55,* 298-302.

Costenbader, V., Swartz, J., & Petrix, L. (1992). Consultation in the schools: The relationship between preservice training, perception of consultative skills, and actual time spent in consultation. *School Psychology Review, 21,* 95-108.

Drasgow, E., & Yell, M.L. (2001). Functional behavioral assessments: Legal requirements and challenges. *School Psychology Review, 30,* 239-251.

Durand, V.M., & Crimmins, D.B. (1988) Identifying the variables maintaining self-injurious behavior. *Journal of Autism and Developmental Disorders, 18,* 99-117.

Ehrhardt, K.E., Barnett, D.W., Lentz, F.E., Stollar, S.A., & Reifin, L.H. (1996). Innovative methodology in ecological consultation: Use of scripts to promote treatment acceptability and integrity. *School Psychology Quarterly, 11,* 149-168.

Erchul, W.P., & Martens, B.K. (1997). *School consultation: Conceptual and empirical bases of practice.* New York: Plenum Press.

Ervin, R. A., DuPaul, G.J., Kern, L., & Friman, P. C. (1998). Classroom-based functional and adjunctive assessments: Proactive approaches to intervention selection for adolescents with attention deficit hyperactivity disorder. *Journal of Applied Behavior Analysis, 31,* 65-78.

Goldstein, A.P., & Martens, B.K. (2000). *Lasting change: Methods for enhancing generalization of gain.* Champaign, IL: Research Press.

Graden, J.L., Casey, A., & Bonstrom, O. (1985). Implementing a prereferral intervention system: Part II. The data. *Exceptional Children, 51,* 487-496.

Gresham, F.M. (1989). Assessment of treatment integrity in school consultation and prereferral intervention. *School Psychology Review, 18,* 37-50.

Gresham, F.M., & Elliott, S.N. (1984). Assessment and classification of children's social skills: A review of methods and issues. *School Psychology Review, 13,* 292-301.

Gutkin T.B., & Curtis, M.J. (1982). School-based consultation: Theory and techniques. In C.R. Reynolds & T.B. Gutkin (Eds.), *The handbook of school psychology* (pp. 796-828). New York: Wiley.

Gutkin, T.B., Henning-Stout, M., & Piersel, W.C. (1988). Impact of a district-wide behavioral consultation prereferral intervention service on patterns of school psychological service delivery. *Professional School Psychology, 3,* 301-308.

Happe, D. (1982). Behavioral intervention: It doesn't do any good in your briefcase. In J. Grimes (Ed.), *Psychological approaches to problems of children and adolescents* (pp. 15-41). Des Moines, IA: Iowa Department of Public Instruction.

Hiralall, A.S., & Martens, B.K. (1998). Teaching classroom management skills to preschool staff: The effects of scripted instructional sequences on teacher and student behavior. *School Psychology Quarterly, 13,* 94-115.

Joyce, B., & Showers, B. (1981). Improving inservice training: The messages of research. *Educational Leadership, 39,* 379-385.

Kern, L., Childs, K. E., Dunlap, G., Clarke, S., & Falk, G. D. (1994). Using assessment-based curricular intervention to improve the classroom behavior of a student with emotional and behavioral challenges. *Journal of Applied Behavior Analysis, 27,* 7-19.

Mannino, F.V., & Shore, M.F. (1975). The effects of consultation: A review of the literature. *American Journal of Community Psychology, 3,* 1-21.

Martens, B. K. (1992). Contingency and choice: The implications of matching theory for classroom instruction. *Journal of Behavioral Education, 2,* 121-137.

Martens, B.K., Eckert, T.L., Bradley, T.A., & Ardoin, S.P. (1999). Identifying effective treatments from a brief experimental analysis: Using single-case design elements to aid decision making. *School Psychology Quarterly, 14,* 163-181.

Martens, B.K., Hiralall, A.S., & Bradley, T.A. (1997). A note to teacher: Improving student behavior through goal setting and feedback. *School Psychology Quarterly, 12,* 33-41.

Martens, B. K., & Kelly, S. Q. (1993). A behavioral analysis of effective teaching. *School Psychology Quarterly, 8,* 10-26.

Martens, B.K., Peterson, R.L., Witt, J.C., & Cirone, S. (1986). Teacher perceptions of school based interventions. *Exceptional Children, 53,* 213-223.

Martens, B.K., Witt, J.C., Daly E.J., & Vollmer, T. (1999). Behavior analysis: Theory and practice in educational settings. In C.R. Reynolds & T.B. Gutkin (Eds.), *Handbook of school psychology* (3rd ed., pp. 638-663). New York: Wiley.

McDougal, J.L., Clonan, S.M., & Martens, B.K. (2000). Using organizational change procedures to promote the acceptability of prereferral intervention services: The school-based intervention team project. *School Psychology Quarterly, 15,* 149-171.

Medway, F.J. (1979). How effective is school consultation?: A review of recent research. *Journal of School Psychology, 17,* 275-281.

Noell, G.H., Witt, J.C., Gilbertson, D.N., Ranier, D.D., & Freeland, J.T. (1997). Increasing teacher intervention implementation in general education settings through consultation and performance feedback. *School Psychology Quarterly, 12,* 77-88.

Noell, G.H., Witt, J.C., LaFleur, L.H., Mortenson, B.P., Ranier, D.D., & LeVelle, J. (In press). Increasing intervention implementation in general education following consultation: A comparison of two follow-up strategies. *Journal of Applied Behavior Analysis.*

Northup, J., George, T., Jones, K., Broussard, C., & Vollmer, T.R. (1996). A comparison of reinforcer assessment methods: The utility of verbal and pictorial choice procedures. *Journal of Applied Behavior Analysis, 29,* 201-212.

Piersel, W.C., & Gutkin, T.B. (1983). Resistance to school-based consultation: A behavioral analysis of the problem. *Psychology in the Schools, 20,* 311-320.

Reschly, D.J. (1988). Special education reform: School psychology revolution. *School Psychology Review, 17,* 459-475.

Ringdahl, J.E., Vollmer, T.R., Marcus, B.A., & Roane, H.S. (1997). An analogue evaluation of environmental enrichment: The role of stimulus preference. *Journal of Applied Behavior Analysis, 30,* 203-216.

Ritter, D.R. (1978). Effects of a school consultation program upon referral patterns of teachers. *Psychology in the Schools, 15,* 239-243.

Sarason, S.B. (1982). *The culture of the school and the problem of change* (2nd ed.). Boston, MA: Allyn & Bacon.

Taylor, J. C., & Romanczyk, R. (1994). Generating hypothesis about the function of student problem behavior by observing teacher behavior. *Journal of Applied Behavior Analysis, 27*, 251-265.

Telzrow, C.F. (1999). IDEA amendments of 1997: Promise or pitfall for special education reform? *Journal of School Psychology, 37*, 7-28.

Touchette, P. E., MacDonald, R. F., & Langer, S. N. (1985). A scatter plot for identifying stimulus control of problem behavior. *Journal of Applied Behavior Analysis, 18*, 343-351.

Watson, T. S., Ray, K. P., Turner, H. S., & Logan, P. (1999). Teacher-implemented functional analysis and treatment: A method for linking assessment to intervention. *School Psychology Review, 28*, 292-302.

Witt, J.C. (1997). Talk is not cheap. *School Psychology Quarterly, 12*, 281-292.

Witt, J.C., Noell, G.H., La Fleur, L.H., & Mortenson, B.P. (1997). Teacher usage of interventions in general education: Measurement and analysis of the independent variable. *Journal of Applied Behavior Analysis, 30*, 693-696.

Yeaton, W.H., & Sechrest, L. (1981). Critical dimensions in the choice and maintenance of successful treatments: Strength, integrity, and effectiveness. *Journal of Consulting and Clinical Psychology, 49*, 156-167.

Ysseldyke, J.E., Pianta, B., Christenson, S., Wang, J., & Algozzine, B. (1983). An analysis of prereferral interventions. *Psychology in the Schools, 20*, 184-190.

Zins, J.E., Kratochwill, T.R., & Elliott, S.N. (Eds.). (1993). *The handbook of consultation services for children: Applications in educational and clinical settings.* San Francisco: Jossey-Bass.

# Examining the Efficacy
# of School-Based Consultation:
# Recommendations for Improving Outcomes

Timothy J. Lewis
Lori L. Newcomer

**SUMMARY.** Schools are faced with the difficult task of educating students who present diverse learning and behavioral challenges. To meet student needs, schools tap the expertise of a variety of specialists who provide services through "pull-out" programs or consultation to general educators. Unfortunately, neither strategy has proved effective to date with respect to children and youth who present significant social behavior problems. A brief review of the literature points to the shortcomings as linked to multiple treatments with varying outcomes and inconsistent implementation of best practices. One option to address the challenges schools face in light of ineffective practices to date is the development of school-wide systems of positive behavior support (PBS). Effective implementation of school-wide systems of PBS will require moving the consultation process from individual cases to working with teams of ed-

Timothy J. Lewis, PhD, is Associate Professor in the Department of Special Education at the University of Missouri-Columbia, 303 Townsend Hall, Columbia, MO 65211.

Lori L. Newcomer, MEd, is a doctoral student in Special Education at the University of Missouri-Columbia, and a behavioral consultant for the Special School District of St. Louis County.

Development of this manuscript was supported in part by a grant from the Office of Special Education Programs, with additional funding from the Safe and Drug Free Schools Program, US Department of Education (H326S980003). Opinions expressed herein are those of the authors and do not necessarily reflect the position of the US Department of Education, and such endorsements should not be inferred.

[Haworth co-indexing entry note]: "Examining the Efficacy of School-Based Consultation: Recommendations for Improving Outcomes." Lewis, Timothy J., and Lori L. Newcomer. Co-published simultaneously in *Child & Family Behavior Therapy* (The Haworth Press, Inc.) Vol. 24, No. 1/2, 2002, pp. 165-181; and: *Behavior Psychology in the Schools: Innovations in Evaluation, Support, and Consultation* (ed: James K. Luiselli, and Charles Diament) The Haworth Press, Inc., 2002, pp. 165-181. Single or multiple copies of this article are available for a fee from The Haworth Document Delivery Service [1-800-HAWORTH, 9:00 a.m. - 5:00 p.m. (EST). E-mail address: getinfo@haworthpressinc.com].

ucators. Key skills and possible measurement strategies to develop and sustain school-wide consultation efforts are discussed. *[Article copies available for a fee from The Haworth Document Delivery Service: 1-800-HAWORTH. E-mail address: <getinfo@haworthpressinc.com> Website: <http://www.HaworthPress.com> © 2002 by The Haworth Press, Inc. All rights reserved.]*

**KEYWORDS.** Behavior consultation, positive behavior support, school-wide systems, challenging behavior

Many classroom teachers are faced with the task of educating children and youth whose primary language is not English, who function at borderline levels of cognitive ability, who present significant learning and language disabilities, and who present a continuum of social and behavioral challenges. Increasing homogeneity among students has created the need for a variety of educational specialists such as speech and language pathologists, special education teachers, curriculum specialists, school psychologists, and school counselors. However, the majority of students, even those currently placed on Individualized Education Plans (IEP), spend most of their school day in the general education classroom environment (U.S. Department of Education, 2000a). Yet it is unrealistic to expect the general education classroom teacher to be able to meet the wide range of student needs without specialist support. To deliver specialist support most schools utilize an "expert" model through "pull-out" programs such as delivering special education programming in segregated classrooms or through consultation to the classroom teacher whereby the specialist creates a plan that the general educator is then expected to implement.

Even within specialized settings the need for expertise delivered through a consultative process continues to grow. Factors such as compliance with federal and state regulations, understanding and implementing best practices, and working with families and multiple agencies create complex school environments that move the case management of students with problem behavior beyond the capacity of a single educator. Unfortunately, educators have historically been the least effective in meeting the needs of children and youth who present significantly challenging behavior problems especially those identified with emotional and behavioral disorders (EBD) (U.S. Department of Education, 1995).

There is a clear knowledge-base with respect to developing effective support plans for children and youth who display problem behavior (Walker, Horner, Sugai, Bullis, Sprague, Bricker, & Kaufman, 1996). Essential strategies include social skill instruction (Gresham, 1998; Mayer, 1995; Peacock Hill Working Group, 1991; Walker et al., 1996), academic restructuring to accommodate individuals (Colvin, Kameenui, & Sugai, 1993; Kameenui & Simmons, 1990; Walker et al., 1996), parent involvement (Conduct Problem Prevention Research Group, 1992; Elliot, 1994a, 1994b; Larson, 1994; Patterson, Reid, & Dishion, 1992; Webster-Stratton & Spitzer, 1996), and multiple opportunities to practice appropriate behavior and receive instructive feedback. The challenge, in light of the increasing complexity in both general and special education classrooms, is to build capacity within schools using existing expert delivery systems to ensure that best practices, such as consultation, are being implemented. However, the limited empirical examinations of the consultation process to date have shown modest success. The purpose of this article is to:

a. review the efficacy of school-based consultation,
b. outline essential strategies that lead to positive outcomes,
c. offer suggestions for re-thinking how consultants are used in schools to increase the likelihood of success.

## EXAMINATION OF CURRENT SCHOOL-BASED CONSULTATION PRACTICES

Consultation is a service delivery model, not a procedure based on a scientific analysis of behavior. Reviews of the literature indicate a limited empirical database on the efficacy of consultation in schools. Researchers that have reviewed the literature draw attention to the methodological flaws that characterize most empirical research in this area (e.g., Fuchs, Fuchs, Dulan, Roberts, & Fernstrom, 1992; Gresham & Kendell, 1987; Gutkin, 1993; Pryzwansky, 1986) and point out that few well-controlled studies have actually been conducted (Kratochwill & VanSomeren, 1985). Only a few group-design studies have been experimental in nature, and much of the single-case designs have involved only one or two subjects (Fuchs et al., 1992), bringing the external validity of these investigations into question. The limited database and methodological flaws further limit the level of confidence in the outcome literature on consultation.

*Measuring the effectiveness of consultation.* Part of the problem in determining the effectiveness of consultation in schools is that it is difficult to measure the efficacy of the process. Gresham and Kendall (1987) identify three areas of importance to school consultation:

 a. changes in consultee's (teacher) classroom behavior,
 b. changes in consultee's knowledge and/or attitudes,
 c. changes in the clients' (students) behavior in the classroom.

Outcome measures more typically reflect the correct implementation of appropriate interventions developed through consultation that brings about desired changes (Watson, Sterling, & McDade, 1997). It remains unclear to what extent the different steps in a consultation model contribute to the effectiveness of the process (Fuchs & Fuchs, 1989) or to successful outcomes in behavior change. The efficacy of consultation is often measured by teacher satisfaction rather than by changes in student behavior or other outcomes (Gresham & Lopez, 1996). Such measures of consumer satisfaction with the consultation process may not be consistent with measures of desired student outcomes. Indeed, there is little empirical evidence that consultation as a delivery model brings about desired student behavior change.

The wide variety of reasons for which a consultant is called in on a case presents another challenge to measuring the efficacy of the process. Just as patients consult with a physician for a multitude of concerns, teachers engage in consultation for a variety of reasons. With such diversity in presenting problems, it is invalid to compare the efficacy of the process across situations. Without a common set of problem behaviors and accurate measures of those behaviors prior to initiating consultation, it is difficult to conduct investigations that lead to rigorous results (Dunson, Hughes, & Jackson, 1994). Other variables that may also impact measures of consultation efficacy are consultant style, teacher acceptance of the consultative model, and compliance with tasks related to the consultation process itself (e.g., completing forms, collecting baseline, participating in interviews).

*Variation in consultation models.* An additional variable that makes evaluating consultation difficult is the variety of approaches used in school settings. Currently, behavioral and mental health approaches are the most commonly used strategies. These approaches are similar in that they use a structured problem solving process, but differ markedly in regard to the relationship between the consultant and the consultee and the focus of interest in problem solving (Macklem & Kalinsky, 2000).

The mental health consultation model has two goals: first, to help the teacher with current problems and second, to help the teacher become more effective in solving similar problems in the future (Macklem & Kalinsky, 2000). Treatment focuses on mental and emotional health as a more important consideration than the maladaptive behavior using an intrapsychic, insight-based, process-oriented approach to behavior change (Cullinan, Epstein, & Lloyd, 1991). Behavior is seen as a symptom of a problem, or an indicator of social or "inner" conflict. Mental health consultation can be either teacher-centered or student-centered. In student-centered consultation, the consultant forms a trusting, working relationship with the student, attempts to evaluate the student and provides treatment recommendations. In teacher-centered case consultation, the consultant works to improve the teacher's skill, knowledge level, and attitudes in an effort to impact the teacher's perceptions and understandings of the problem behavior. The mental health model is based on four assumptions:

a. the consultant can alter the teacher's perceptions,
b. a change in perceptions will result in a change in teacher behavior,
c. a change in the teacher's behavior will affect the student's behavior,
d. a change in the teacher's behavior will generalize to other problem situations. (Sugai & Tindal, 1993)

Behavioral consultation is based on behavioral and social learning theories. Behavior is viewed as functionally related to factors within the environment. The behavioral consultant works with the teacher to identify the interactions between the student's behavior and the environmental stimuli that occasion and maintain problem behavior. The behavioral consultation approach consists of:

a. observing behavior and setting,
b. establishing a baseline rate of problem behavior,
c. analyzing Functional Behavioral Assessment (FBA) and baseline data,
d. setting student behavior objectives,
e. implementing intervention,
f. evaluating outcomes,
g. using systematic decision-making procedures to adjust the program.

Through this systemic process a corollary outcome of behavioral consultation is that the teacher will acquire specific skills and knowledge to handle the problem behaviors differently (Sugai & Tindal, 1993). Rooted in a behavior analytic perspective, the focus is on changes in the teacher's behavior, the student's behavior, and the environment. Emphasis is placed on student and teacher behaviors that are accessible, observable, and changeable with an instructional approach to behavior change.

*Integrity of treatment in the absence of the consultant.* One of the biggest challenges to successful outcomes for students through consultation is the failure on the school's part to implement and sustain consultation developed intervention plans. In any approach to consultation in schools, the goal is to assist teachers to acquire new skills, develop support plans, and implement procedures. Once the desired changes in behavior occur, the consultant withdraws from the situation. The assumption is that the teacher has learned new skills that can be maintained over time and generalized to other students and situations. What is all too typical is for the intervention and support to fade away once the consultant is no longer directly involved. In practice, treatment integrity hinges largely on the teacher's acceptance and consistent implementation of the intervention. The integrity of consultation procedures and behavioral interventions are central to treatment efficacy, yet a major barrier to effectiveness in consultation is loss of integrity in implementation. Studies suggest that only half of teacher consultees actually implement treatment plans, with even fewer implementing them consistently (Macklem & Kalinsky, 2000; Noell & Witt, 1996). In a recent review of data from two federally funded grants involving 22 cases, data on the integrity with which treatments were implemented by consultees were available for less than 50% of cases (Sheridan, Colton, Fenstermacher, Lasecki, & Wilson, 1996). Another recent study reported that while teacher self-report of integrity of intervention was 54%, teachers implemented the treatment as planned only 4% of the time (Wickerstrom, Jones, LaFleur, & Witt, 1998). There is a clear tendency for treatment integrity to fade once the consultant is no longer involved. Noell and colleagues (1997) found that with daily feedback provided by the consultant, treatment integrity can improve. However, in the absence of such feedback and support, treatment integrity began to deteriorate after only two to four days. Although we know that treatment integrity is an issue, we do not have a clear picture as to why teachers do not consistently implement interventions as planned.

*Current status of the school-based consultation process.* To date, little is known about the extent to which teachers actually implement recommended interventions following consultation (Noell & Witt, 1999).

Even more disturbing, there are considerable data to suggest that teachers do not consistently generalize what they learn from participating in the consultation process to other situations and students (Noell & Witt, 1996). The time and effort expended in the consultation process is considerable and costly for both consultants and consultees with little evidence of the efficacy of the process. At best, consultation can be characterized as having limited impact on student and staff behavior. However, as indicated above, there are variables that, if addressed, could increase the likelihood of success. In addition, the failure of consultation is not that the process itself is inherently flawed, rather, current school systems are not designed to support the consultative process. To improve outcomes for students, we must look beyond the current case-by-case consultative process and specifically

a. develop and use consultation practices that develop behavior support plans that reflect current best practices,
b. develop clear outcome measures across students,
c. build capacity within schools to implement and sustain effective practices developed through the consultation process.

## *KEY FEATURES OF EFFECTIVE CONSULTATION*

While all noted features of effective consultation have yet to be empirically defined, certain critical elements, largely based on behavioral approaches to consultation appear to contribute to improved outcomes for students. Those features in which there are some data to support usage are briefly described below.

*Data-based decision making.* Data collection procedures that are direct and formative facilitate the identification of the problem and help to determine the objective of the consultation. Based on operationally defined behaviors, data analysis can minimize bias and inaccurate perceptions and focus attention on the specific problem behaviors and the settings in which they occur, leading to efficient and timely intervention decisions. A data-based approach also facilitates clear communication between the consultant and teacher regarding outcomes and intervention effectiveness (Sugai & Tindal, 1993).

*Working in teams.* Students rarely interact with only one adult in the school environment. Several teachers, specialists, support personnel, and staff typically are directly involved in a student's school day. Each of these individuals brings information to the decision-making process, and should be considered part of a team in the development of any intervention or support plan. Through their participation, the unique values and culture of the school and community are considered in determining a course of action. Assembling the critical players to participate in the process helps to promote support plans and interventions that are compatible with existing routines and settings and that match the skills and resources of those who are responsible for implementation (O'Neill et al., 1997; Vaughn, Hales, Bush, & Fox, 1998).

*Consultant skill.* The skills the consultant brings to the process is another critical feature of effective consultation. Rhoades and Kratochwill (1992) report that teachers appear to want a consultant to take a directive role in problem-solving when collaborating with them. While the literature supports a collaborative approach to consultation, the consultant must posses a level of expertise and fluency in both process and content. In addition, consultants must be fluent in terms of current best practices with respect to behavior changes such as FBA and PBS. Additionally, the consultant must be well-versed in academic instruction and interventions, curriculum modification and adaptation, use and interpretation of assessment methods, classroom assessment and management, behavioral instruction and behavior management (Sugai & Tindal, 1993).

*Implementation integrity.* An essential feature of effective consultation is the competent and consistent implementation of empirically validated practices. Quick fixes and claims of "cures" can be alluring in the face of challenging behaviors. However, the adoption of unproven methods can distract and prevent the implementation of other research-based interventions. More importantly, practices must be implemented accurately and consistently (Noell & Witt, 1996). To accomplish this objective, a contextual "goodness of fit" between the problem context and support plan must be established whereby the consultant not only has expertise in plan development, but must also "read" the school environment and develop strategies to ensure that plans

a. fit the natural routines of the setting,
b. are consistent with the values of the people in the setting,
c. are efficient in terms of time and resources,
d. are matched to the skills of the people who will carry out the procedures,
e. produce reinforcing short-term results. (O'Neill et al., 1997)

## MOVING THE CONSULTATION PROCESS
## IN NEW DIRECTIONS

Educators are faced with a dilemma. The need for specialized expertise across the school environment to address problem behavior continues to increase. Current "pull-out" programs have failed to significantly impact student behavior. Providing consultation services within the existing educational environment has also failed to show significant impact. Based on this brief review of why consultation has failed to show success, several key factors have consistently emerged in the literature. First, too many different models are used under the name "consultation." This may be especially relevant in looking at mental health models whose outcomes are often more directed at impacting teacher perception than directly altering student behavior. Second, the process itself may not fail, rather, we have yet to identify sensitive measures that will produce unequivocal results through empirical analysis. From a research perspective, this does appear to be the case. However, the applied focus of consultation, which is behavior change, has also failed to show consistent positive outcomes. Third, the consultant does not have the necessary skills to develop effective plans in concert with the consultee. While this may be the case in some instances, there is a clear body of literature that points to effective practices such as the use of FBA, instructional-based interventions, and appropriate academic accommodations. It is a reasonable assumption that, if consultation efficacy were the focus of an empirical study, investigators would only include those consultants who had a minimal level of expertise with current best practices. Finally, the issue is not that the consultation process fails because of a lack of expertise on the consultants' part or that we are unable to measure student outcomes, rather, interventions simply are not implemented with a high degree of integrity in the absence of the consultant. Based on our work in developing school-wide systems of support, this factor appears to be the most relevant in understanding why the consultation process fails to improve student behavior (Lewis, Colvin, & Sugai, 2000; Lewis, Newcomer, Kelk, & Powers, 2000; Lewis, Sugai, & Colvin, 1998).

*System consultation.* Building on the assumption that consultation fails because the school system does not support and sustain recommended best practices, we advocate re-thinking the current school consultation process. In essence, the consultant role should be one of building capacity within schools to:

a. ensure that all educators implement best practices with respect to positive behavior support,
b. assist teams of educators to design, implement, and sustain school-wide systems of support,
c. continue to assist with traditional plan development for individual students.

By expanding the role of consultant to include the first two points, schools will increase the likelihood that all educators within the school will have the skills to implement treatment programs with a higher degree of integrity. The goal is to move from "an expert" model who offers a plan and then leaves, to developing "expertise" across educators within the school building.

*Key features of school-wide systems of positive behavior support.* A recent trend in addressing behavioral challenges in schools is developing a continuum of positive behavior supports with the central focus on increasing appropriate behavior versus simply reducing problem behavior (Sugai et al., 2000; U.S. Department of Education, 1998, 2000b; Walker et al., 1996). The first level of the continuum are "universal" strategies that focus on all students and all adults within the school building. Universal strategies include establishing a common set of positively stated expectations, teaching students how to meet the expectations, recognizing and celebrating student social behavioral progress, and insuring consistency among all adults within the school (Colvin, Kameenui, & Sugai, 1993; Lewis & Garrison-Harrell, 1999; Lewis & Sugai, 1999). The second level of the continuum are "small group" or "targeted" strategies. These secondary strategies are designed to provide additional practice and support for those students who continue to engage in problem behavior even though universal strategies are in place. Example strategies at this level include using mentors, check-in/out procedures, self-management, and more intensive small group social skill training (Kerr & Nelson, 1998). The third level of the continuum focuses on "individual" students. The cornerstone of developing effective individual student PBS plans is a comprehensive FBA (Gable, Quinn, Rutherford, & Howell, 1998; O'Neill et al., 1997; Sugai et al., 1999). Once hypotheses are developed as to how student problem behavior is functionally related to the teaching environment, plans must be developed that teach a pro-social replacement behavior that results in the same or similar outcome as the problem behavior, alter the learning environment to allow the student to practice the replacement behavior successfully, and outline related support structures in the school, home, and community.

The intended outcome of school-wide systems of PBS is to prevent problem behavior, intervene early when problem behaviors are first noted, and provide comprehensive individual behavior support plans. The central theme of school-wide systems of PBS is on teaching appropriate behavior, building multiple opportunities to practice appropriate social skills and receive feedback on their use, and altering environments so that they support students who display behavioral challenges. In order to build school-wide systems of PBS schools must

   a. form teams of educators who design and oversee the process,
   b. use data, such as discipline reports, absences, referrals to specialized services, to guide and inform decisions,
   c. train and support all adults within the school building to high levels of fluency on key strategies,
   d. build expertise across faculty to deal with challenges along the continuum,
   e. involve families and community agencies,
   f. develop strategies to maintain systems over time.

Creating such systems will necessitate a "re-thinking" of school discipline and instructional strategies which, in turn, will necessitate a re-thinking of how we use expertise in a consultative capacity (Lewis & Daniels, 2000).

*Essential school-wide consultation skills.* Moving the role of consultant from contact with individual teachers or small groups of educators to assisting teams in building a continuum of behavior support will require additional sets of skills. Building on what has currently been identified in the consultation literature as essential for success and key features of school-wide systems of PBS, Table 1 provides an overview of basic skills needed to work with school systems. Possible outcome measures to ascertain the degree to which each variable is in place are also provided. Ultimately, larger school outcome measures (e.g., discipline reports, referrals, specific setting behavior problems, individual student plans) should be used to measure the success of any consultation effort with respect to school-wide systems. The overall focus, as can be seen in Table 1, is moving the consultant from the role of providing direct technical assistance through short-term interactions to one of long-term partnerships with school teams. The school team personnel then become the ones to build direct and indirect plans to support educators and families who work with students with problem behavior.

TABLE 1. Consultant skills necessary to build and sustain school-wide systems of positive behavior support.

| Essential Consultation Skill | Example Outcome Measures |
|---|---|
| Mastery of key features of universal systems of support (e.g., social skill instruction, instructional strategies, basic classroom management) | • School surveys on presence/absence of key features (e.g., Lewis & Sugai, 1999)<br><br>Student behavioral reports (e.g., office referrals, number of in-school suspensions) |
| Mastery of key features of small group/targeted systems of support (e.g., self-management, social skill generalization strategies, informal FBAs, basic behavior management) | • School surveys on presence/absence of key features<br>• Case studies<br>• Student behavioral reports<br>• Teacher/Parent surveys |
| Mastery of key features of individual student systems of support (e.g., FBA, behavioral support plans, collaborating with families and community agencies) | • PBS plan based on FBA outcomes<br>• PBS plan in compliance with federal regulations (if student is on IEP)<br>• Individual student data within problem setting and generalized setting<br>• Parent and community surveys |
| Fluent with basic behavioral principles (e.g., learning theory, identifying functional relationships in behavioral patterns, reinforcing/aversive stimuli) | • Developed systems emphasizes an instructional approach<br>• Reinforcement rates of student behavior<br>• PBS plans focus on teaching and supporting replacement behavior<br>• PBS plans based on empirically proven practices |
| Establish school data collection systems (from all school to individual student) and guide educators through decision making process to inform practice at each of the three levels of intervention | • School wide systems allow educators to target problem areas and specific students<br>• Data system allows for periodic evaluation of the success of the system<br>• Individual student data allow for instructional decisions and evaluation of plan effectiveness |
| Train groups of educators from varying disciplines on effective behavioral strategies | • School team plans reflect key principles<br>• Educators able to implement school plan in their respective settings with a high degree of integrity (e.g., Sugai Lewis-Palmer, Todd, & Horner, 1999) |
| Provide direct technical assistance to school teams including basic organization to work efficiently as a team | • School teams accomplish goals<br>• School teams impact the system across the continuum (system data)<br>• Teams able to provide sufficient information and support to allow teachers to implement procedures (Sugai et al., 1999) |
| Assist in building communication systems between school teams and the larger school staff | • Permanent product review such as faculty meeting agenda, memos, training materials |

| Essential Consultation Skill | Example Outcome Measures |
|---|---|
| Build "expertise" among team members and other school personnel to reduce reliance on consultant and other specialists | • Reduction in student problem behavior<br>• Reduction in referral rates to specialists |
| Work with school teams to develop collaborative partnerships with families and community agencies | • Reduction in student problem behavior<br>• Consumer satisfaction surveys |

## CONCLUSION AND RECOMMENDATIONS

The need remains, and the demand will grow for specialist expertise in meeting the challenges of diverse learners, especially in the area of social behavior problems. The concern is to deliver expertise that will not only impact the student, but also build skills and capacity across educators and families. To date, school consultation has not been demonstrated to be highly effective in meeting the specialized needs of students and educators. The lack of efficacy can be traced largely to the varying methods and purposes of school consultation and the limited implementation fidelity following plan development. A parallel situation exists in the examination of the efficacy of educators to meet the social behavioral needs of students at risk and those with disabilities in that outcome data to date are very poor. The failures to meet the needs of at-risk students and students with disabilities can also be traced to multiple uncoordinated intervention methodology with varying outcomes and the lack of systemic intervention along a systemic continuum.

An emerging strategy to improve schools' abilities to meet the needs of at-risk students and students with disabilities is to build a school-wide system of behavioral support (Sugai et al., 2000). However, building school-wide systems and complex individual support plans will continue to require specialist expertise. By moving the focus from an expert model on a case-by-case basis and building expertise across school environments, the current weaknesses of the consultation approach may be alleviated. First, by building capacity within schools, the need for pull-out programs and individual support plans will be lessened, thereby allowing educators and consultants to focus more time on fewer high need students. Second, by creating systems whereby all educators become fluent in effective behavior management, you increase the likelihood that small group and individual student plans will be implemented with integrity. Finally, by focusing efforts on creating capacity, schools should be able to maintain treatment gains in the absence of the specialist.

An additional advantage to moving the consultation process from a case-basis to a systems level would be the generation of better efficacy data. Central to the systems approach of PBS is the collection and use of student and teacher data. Formative data collection would allow the field to conduct better evaluations with respect to consultation efficacy. Building in data points that reflect implementation should also be included to better pinpoint those variables that account for success and failure. Clearly, more research on the school consultation process is warranted.

## REFERENCES

Colvin, G., Kameenui, E., & Sugai, G. (1993). Reconceptualizing behavior management and school-wide discipline in general education. *Education and Treatment of Children, 16*, 361-381.

Conduct Problems Prevention Research Group. (1992). A developmental and clinical model for the prevention of conduct disorders: The FAST Track Program. *Development and Psychopathology, 4*, 509-527.

Cullinan, D., Epstein, M. H., & Lloyd, J. W. (1991). Evaluation of conceptual models of behavior disorders. *Behavioral Disorders, 16*, 148-157.

Dunson, R. M., Hughes, J. N., & Jackson, T. W. (1994). Effects of behavioral consultation on student and teacher behavior. *Journal of School Psychology, 32*(3), 247-266.

Elliot, D. S. (1994a). *Youth violence: An overview*. Center for the Study and Prevention of Violence, Boulder, CO.

Elliot, D. S. (1994b). Serious violent offenders: Onset, developmental course, and termination–The American Society of Criminology 1993 Presidential Address. *Criminology, 32*, 1-21.

Fuchs, D., & Fuchs, L. S. (1989). Exploring effective and efficient prereferral interventions: A component analysis of behavioral consultation. *School Psychology Review, 18*, 260-283.

Fuchs, D., Fuchs, L. S., Dulan, J., Roberts, H., & Fernstrom, P. (1992). Where is the research on consultation effectiveness? *Educational & Psychological Consultation, 3*(2), 151-174.

Gable, R. A., Quinn, M. M., Rutherford, R. B., & Howell, K. (1998). Addressing problem behaviors in schools: Use of functional assessments and behavior intervention plans. *Preventing School Failure, 42*, 106-119.

Gable, R. A., Sugai, G., Lewis, T. J., Nelson, J. R., Cheney, D., Safran, S. P., & Safran, J. S. (1998). *Individual and systemic approaches to collaboration and consultation.* Reston, VA: Council for Children with Behavioral Disorders.

Gresham, F. M. (1998). Social skill training: Should we raze, remodel, or rebuild? *Behavioral Disorders, 24*, 19-25.

Gresham, F. M., & Kendell, G. K. (1987). School consultation research: Methodological critique and future research directions. *School Psychology Review, 16*, 306-316.

Gresham, F. M., & Lopez, M. F. (1996). Social validation: A unifying concept for school-based consultation research and practice. *School Psychology Quarterly, 11*, 204-227.

Gutkin, T. B. (1993). School-based consultation research: Current status and possible future directions. In J. E. Zines, T. R. Kratochwill & S. N. Elliott (Eds.), *Handbook of consultation services for children.* San Francisco: Jossey-Bass.

Kameenui, E. J., & Simmons, D. C. (1990). Designing classroom management strategies within the context of instruction. In *Designing instructional strategies: The prevention of academic learning problems.* Englewood Cliffs, NJ: Macmillan.

Kerr, M. M., & Nelson, C. M. (1998). *Strategies for managing behavior problems in the classroom.* Upper Saddle River, NJ: Prentice-Hall.

Kratochwill, T. R., & VanSomeren, K. R. (1985). Barriers to treatment success in behavioral consultation: Current limitations and future directions. *Journal of School Psychology, 23*, 225-239.

Larson, J. (1994). Violence prevention in the schools: A review of selected programs and procedures. *School Psychology Review, 23*, 151-164.

Lewis, T. J., Colvin, G., & Sugai, G. (2000). The effects of precorrection and active supervision on the recess behavior of elementary school students. *Education and Treatment of Children, 23*, 109-121.

Lewis, T. J., & Daniels, C. (2000). Rethinking school discipline through effective behavioral support. *Reaching Today's Youth, 4*, 43-47.

Lewis, T. J., & Garrison-Harrell, L. (1999). Effective behavior support: Designing setting specific interventions. *Effective School Practices, 17*, 38-46.

Lewis, T. J., Newcomer, L., Kelk, M., & Powers, L. (2000). Preventing and addressing aggressive and violent behavior through individual systems of positive behavioral support. *Reaching Today's Youth, 5*, 37-41.

Lewis, T. J., & Sugai, G. (1999). Effective behavior support: A systems approach to proactive school-wide management. *Focus on Exceptional Children, 31*(6), 1-24.

Lewis, T. J, Sugai, G., & Colvin, G. (1998). Reducing problem behavior through a school-wide system of effective behavioral support: Investigation of a school-wide social skills training program and contextual interventions. *School Psychology Review, 27*, 446-459.

Macklem, G. L., & Kalinsky, R. (2000). *School consultation: Providing both prevention and intervention services to children and school staff.* Paper presented at the National Association of School Psychologists, New Orleans, Louisiana. (ERIC Reproduction Service No. ED 444 103).

Mayer, G. R. (1995). Preventing antisocial behavior in the schools. *Journal of Applied Behavior Analysis, 28*, 467-478.

Noell, G. H., & Witt, J. C. (1996). A critical re-evaluation of five fundamental assumptions underlying behavioral consultation. *School Psychology Quarterly, 11*, 187-188.

Noell, G. H., & Witt, J. C. (1999). When does consultation lead to intervention implementation?: Critical issues for research and practice. *Journal of Special Education, 33*, 29-35.

Noell, G. H., Witt, J. C., Gilbertson, D. N., Ranier, D. D., & Freeland, J. T. (1997). Increasing teacher intervention implementation in general education settings through consultation and performance feedback. *School Psychology Quarterly, 12*, 77-88.

O'Neill, R.E., Horner, R.H., Albin, R.W., Sprague, J.R., Storey, K., & Newton, J.S. (1997). *Functional assessment and program development for problem behavior: A practical handbook*. Pacific Grove, CA: Brooks/Cole.

Patterson, G. R., Reid, J. B., & Dishion, T. J. (1992). *Antisocial boys*. Eugene, OR: Castalia Press.

Peacock Hill Working Group. (1991). Problems and promises in special education and related services for children and youth with emotional or behavioral disorders. *Behavioral Disorders, 16*, 299-313.

Pryzwansky, W. (1986). Indirect service delivery: Considerations for future research in consultation. *School Psychology Review, 15*, 479-488.

Rhoades, M. M., & Kratochwill, T. R. (1992). Teacher reactions to behavioral consultation: An analysis of language and involvement. *School Psychology Quarterly, 7*(1), 47-59.

Sheridan, S. M., Colton, D. L., Fenstermacher, K., Lasecki, K., & Wilson, K. (1996). *Efficacy of conjoint behavioral consultation as a vehicle for inclusion*. Paper presented at the American Psychological Association, Toronto. (ERIC Reproduction Service No. ED408 515).

Sugai, G., Horner, R. H., Dunlap, G., Hieneman, M., Lewis, T. J., Nelson, C. M., Scott, T., Liaupsin, C., Sailor, W., Turnbull, A., Turnbull, H. R., Wickham, D., Wicox, B., & Ruef, M. (2000). Applying positive behavior support and functional behavioral assessment in schools. *Journal of Positive Behavior Interventions, 2*, 131-143.

Sugai, G., Lewis-Palmer, T., Todd, A.W., & Horner, R. (1999). *Systems-wide evaluation tool (SET)*. Eugene, OR: University of Oregon.

Sugai, G., & Tindal, G. (1993). *Effective school consultation: An interactive approach*. Pacific Grove, CA: Brooks/Cole Publishing Company.

Tolan, P., & Guerra, N. (1994). *What works in reducing adolescent violence: An empirical review of the field*. Center for the Study and Prevention of Violence, Boulder, CO.

U.S. Department of Education (1995). *The condition of education, 1995*. Washington, DC: National Center for Education Statistics.

U.S. Department of Education (1998). *Early warning timely response: A guide to safe schools*. Washington, DC: Author.

U.S. Department of Education (2000a). *22nd Annual Report to Congress*. Washington, DC: Author.

U.S. Department of Education (2000b). *Safeguarding our children: An action guide*. Washington, DC: Author.

Vaughn, K., Hales, C., Bush, M., & Fox, J. (1998). East Tennessee State University's "Make a difference" project: Using a team-based consultative model to conduct functional behavioral assessments. *Preventing School Failure, 43*, 24-30.

Walker, H. M., Horner, R. H., Sugai, G., Bullis, M., Sprague, J. R., Bricker, D., & Kaufman, M. J. (1996). Integrated approaches to preventing antisocial behavior patterns among school-age children and youth. *Journal of Emotional and Behavioral Disorders, 4*, 193-256.

Watson, T. S., Sterling, H. E., & McDade, A. (1997). Demythifying behavioral consultation. *School Psychology Review*, *26*, 467-474.

Webster-Stratton, C., & Spitzer, A. (1996). Parenting a young child with conduct problems. In Ollendick, T.H. & Prinz, R.J. (Eds.) *Advances in Clinical Child Psychology, Volume 18*. (Ch.1 pp. 1-61) Plenum Press: New York.

Wickerstrom, K. F., Jones, K. M., LaFleur, L. H., & Witt, J. C. (1998). An analysis of treatment integrity in school-based behavioral consultation. *School Psychology Quarterly*, *13*, 141-154.

# Index